DEBUNKING GLENN BECK

DEBUNKING GLENN BECK

HOW TO SAVE AMERICA FROM MEDIA PUNDITS AND PROPAGANDISTS

~

Karl Rogers

Foreword by Harvey Sarles

 PRAEGER

AN IMPRINT OF ABC-CLIO, LLC
Santa Barbara, California • Denver, Colorado • Oxford, England

Library of Congress Cataloging-in-Publication Data

Rogers, Karl, 1967–
Debunking Glenn Beck : how to save America from media pundits and propagandists / Karl Rogers ; foreword by Harvey Sarles.
    p. cm.
Includes bibliographical references and index.
ISBN 978-1-4408-0029-0 (hbk. : alk.paper) – ISBN 978-1-4408-0030-6 (ebook)
1. United States—Politics and government. 2. Democracy—United States. 3. Beck, Glenn. I. Title.
JK31.R57 2011
320.973–dc23   2011032648

ISBN: 978-1-4408-0029-0
EISBN: 978-1-4408-0030-6

15 14 13 12 11   1 2 3 4 5

This book is also available on the World Wide Web as an eBook.
Visit www.abc-clio.com for details.

Praeger
An Imprint of ABC-CLIO, LLC

ABC-CLIO, LLC
130 Cremona Drive, P.O. Box 1911
Santa Barbara, California 93116-1911

This book is printed on acid-free paper ∞

Manufactured in the United States of America

For My Mother and Father

There is nothing that obtains so general an influence over the manners and morals of a people as the press; from that as from a fountain the streams of vice or virtue are poured forth over a nation.

—Thomas Paine

Contents

FOREWORD

Glenn Beck is the "star" of this book's title. But the book itself is more deeply an analysis and discussion of America: What is democracy and how does it "work"? Where did it come from? Where is it at right now . . . and why? How can we—the citizens—extend this land of "We, the People" into a strong and meaningful future?

Or can we? Beck's America is quite different—and quite oppositional—to the actual America, which should include all the people. He is clever, a public star on television, in his several books, and wherever else he appears. His ability to use his skills to effectively "redraw" America's history to suit his wishes, especially, and to draw or represent the really rich, the corporations, is amazing, popular, and powerful.

"We, the People" are in the midst of a New Gilded Age in which the very few, very rich control our economy. This is the third such time in the past century—and the temptation for the very rich, as well as their followers and heirs, is to share in the great riches and accompanying power that the very few control. We've seen most of this before: the "robber barons," the Great Depression as the earlier Gilded Ages lost their sheen, and the collapse of our economy a couple of years ago.

In the oligarchy or plutocracy in which we find ourselves, very few control the money, politics, and power to promote the ability of the oligarchs to fund and try to justify their positions. The really rich are extremely powerful and will use almost any means to keep this all going. And the very idea of the corporation has been on the rise and has gained power as we all watch . . . and do little.

Just who is Glenn Beck in this situation? Well, he is a "front man"—"star" or "hottie"—who has very cleverly used the stages or grandstands that the medium of television has provided. He looks and sounds really "good"—as he attempts to convince us that he knows how the world really is . . . or should be. And he keeps telling us that he knows all there is to know, and that most everyone who opposes him is simply wrong. Anyone who opposes him, he claims, is a socialist, a Marxist, an anarchist, or anti- the "proper" America—his America.

And who is the author of this book? Karl Rogers is a philosopher by education and one of the most interesting thinkers I've ever met. He is a student of the world, and especially of the very nature of democracy, because he thinks democracy is the best—perhaps only—direction for a good and decent world. He is deeply concerned that education and democracy are taken too much for granted, that most of "We, the People" are not educated toward their study and understanding. We are accustomed to relying on some vague trust that our government will continue to "work" fairly much in our behalf. Or we seem to believe that there's nothing much we can do about it. Money, success—let's all try to get our kids into Harvard or Yale, where the connections to Wall Street and Washington are greased every day.

Thus the "debunking" of Glenn Beck proceeds with an ongoing examination of the history and operation of American democracy and of the Founding Fathers—what they thought and wrote, and why. (I hope readers of this book can become more committed to knowing, and thence doing, what democracy "needs" in any/every moment, that we all have a copy of the U.S. Constitution very near to our reading places, and that we read the Constitution and its amendments as we read this book, and rethink who we are and what a democracy is as we actually try to live it.)

The Constitution begins with the Preamble: "We, the People." Democracy is the people, we . . . us. How to bring us all together? How do we retain the sense of our own individual power, even as the world changes? Thomas Jefferson and his colleagues wondered this, too—just as they were the first to declare their/our independence from monarchy. But the temptation toward monarchy—people, power, corporations—always hovers, and we have to study each moment and restate and restore our independence, each of us, all of us. Thus central to this book is a study of America—how it is and has to be in order to remain an (active) democracy.

We began with a society in which the richer men reigned. Slaves were not people, nor were the natives—Indians—nor were women. The militia—against the British—in some ways led to our independence. Then the Civil War: America is the only nation that retains a sense of itself even after it fought a powerful internal battle. Then there were the Thirteenth to Fifteenth Amendments, for the most part ending slavery.

We got out of the messes of the Gilded Age twice in the past century. So many of our (now) citizens immigrated here during those/these times, when immigration meant cheap labor. In the long run, it worked pretty well. Most of the time, for most of us.

Thinking sometimes changes, too. And now we are reading this book. In each chapter, Karl "takes on" Glenn Beck, attempting to present, clarify, and specify what Beck is up to—and to present the history and facts of America in all its complexities, which Karl presents and unpacks very well. Who were the major Founding Fathers? How did they write and think? What did they have on their minds for the first nation to overthrow monarchy and to form a nation of "We, the People"? Who are we and how do we keep the nation "going" in various times and circumstances? Especially right now, as the gilded, so-rich corporate powerful think they deserve all there is. We . . . the people? Bah!

Karl literally debunks Beck's thinking. Not to beat him up or accuse him of stupidity, but to get us to think: Who are we? Where are we going? During all this, the foundations of a living democracy emerge, are present, and often "shine."

Glenn Beck and his strategies must be understood critically by seeing how Beck deals with (or "dismisses") the Constitution. Karl shows how Beck's claims to owning a proper understanding of America resides in "twistifications" of the Constitution and a tossing-off of our history, as if Beck knows all there is to know about America and his version is obvious and true. Democracy? Huh?

As Karl makes evident, Beck doesn't take the Constitution or our history seriously. Beck lays out the America—then and now—that he wants to exist. In particular, he represents the America that is run, controlled, by corporate thinking and acting, which is, for him, the "proper" and most powerful America, the only America. For the rest of us, he mostly creates or "makes up" the whys and wherefores that will keep America ruling and controlling the world.

People, power. Beck focuses on power as being the "true" America—his corporate view of America—focusing on present-day "moneyed" viewings. He doesn't pay too much attention to slavery (to women?); instead, he "twistifies" documents and characters to lend credence to what he wants—and uses them to lead us to the America in which the rich are those who most "deserve" to be rich (the smart, clever, and successful—anyone who counts in the world). Only the corporate and powerful should count, lest we "lose our way." Questions of what is a citizen, the common good or common welfare, the power of each person, habeas corpus—blah!

Karl concludes that Beck's message erodes the belief in the possibility of good government and democratic participation. This risks causing a level of public apathy that will erode the political institutions upon which the possibility of good government and democracy are founded. The American people need a progressive message calling for "We, the People" to claim their government and their country through grassroots movements.

The time is now—for America and perhaps the larger world—for "We, the People" to claim their governments and countries.

Toward a thoughtful read!

—Harvey Sarles

Harvey Sarles is a professor of cultural studies and comparative literature at the University of Minnesota. He is also the founder and a director of the John Dewey Center for Democracy and Education.

PREFACE

Radio and television show host Glenn Beck is a controversial figure. He has made his fortune from being a media pundit and propagandist. Describing himself as only "a rodeo clown" and an entertainer in search of ratings, he has regaled his listeners and viewers with exposés about government conspiracies and plots.[1] Declaring that progressives are secretly attempting to impose socialism on America, he denounces any kind of "social justice" as being the path toward National Socialism and/or communism. While advocating his brand of "conservative libertarianism" and claiming that he is on a mission from God to restore America to its founding principles, Glenn Beck has become a household name and best-selling author. When I first saw him on television, I thought that his own description of himself as a rodeo clown was about right. I watched his show with some amusement, thought "this guy is nuts," and gave him no more thought.

Some time later, I was on a flight to Alaska and noticed that the man sitting next to me was reading a book by Glenn Beck called *Arguing with Idiots: How to Stop Small Minds and Big Government.*[2] We struck up a conversation. I asked him what he thought of the book. He said it was okay. He passed it over to me. Flicking through it, I was disappointed with its general silliness, as it trotted out cliché after cliché interspersed with cartoons and random comments. I passed the book back.

However, over the next few weeks, I started watching his show. My first impression was that his "logic" tended to leap about—in what he terms his A.D.D. moments—but it conformed to the same formula and was easy enough to follow. Beck takes a proposed policy, say, public health care, and associates it with an ideology, such as communism, and then, via that ideology, he connects it with some of the extremes that have been done in the name of that ideology, say, Soviet gulags. Hence, according to this "logic," if you want a taxpayer-funded system of health care to provide subsidized prescriptions for children or the elderly, then you are on the slippery slope toward a totalitarian police state and labor camps. Using this "logic," he has argued that Christians or progressives who want any degree of "social justice" in America are on the path to National Socialism, concentration camps, and attempted genocide. He has urged Christians to leave any church in which the pastor or priest advocates any kind of "social justice." He has also called progressivism a cancer that needs to be cut out and eradicated. These claims seem to be rather implausible, but it left me wondering whether any people were buying into any of it.

Reluctantly and with some embarrassment, I bought his book and read it from cover to cover. I found it to be so full of distortions, half-truths, and assertions that it led me to decide to write a book in response to it.

I don't think that Beck is "nuts." He is an entertainer. His show is all about ratings to gain advertising revenue and make money. It is a commercial endeavor. Beck has a multimillion-dollar business, with his TV and radio shows, his websites, his books, and his public performances. And, after all, he is largely preaching to the choir. His audience tends to be members of the conservative right, self-proclaimed libertarians, and conspiracy theorists, and Beck tells them what they want to hear. They lap it up.

What's the problem, then? If I don't like his show, I can always turn off the TV or change the channel, right? So why should I care?

Increasingly, mass media has dominated public debate in America. With intensified media consolidation, TV, radio, and newspapers give voice to the interests of fewer people—the owners of media corporations. While media pundits represent themselves as reflecting the concerns and views of their audience, they express and represent the message and interests of their employers. The Internet has become factionalized, with people only interested in sites that reinforce their own opinions and views, when they are not indulging in gossip or pornography. What has happened to the promise of the Great Conversation? Where are public debates and the frank exchange of views? It seems to me that they have all but disappeared. Media pundits and propagandists have taken over. They preach to the converted, and their distortions and lies are disseminated unchallenged to reinforce the views of people who already want to believe them. In cable TV newspeak this is called *narrowcasting*. It refers to the deliberate formatting of TV talk shows and news to appeal to a targeted and politicized audience to reinforce their already held beliefs and assumptions.

Under such circumstances, public debate is almost impossible, and the breeding ground for extremism is fertile. And without public debate, democracy is stifled and the public merely become the pawns of media control and propaganda. Glenn Beck provides us with an example of how corporate media attempt to stifle public debate and manipulate public opinion.

In order to understand Glenn Beck, he must be situated within the wider context of Fox News and the conservative right-wing media strategy of divide and conquer among the American working and middle classes. A divided citizenry, at odds with even the idea that government can be a force for good, expecting corruption and incompetence to be the inevitable outcome of politics, remain powerless in the face of the relentless rise of unrestrained corporate power and the corporate takeover of the American government. We are already well past the dawn of the construction of a New Gilded Age. What is Beck's strategy? He is largely preaching to the converted, reinforcing their views and prejudices, aiming to convince his audience that *any* kind of progressive change or reform is a part of some Marxist or revolutionary plot to gain governmental control over America and destroy it. Hence, any kind of finance reform to protect consumers and prevent the kind of irresponsible practices that led to the 2008 financial crisis is represented as an attempt to control the financial sector. Any kind of reform to provide all Americans with affordable health care is represented as an attempt to control the lives of Americans, to set up "death panels," and to ration health care (ignoring the fact that private insurance rations health care to those who can afford it). Any support of trade unions and organized labor, to help workers gain better wages and working conditions, is represented as an attempt to take over industry. Any call to reduce military spending in order to balance the budget or reduce the national debt is represented as an attempt to destroy the military and subvert the people who defend the Constitution. Any attempt to improve people's lives by providing public education, affordable housing, public transport, unemployment welfare, or social security is represented as a plot to increase dependency on government. Calls to preserve *Net Neutrality* to protect the Internet from being taken over and controlled by corporations (as well as by the government or anyone else) are represented as part of an attempt at governmental control over the media. Any law to improve the quality of food, air, or water by reducing pollution and unsanitary practices is represented as totalitarian and oppressive government regulation.

Beck describes American progressive youth movements and American trade unions as part of a Marxist plot to take over the world through "democratic revolution."[3] He claims that progressives are radicals "infesting" education and unions, to the extent that "our society is riddled with them," and that they aim to overthrow the capitalist system. Hence Beck urges his viewers to wake up, open their eyes, and "think out of the box." "The Revolution Is Now!" he tells us.[4] His strategy is to scare his viewers, to make them afraid of anything that will change the status quo, but leave them feeling powerless to stop that change—apart from stocking up on canned food, ammunition, and buying gold. By urging support of the Tea Party, he offers his audience "hope" to "restore honor" and "take back government," but he is supporting pro-corporate candidates and the same corporate forces that are overtaking government and using it as their instrument. In other words, his whole anti-government rhetoric is directed toward terrifying his audience that all social and political reforms are bad, and it is best to support business as usual by supporting the Tea Party, while at the same time leaving his audience feeling that this somehow puts them in touch with the foundations of the American Revolution and the Republic, as presented to them by Glenn Beck.

The Tea Party is the means by which people who were disenfranchised by government and the bailout of banks were funneled back into the Republican Party. Beck's strategy is not to return America to its foundational principles but to preserve the status quo wherein corporations are able to consolidate further their control over finance, the Federal Reserve, health care, industry, wages, working conditions, and the media. His strategy is to conceal the corporate consolidation of control over government (and the military) by misdirecting people from the source of their disenfranchisement. This is why he tells us about the leftist plot by Marxists and anarchists to infiltrate the government and destroy America, a plot that must be stopped by the conservative and libertarian right in the Tea Party in order to restore the rule of the "free market" (which is dominated by corporations). His strategy is to conceal the extent that corporatism is the cancer destroying America by telling us a spook story of impending revolution and anarchy, thus presenting corporatism as the solution to America's problems. Hence, what lies behind Beck's "conservative libertarian" rhetoric is a corporate ideology that aims to conceal the rise of the corporate state behind the mask of its opposite—radical left conspiracy—which can only be prevented by supporting the Tea Party (which, of course, preserves the corporate hegemony).

Perhaps one of the most disturbing episodes of his TV show, "The War Room," was one of his earliest with Fox News. In it, Beck "speculated" on the possibility of mass insurrection to overthrow the government and gave us a picture of the "worst case" scenario for 2014.[5] While he repeatedly distanced himself from any claim to be making a prediction—instead he claimed to be only exploring possibilities and "thinking through the unthinkable"—he also repeatedly connected his narrative to the present by saying that this is beginning now and referred to past predications of his that had come to pass. Topped and tailed with caveats distancing himself from his "speculations," probably for legal reasons, Beck described the collapse of American cities, the imposition of martial law, financial meltdown, hyperinflation, the clampdown on free speech (Beck cited the 2002 Bipartisan Campaign Reform Act as an example), the rise of street gangs, and civil war. He told us about looming civil unrest, militias, and insurrection, and describes "the bubba effect," whereby isolated, self-reliant, armed, and paranoid communities of alienated and disenfranchised people will rise up to defend themselves against tyrannical government (and wayward Mexicans). All of this was blamed on the incompetence of the government, the bailouts, and a lack of border control.

Arguably, Beck's anti-government rhetoric could be construed as a call for insurrection and the violent overthrow of the government, but he distances himself from the charge of sedition with claims that this is "speculation" and by stating that he hopes this does not happen. In "The War Room," we can see how panic and hysteria are important parts of Beck's narrative. He needs to convince his audience that a crisis is at hand, that the world will never be the same again, that a revolution is happening—a growing state of chaos and destruction—and that martial law and societal collapse are imminent. This feeds into people's own sense of alienation and anxiety but misdirects it into blaming an imaginary conspiracy. He calls it "the perfect storm," whereby covert revolutionaries in the government create the crises they can then offer solutions for. His task is to intensify the degree of frustration and fear among his increasingly polarized and factionalized audience—to create a "them-and-us" struggle for survival—which increases mistrust and further damages the possibility of public debate and discourse. This is worrying after incidents such as Byron Williams's failed attempt to shoot people at the Tides Foundation, which Williams confessed to be as a result of listening to and believing Glenn Beck's exposé of this nonprofit organization as a front for conspirators plotting to undermine America.[6] It is also worrying when, unperturbed by his possible influence on Williams, Beck continues to target Frances Fox Piven, a seventy-nine-year-old professor of sociology, even though she has received death threats, arguably as a result of his accusations.[7]

Beck's anti-government rhetoric—linking progressives, radicals, and revolutionaries—claims that the U.S. government under the Obama administration has seized control over the finance sector, health care, industry, welfare, the media (citing Net Neutrality as being an FCC plot for government control), and food prices (citing the 2010 Food Safety Modernization Act), with only the military resisting government control (apparently, according to Beck, the military should not be under government control). Without any hint of irony, in a hushed voice, Beck implores every service man and woman to remember their oath to the Constitution. (Wouldn't that be the same Constitution that places the military under the control of Congress and the president in times of war?) It seems that, according to Beck, progressives have been acting as a fifth column within the government, plotting to control every aspect of every American's life. Glenn Beck has twisted the meaning of "regulation" to mean "control," as if placing enforceable standards on the quality of drinking water means that the government controls America's water supply. Hence, although the idea of Net Neutrality means to prevent anyone from controlling the Internet, it means the opposite according to Beck because it does not let powerful corporations do what they please with the Internet. Yet he does not explicitly state this. Instead, he misrepresents Net Neutrality as an attempt at government regulation of the Internet—the imposition of the Fairness Doctrine. Similarly, although the 2010 Food Safety Modernization Act actually gives agribusiness control over food production and supply by making it even harder for small farms to compete, Beck tells us that it is a government takeover of food in order to raise prices and cause riots. Hence, when food prices rise due to the reduction in market competition, Beck can blame left-wing conspirators within the government. Time and time again, Beck misrepresents the U.S. government in terms of a covert Marxist plot, as a red cape to distract the people, the bull, from the sword of unrestrained corporate power. Behind the government stand cartels of corporations carving up the country, not shady Marxist conspirators.

While this book is an attempt to challenge the distortions made by Beck—an example of a contemporary media pundit and propagandist—it is not my intention to attack him as a person. He is as entitled to enjoy his First Amendment rights to free speech as anyone else is. However, Glenn Beck is a symptom of what has gone wrong with mainstream media. My intention in this book is to discuss and critique his ideas and arguments. A growing number of books have been written about Glenn Beck.[8] These books have largely dealt with the phenomenon of Glenn Beck: his background and rise to fame. Other books have discussed him in relation to Fox News and/or media in general. However, none of these books have given a detailed and critical analysis of his message and arguments. In *Debunking Glenn Beck*, the ideas and ideology at work in Beck's arguments are discussed in detail and critically analyzed. This book shows how he has distorted the meaning of the Constitution, American history, and the facts and aims of progressivism. The book concludes by explaining how Americans can revitalize public debate and democracy in America.

I hope that you enjoy it.

1

TWISTIFICATIONS AND THE CONSTITUTION

The word "twistification" was coined by Thomas Jefferson to describe how he believed John Marshall, the Supreme Court's first chief justice, misinterpreted the Constitution. Appointed to the Court by the outgoing president, John Adams, Marshall was a thorn in President Jefferson's side and was chief justice for thirty-five years. He famously (or infamously, depending on one's point of view), during the *Marbury v. Madison* case of 1803, established the legal principle of judicial review by pronouncing, "It is emphatically the province and the duty of the judicial department to say what the law is."[1]

Jefferson considered this to be the first of many of Marshall's twistifications. I shall return to the notion of judicial review later in this chapter, but the word twistification appropriately conveys how Glenn Beck interprets the Constitution. Despite the pretense that he sticks by the letter of the Constitution and understands it in terms of its original meaning, Beck has produced a number of his own twistifications.[2] Let's take a look at some of these.

INTERPRETING THE CONSTITUTION

Beck claims that "maybe the problem is that the entire Constitution is written in *English*—a language that is very difficult for the average idiot to comprehend," and so he translates the Constitution for us in order to leave "no doubt what our Founding Fathers really intended."[3] But how does Beck know what "the Framers" meant or intended? Did he hold a séance? He does not tell us. Instead, he presumptuously channels their intentions to us.

Consider the Preamble:[4] "We the People of the United States, in order to form a more perfect union, to establish justice, insure domestic tranquility, provide for the common defense, promote the general welfare, and secure the blessings of liberty to ourselves and our posterity, do establish to ordain and establish this Constitution for the United States of America."[5] Beck tells us that this clearly allows for the military and demonstrates religious sensibilities, but that it does not mean any kind of welfare state. Maybe this is true. Maybe it is not. But if we look at the wording of the Preamble, we see that the phrase "common defense" is used rather than the word "military," and that no direct mention of any religion or deity is invoked (beyond the use of the word "blessings") yet "promote the general welfare" is specifically included as a responsibility or duty of "the union." Perhaps there is some room for interpretation here. But according to Beck, interpretation is unnecessary and he has given us the true meaning. Oddly enough, according to Beck, the Preamble completely endorses his own conservative policies regarding national defense, opposition to any kind of public welfare provision, and the belief that the United States was founded as a Christian country (and therefore we can ignore the separation of Church and State). Beck's twistification here is to interpret the Constitution in a way that coincides with his own political agenda, regardless of the actual wording, and assert that his is the only legitimate interpretation. This "cherry picking" is a typical tactic of conservative media pundits and propagandists. They focus on particular interpretations of key phrases or sections of the Constitution, then interpret them as fully endorsing their own political stance (or, at least, their employer's political stance), and they simply ignore any other interpretations, phrases, or sections of the Constitution that problematize or even contradict their viewpoint.

Clearly, Congress and the Supreme Court have a great deal of latitude regarding how to interpret what phrases such as "the general welfare" mean. But what did it mean for the Founders? Beck repeatedly tells us that only an idiot would think that the Founders meant a taxpayer-funded system of public welfare or services. Beck tells his listeners, viewers, and readers that progressive ideas such as social justice run contrary to the founding principles of America. Such ideas promote redistribution of wealth and collectivism, which Beck tells us are cancers eating away at American values and society. However, if we take a look at the writings of Thomas Paine—one of the Founders and one of Beck's heroes—then we can see that, once again, things are not quite as cut and dry as Beck would have us believe. In his pamphlet *Agrarian Justice* (1795), Paine developed the ideas put forth in his *Rights of Man* (1791).[6] He criticized how private land ownership denies the majority of people the means of independent survival and proposed a taxpayer-funded system of public welfare for landless Americans. He advocated that landless adults (men and women) over the age of twenty-one be paid a basic income ("the sum of 15 pounds sterling") as a compensation "for the loss of his or her natural inheritance, by the introduction of the system of landed property," paid as "a right, and not a charity" from "a national fund." The "sum of ten pounds per annum, during life, to every person now living, of the age of fifty years, and to all others as they shall arrive at that age." He also proposed an invalidity benefit of ten pounds to be paid to blind persons annually. The "national fund" was to be accumulated through property taxes or a "ground-rent" paid at the moment of inheritance—an inheritance tax equal to the value of the land as it would be in its natural (uncultivated) state. Paine not only explicitly considered his proposal to be a form of redistribution of wealth and social justice, but he also considered it to be conducive to the "general welfare" of the public and for the benefit of civilization. Could this mean that Thomas Paine—Beck's hero—was a progressive?

Perhaps Paine should be treated as an exception—being something of a radical thinker. However, Beck tells us that the Framers did not have in mind such progressive ideas as publicly funded education and that only an idiot would think they would consider education and "the pursuit of happiness" to be the business of government. Clearly, these are private matters. I shall discuss public education in chapter 3. However, for now, let's take a look at the following quotation: "Whereas in all well regulated Governments, it is the indispensable duty of every Legislature to consult the Happiness of a rising Generation, and Endeavour to fit them for an honorable Discharge of the Social Duties of Life, by paying strictest attention to their education."

Which un-American progressives came out with such a cancerous outrage against the founding principles of America? These were the remarks of the North Carolina legislature, made on November 12, 1789, as they chartered the University of North Carolina. This was the same legislature that ratified the Bill of Rights on December 11, 1789. While this was the action of a state government, it clearly seems that, for the North Carolina legislature, government could not only be a force for good and provide for the general welfare and public happiness, but it was its "indispensable duty" to do so. It seems that Beck is not as attuned to the foundations of America as he would like to believe. Or, at least, like us to believe.

Actually, the Framers were divided on the question of how to interpret the meaning of "the general welfare." James Madison wrote in his article "General View of the Powers Conferred by the Constitution" that the Constitution clearly specifies the power of Congress to raise taxes for a common treasury to pay for the common defense and general welfare of the union, and in his "The Alleged Danger from the Powers of the Union to the States Governments Considered" that these taxes should be raised from individual citizens.[7] In "The Influence of the State and Federal Governments Compared," Madison argued that the power of Congress to collect and decide how to spend taxes should not be limited by the states because the legislatures of the states are not likely to put the national interests ahead of those of their state.[8] For Madison, the Constitution sufficiently qualified the congressional power to tax, but this power must be limited to congressional powers enumerated in the Constitution. This has been termed as the *narrow interpretation* of "the general welfare." Hence, as president, he vetoed the 1817 Public Works Bill because he considered the improvement of state infrastructure, such as roads and canals, to be the responsibility of the states, not the federal government.

Alexander Hamilton argued that a powerful federal government was essential for the welfare and prosperity of the union, particularly for the small states.[9] In his article "The Necessity of a Government as Energetic as the One Proposed to the Preservation of the Union," he argued that it was in the national interest that how much the people were taxed and how those taxes were to be spent for the common defense and the general welfare were exclusively the powers of Congress. And in "Concerning the General Power of Taxation," he stated that it was the exclusive power of the federal government to decide which laws were necessary and how to execute them properly, while it was the obligation of the people to hold their government accountable to them and the Constitution.[10] Hamilton argued that the states should not abridge the federal government's power to collect taxes for "the general welfare."[11] For Hamilton, it was entirely up to the discretion of Congress to determine what constituted "the general welfare" and that this term could include education, agriculture, manufacturing, and commerce, providing that they were uniformly developed throughout the union rather than in one particular region or state. This has been termed the *broad interpretation* of "the general welfare."

President George Washington and President John Adams agreed with Hamilton's broad interpretation, while President Jefferson agreed with Madison's narrow one. For example, Jefferson considered the establishment of a national bank to be unconstitutional.[12] However, since that time, the Supreme Court has tended to adopt the narrow interpretation, until 1936, when it struck down parts of the 1933 Agricultural Adjustment Act as being unconstitutional for violating the Tenth Amendment and President Roosevelt threatened to put more Supreme Court judges on the bench.[13] Since 1936, the Supreme Court has followed the broad interpretation, which means that the Court accepts that Congress has the power to decide what "the general welfare" is and fund its provision as it deems fit. Furthermore, the Supreme Court accepts that the federal government has the right to withhold federal funds in order to coerce the states into accepting federal conditions and standards.[14] It remains to be seen whether or not this view changes in relation to states' rights challenges to the constitutionality of the 2010 Health Care and Education Reconciliation Act.

IS THE CONSTITUTION A STATIC TEXT OR LIVING DOCUMENT?

After chastising idiots for not reading the Constitution properly, Beck goes on to inform us that Article I, Section 9, Clause 1—"The Migration and Importation of such Persons as any of the States now existing shall think proper to admit, shall not be prohibited by the Congress prior to the Year one thousand eight hundred and eight, but a Tax or duty may be imposed on such Importation, not exceeding ten dollars for each person"—refers to immigration. He says that "the Founders actually put a price tag on coming to this country; $10 per person. Apparently they felt like there was actually a value to being able to live here. Not anymore. These days we can't ask *anything* of immigrants—including that they abide by our laws."[15]

This is quite a twistification! Clearly Beck needs to do some further reading if he wants to understand the original meaning of this clause. In eighteenth-century English, the meaning of the phrase "importation of such persons" refers to the slave trade, not immigration. This clause states that Congress will not prohibit the slave trade for twenty years and that it will not tax the importation of slaves by more than ten dollars per head. Immigrants were not taxed at all! It seems that Beck is not as attuned to the intent of the Framers and plain (eighteenth-century) English as he would like us to believe.

Actually, Beck downplays slavery in the Constitution. He is rather annoyed with anyone who even mentions that slaves were only treated as three-fifths of free persons in Article I, Section 1, Clause 3, which reads:

> Representatives and direct Taxes shall be apportioned among the several States which may be included within this Union, according to their respective Numbers, which shall be determined by adding the whole Number of free Persons, including those bound to Service for a Term of Years, and excluding Indians not taxed, three-fifths of all other persons.

Beck asserts that only an idiot would think that for the Founders this had anything to do with their estimation of the value of a slave's life in comparison with a free person's life. With an astounding twist of logic, he goes on to claim that many of the Founders actually wanted to eliminate slavery, but their hands were tied, and the three-fifths ratio was actually doing the slaves a favor!

Let's take a look at this twistification. Beck claims that the Framers agreed on this compromise to limit the power of the southern states and ensure that the abolition of slavery remained on the table. However, this is a gross oversimplification. Yes, the three-fifths compromise (as proposed by delegates James Wilson and Roger Sherman at the Philadelphia Convention of 1787) was agreed to in order to prevent the southern slave-owning states from using the number of their slaves to increase their proportion of representation and thereby dominate the House of Representatives. In turn, the southern states gained more representation than they otherwise would have had if the number of slaves had been excluded completely. However, this was not the only issue at stake. The northern states also wanted to tax the wealth of the southern states and thereby wanted slaves to be included in the number of persons for each of the slave-owning states (this is why the "Indians not taxed" are excluded from consideration altogether). Despite Robert Morris's protest that slaves should be either counted as whole persons or excluded completely, the delegates of free states wanted slaves counted as half a person, and the delegates of slave-owning states wanted them counted as three-quarters. The compromise was arrived at to achieve a balance between apportioning representatives and direct taxation according to the population of the states.[16] This had little to do, if anything, with keeping the elimination of slavery on the table.

It also needs to be remembered that, at that time, only white male property owners were able to vote (about 15 percent of the population).[17] The representatives of the state legislatures sent to the House of Representatives were all white male property owners. For the slave-owning states, the representatives were also predominantly slave owners. So not only was it the case that slaves were unable to vote, but the representatives of their state were among the same people who owned the slaves. And due to raising direct taxes in proportion to each state's population, the northern states also benefited greatly from the wealth produced by slave labor in the southern states. Talk about taxation without representation! Effectively, a slave paid a 100 percent income tax, while any hope of emancipation rested with the same people who had enslaved him in the first place, and made a tidy sum doing so, either directly or indirectly. As it was, even with this compromise, the interests of slave owners were disproportionately represented in the House of Representatives, in the presidency, and in the Supreme Court until the commencement of the Civil War in 1861. Regardless of what the Framers may or may not have intended, this compromise managed to keep the abolition of slavery off the table for over three-quarters of a century, and would have continued to do so if it had not been for the Civil War. Far from securing the future possibility of abolishing slavery, the three-fifths compromise benefited slave owners, reduced the tax burden on the northern states, and would have allowed for the institution of slavery to continue in perpetuity had it not been for the Civil War and the military defeat of the Confederacy, which placed the southern states under martial law and forced them to ratify the Thirteenth and Fourteenth Amendments as a condition for rejoining the union.

It is significant that just prior to the outbreak of the Civil War, the Corwin Amendment to the Constitution (which would have been the Thirteenth Amendment) prohibited Congress from ever abolishing slavery. It passed both the House and Senate by a two-thirds majority and was endorsed by President Buchanan and President Abraham Lincoln. It was set for ratification by the states until the events of the Civil War interrupted its ratification. The postwar passing of the Thirteenth Amendment (ratified in 1865) made the Corwin Amendment moot.

Of course, I am not suggesting that Beck is advocating the restoration of the three-fifths ratio. My point is that the Constitution is a historical document that has undergone changes and that Beck's attempts to downplay how the original document protected the institution of slavery amounts to revisionism. As well as twisting the meaning of Article I, Section 9, Clause 1, which specifically prohibited Congress from even discussing the abolition of the slave trade for twenty years and allowed the U.S. Treasury to profit from taxing it during that time, Beck conveniently forgets to mention Article IV, Section 2, Clause 3 of the Constitution, which reads, "No person held to Service or Labor in one State, under the laws thereof, escaping into another, shall, in Consequence of any Law or Regulation therein, be discharged from such Service or Labor, but shall be delivered up on the Claim of the Party to whom such Service or Labor may be due."

In other words, even if a slave managed to escape into a free state from a slave-owning state, the authorities of the free state had a constitutional obligation to return the person to his or her "owner." Such was the concern of the Framers for the plight of the slaves! So, if we take the trouble to read the Constitution in plain English, we can see that, regardless of any claims about their intentions, it seems that the Framers went to a great deal of trouble to secure and protect the institution of slavery while allowing the union to profit from revenues obtained from slave labor. It seems that, to paraphrase George Orwell, for the Framers, all men were equal, but some men were less equal than others. About three-fifths, I'd say.

However, Beck assures us that many of the Founders wanted to abolish slavery but were unable to. He claims it is unfair for us to morally judge them. Let's take a look at this plea.

Indeed, as Beck points out, Madison was opposed to slavery and seems to have been consistently so throughout his adult life (but he was born into a tobacco plantation–owning family, inheriting and owning the land when he came of age, and presumably he commercially benefited from slave labor). Madison's efforts against slavery were largely confined to writing down his moral struggle with it in relation to the needs of "the union." He considered the question of emancipation of slaves to be important but subordinate to the need for a strong union. Beck seems to sympathize with Madison, but would he apply the same logic to "nation building" in other countries? Consider the Soviet Union, for example. Beck has (quite rightly) opposed and denounced Stalin's policy and methods of "agricultural collectivization" in the Soviet Union during the late 1920s and early 1930s. Yet the effective enslavement of the peasantry, so as to export the grain (to the West, incidentally) to finance the industrialization of the Soviet Union, was justified by Stalin and the Communist Party as being historically necessary to strengthen the Soviet Union. However, just as we can condemn the enslavement of the peasantry in the USSR, so we can condemn slavery in the United States. Nation building is not a sufficient moral justification for the use of slave labor.

Furthermore, we can imagine Beck's reaction if President Barack Obama announced that, in order to maintain a strong federal government and help pay off the national debt, executives in the finance sector would be clothed, fed, and housed but have to pay an income tax of 100 percent. Beck considers it a moral outrage that the House of Representatives even proposed that AIG executives pay 90 percent tax on their bonuses they received after AIG was bailed out by the taxpayers, which he considers to be a "bill of attainder."[18] And we can imagine his reaction if, in the name of affirmative action, the federal government proposed that the white population were only allowed three-fifths representation in the House of Representatives! Despite Beck's protests to the contrary, Madison can be held morally accountable for his judgment that preserving "the union" took precedence over the abolition of slavery. Madison may well have been opposed to the slave trade, but he was also complicit in its constitutional institution. He wrote and signed the articles that protected the institution of slavery and allowed the federal government the right to gain revenue from it, and Madison was opposed to the Bill of Rights as being "unnecessary" because the articles were sufficient.

John Adams was opposed to slavery, did not own slaves, and he wrote uncompromising words about his loathing of slavery. However, in 1777, he spoke out against a bill to emancipate slaves in Massachusetts, and he was opposed to enrollment of slaves and freed slaves in the Continental Army because this was a "divisive issue" that would be opposed by the southern states. Again, he put the political needs of preserving "the union" before the equality and freedom of human beings. He was also the first president to sit in the White House, built by slave labor and completed in 1800.

Benjamin Franklin wrote extensively calling for the abolition of slavery. He too, however, put the question of slavery aside for the sake of the union, and it wasn't until toward the end of his life that, in 1785, he freed both of his slaves and became president of the Pennsylvania Abolition Society.

Hamilton had an even more morally ambiguous position in regard to slavery. He advocated allowing slaves to fight for their freedom by serving in the Continental Army, he openly opposed slavery and declared human beings to be equal regardless of skin color, he supported legislation that banned the export of slaves from New York, he supported Toussaint L'Ouverture and the free government in Haiti after the slaves overthrew the French-backed slave owners, he paid his servants rather than use domestic slaves, and he refused to support the forced deportation of freed slaves. But he also supported prohibiting congressional discussions of the abolition of slavery. Further, in 1785 he personally returned a fugitive slave to Henry Laurens of South Carolina, and he supported then President Washington's 1791 authorization of supplying the slave owners in Haiti with arms and money, before they were overthrown.

However, there is an argument that these men were men of their time, and it is unfair to charge them with hypocrisy. The ambiguity and contradictions of their actions and words were the ambiguity and contradictions of the time period and circumstances in which they found themselves. Of course we should confront the question of their complicity in the continuance of slavery for the sake of preserving the union, but this becomes part of a broader question of how the wealth of the United States of America was founded on slavery and how these men were fairly powerless to do much about it without undermining the union and the new nation. This is a question of the moral ambiguities and contradictions inherent in the origins of the United States of America.

However, for Washington and Jefferson, the charge of hypocrisy can be made. These men were strong public advocates of equality among men, expressed abhorrence about slavery, and yet were slave owners. Of course, Washington and Jefferson are two of Beck's heroes, so he is quick to make light of this charge. He admits that Washington and Jefferson owned slaves, but he points out that they opposed the slave trade. Were they hypocrites? To deflect the charge of hypocrisy against Washington and Jefferson, Beck tries to draw an analogy between hiring immigrant labor today and using slave labor in the eighteenth century. He says that in two centuries from now, if people were to decide that hiring undocumented migrant workers to mow their lawns or care for their children was immoral, then those people would be looked back on as racist hypocrites.[19] Beck seems to think that it will be easy to make those accusations, but he objects that no one is making them either now or in the eighteenth century.

One problem with this analogy is that people *were* making those accusations back in the eighteenth century. The movement for abolition existed and people considered it to be morally wrong and unchristian then. Another problem with this analogy is that people today would only be hypocritical if they said hiring illegal immigrants was wrong but still hired illegal immigrants. People who do not claim to be opposed to hiring illegal immigrants and are happy to hire them might be considered immoral in the future, and they might even be charged with breaking the law today, but they cannot be called hypocritical. Also, by trying to make a moral comparison between illegal immigration and slavery, once again Beck is confusing the migration and importation of persons. There is not any moral equivalence between enslaving people through violence and giving someone a job without checking their documents. Anyone in the future who condemns hiring undocumented migrant workers as cheap labor will almost certainly be scathing of people who used slave labor! So regardless of Beck's twistifications, Washington and Jefferson remain open to the charge of hypocrisy.

Let's briefly take a look at Washington. There is no question that he was a slave owner. By 1799, the year of his death, there were over three hundred slaves working on his Mount Vernon estate. Despite writing privately about his desire to see the abolition of slavery, he made very few public remarks on this issue. When he did write or speak publicly on the question of emancipation, he considered slavery to be *necessary* for the stability and growth of the newly formed nation and largely held that slavery would come to an end *eventually*. At the beginning of the War of Independence, Washington would not permit slaves or freed slaves to serve in the Continental Army; he reversed this decision after the British Lord Dunmore proclaimed that any slave who ran away from the rebels' lands and fought for the British would be given their freedom. Washington declared that Dunmore's proclamation violated private property rights and termed Dunmore as "an arch-traitor to the rights of humanity."[20] During the war, Washington wrote privately to his tobacco plantation manager that he wished "to get quit of negroes" and wrote to his friends that he wished to see the abolition of slavery to occur by "slow, sure and imperceptible means" but, after the war, he continued to buy slaves until 1798, and he continued efforts to recapture runaways from his Mount Vernon estate.[21]

During his presidency, he supported and authorized loans and the sale of weapons to the French slave owners in Saint-Dominigue (now called Haiti). He signed the 1790 Naturalization Act, which permitted only white persons to become citizens of the United States, specifically barring freed slaves from becoming citizens. He also signed the 1793 Fugitive Slave Act, which authorized runaway slave hunters to enter free states, recapture the slaves, and return them to their "owners." He could have vetoed either of these bills. After his presidency, he returned to Mount Vernon and started building a whisky still. While he continued to use slave labor to tend to and harvest the cereal, the still itself was a modern still and was not labor intensive. He employed workers for this. This left him with an "oversurplus" of slaves, as he termed these people, but he decided to keep these slaves rather than sell them and break up families. However, despite a 1782 Virginia law permitting the emancipation of slaves, Washington did not free any slaves during his lifetime.[22] Even if we accept that he was morally opposed to the slave trade, his actions show that he both took advantage of slavery and helped secure its practice. That is hypocrisy, by any standard, now or then.

Washington has been praised for signing the 1787 Northwest Ordinance (drafted by Jefferson) which, among other things, abolished slavery in the territories of Ohio, Indiana, Michigan, Illinois, and Wisconsin and protected tribal lands from invasion, trespass, and theft.[23] However, in practice, this was little more than a political move to balance the power of the slave-owning states, which were increasing the number of slaves and the number of representatives in Congress. When the tribes refused to permit settlements on their tribal lands, Washington assigned a new army under the command of General Anthony Wayne to defeat "the Indians not taxed" and force them off their lands.

Jefferson's position on slavery was complicated, inconsistent, and contradictory. He was a vocal opponent of the slave trade and tried unsuccessfully to legislate the emancipation of slaves in the Virginia General Assembly in 1769 and at the Continental Congress in 1784 (where he was defeated by a single vote). Yet he also bought, sold, and acquired many hundreds of slaves throughout his life (he owned over 260 slaves by 1822). He was the author of the Northwest Ordinance and the abolition of slavery in those territories, but as president, he did not veto Congress' suspension of abolition in the Northwest Territories, allowing each newly formed state to decide for itself whether or not to permit slavery. He campaigned for and in 1807 signed into law the abolition of the slave trade throughout the territories of the United States of

America. Yet only three years earlier, President Jefferson had opposed the anti-slavery revolt in Haiti, refusing to recognize their independence and imposing an embargo while making no provision for abolition or the prohibition of importation during the Louisiana Purchase (which aided France with the sum of $15 million). As secretary of state during Washington's presidency, in 1790 Jefferson had issued the French slave owners in Saint-Dominigue forty thousand dollars in emergency relief and one thousand weapons to help suppress the slave revolt (Washington later repaid the French slave owners four hundred thousand dollars for loans granted during the War of Independence). It has been argued that Jefferson's own debts prevented him from freeing his slaves, but in 1817, he refused the money to pay off debts left to him in the will of Thaddeus Kosciuszko (a general in the War of Independence) to allow Jefferson to free his slaves. After Kosciuszko's death, Jefferson refused this money, citing that he was "too old and tired."[24]

How can we understand such contradictory and inconsistent actions? If we take a look at his writings, such as his 1781 *Notes on the State of Virginia*, we can see that Jefferson was deeply racist.[25] He declared black people to be inferior to white people in intellect, morality, and physical appearance. He considered the nature of Africans and their descendants to be fixed and that the only possible way of improving their intellectual and moral capabilities was through mixed breeding with the white race. He also argued that slavery not only caused suffering and injury to black people but also harmed white people by making them brutal, surly, and lazy, unfit to be citizens of the Republic. He called for the emancipation of all slaves, arguing that equality of rights was not dependent on equality of ability, but also for their deportation back to Africa or their exchange for white settlers from other countries. His concern was that if freed slaves were to remain in America, racial tensions would inevitably lead to a race war, which would result in the annihilation of one race by the other. It was for this reason that he opposed the slave revolt in Saint-Dominigue.[26] He thought that, if it were successful, it would lead to slave revolts in the United States of America.

However, Jefferson changed many of his views after reading Henri Gregoire's 1808 book *An Enquiry Concerning the Intellectual and Moral Faculties and Literature of Negroes*, which refuted many of Jefferson's claims regarding the inequalities between Africans and Europeans.[27] Henceforth, Jefferson considered Africans to be potentially equal to Europeans in intellectual and moral capabilities, and he recognized that the intellectual and moral inequalities between American blacks and whites were due to upbringing and circumstances. He still maintained, however, that free white and black men could not live under the same government, due to the inequities and evils involved in the history of slavery. He insisted that peaceful emancipation and deportation was the only solution. While his attitude toward Africans and their American descendants did change throughout his life, as he worked for the end of the slave trade and the emancipation of slaves, he also remained quite trapped by the attitudes and ideas of his time.[28] He died on July 4, 1826. He had only freed two of his slaves (he also allowed another two to leave) during his lifetime.[29] He freed five in his will. The rest of his slaves were auctioned to pay off his debts.

My purpose in mentioning the above is not to vilify or condemn these men, but to show that they were men, caught up in the circumstances and attitudes of their time, possessed of attitudes that even in their own time were beginning to be considered immoral and outdated. The Constitution reflects the attitudes and aspirations of the people who wrote it. It is not a document written by "demigods"—as Jefferson termed the Philadelphia Convention delegates—but by men, warts and all. It is not a sacred text, to be followed and obeyed blindly, but should express the ideals and attitudes of the people for whom it is meaningful as *their* Constitution. It requires interpretation and debate, admits a plurality of views, and, from time to time, requires amendment. Just as the Thirteenth, Fourteenth, and Fifteenth Amendments made the slavery clauses of Article I obsolete by abolishing slavery and giving all men equal rights under the law (although this was not extended to women until 1920 by the Nineteenth Amendment), so the Constitution changes along with changes in society. It should be understood as a living document that reflects the shared attitudes and ideals of the vast majority of people of the United States of America.

Beck denounces the claim that the Constitution is a living document, open to interpretation and change depending on changes in American society, values, and circumstances. He considers that to be a progressive view and, as such, part of the cancer that is undermining the foundational principles of America. He often claims that the Founders did not intend for the Constitution to be changed and that modern Americans should remain true to its original meaning. However, if we look at Jefferson's views on the matter, we can see that at least one Founding Father was committed to the view that the Constitution should be open to change.

In his 1816 letter to Samuel Kercheval, Jefferson argued that the Constitution should be rewritten every generation (every nineteen or twenty years) because "the dead have no rights" and the living should choose for themselves the form of government best suited to their own happiness and good.[30] In a 1789 letter to Madison, Jefferson argued that people have no right to impose laws on future generations. Imposing unalterable laws on future generations or being unquestioningly loyal to the laws of the past would suppose that "the earth belongs to the dead and not the living."[31] As he wrote in his 1824 letter to John Cartwright, "A generation may bind itself as long as its majority continues in life; when that has disappeared, another majority is in place, holds all the rights and powers their predecessors once held and may change their laws and institutions to suit themselves. Nothing then is unchangeable but the inherent and unalienable rights of man."[32] It seems that, according to Jefferson, at least, the Constitution should be rethought and rewritten by every generation.

Of course, the process of amending the Constitution should be long and drawn out, as described in Article V, in order to give people time to deliberate properly such changes and that these genuinely represent the deliberations of the vast majority of people, otherwise the Constitution would simply be rewritten with every changing whim or fashion and would cease to be a constitution at all. In my view, however, the processes involved in deliberating and amending the Constitution should not be limited to state and national legislatures, just as the process of interpretation should not be limited to being the purview of the Supreme Court. The processes of deliberating, interpreting, and amending the Constitution needs to be more democratic and involve the citizenry if it is to be truly an expression of the people. It needs to be noted that the word "democracy" is not used in the Constitution. Not once. In the last chapter of this book, chapter 12, I shall discuss democracy and the Constitution, as well as the nature of public debate in America, and look at how the citizenry can and should become directly involved in debating, ir preting, reinvigorating, and reclaiming the Constitution through a   il convention.

DEMOCRACY AND THE CONSTITUTION

What does Beck have to say about democracy and the Constitution? Not a great deal, but he does have some quibbles. So let's take a look at these. One of them is with the first clause of Article I, Section 3: "The Senate of the United States shall be comprised of two Senators from each State, chosen by the Legislature thereof for six years; and each Senator shall have one vote."

Of course, Beck immediately wants to justify this provision as being the prudent choice of those wise old Founding Fathers.[33] First, he claims that the provision was necessary to persuade the states to ratify the Constitution. But why would this be the case? There never was any question of "the people" being allowed to vote. The original Constitution only allowed white landowners to vote for representatives in the state legislature. It was simply the case that the states with low populations wanted representation equal to that of states with high populations (as they already had in the Articles of Confederation). The Framers—especially Madison—were staunchly anti-democratic, considering democracy to be tantamount to mob rule, and that government should represent those people with a stake in society, that is, landowners. The landless, uneducated, and unwashed (or unperfumed, more to the point) masses couldn't possibly have anything constructive to offer government. As Madison put it, "democracies have ever been the spectacles of turbulence and contention: have ever been found incompatible with personal security or the rights of property . . . have in general been as short in their lives as they have been violent in their deaths."[34]

Adams considered Paine's ideas to be "so democratical" that they could only "produce confusion and every evil work."[35] It is quite telling that when Jefferson and Madison formed the Republican Party (nothing to do with the modern Republican Party) in opposition to the Federalists, their party was called "the democrats" by the opposition—as an insult! The Democratic-Republican Party, as it came to be known, only changed its name to the Democratic Party in 1844. (It is interesting to note that the Framers had not written the possibility of political parties into the Constitution. This caused serious problems for the election of the president and vice president in the 1800 election between Adams, with Charles Pickney, running on the Federalist Party ticket, and Jefferson, with Aaron Burr, running on the Republican Party ticket. The Twelfth Amendment was ratified in 1804 to resolve this oversight.)

Beck's second justification for this "seemingly undemocratic" clause was that the Framers wanted senators to be able to vote in accordance with their conscience rather than "pandering to any specific group of voters."[36] Is Beck saying that the Framers wisely prevented senators from being accountable to the people of each state because otherwise they would have to do what those people wanted rather than what the senators wanted? Who was the legislature supposed to represent? Whose opinions was it supposed to voice? Beck's position makes me wonder how he would react if a senator today informed the media that Congress knows best and the ordinary American people should just shut up and let them get on with it. My guess is that he might accuse that senator of being out of touch or a spokesman for Big Government. However, according to Beck, in the eighteenth century, the people of the various states would have just constituted "special interest groups," whereas, of course, the landowning white men who comprised the state legislatures and elected their senators (from among themselves) could never be described as a special interest group that was pandered to!

As Beck reluctantly admits, this supposedly well-intended measure was a disaster.[37] Infighting among the state legislatures resulted in seats not being filled in the Senate, and as he points out, this was eventually changed by the Seventeenth Amendment (ratified in 1913), which ensured senators were elected by the people. However, Beck asks whether term limits for senators should be considered to counterbalance this progressive measure. One might even suspect that Beck wishes the Seventeenth Amendment to be repealed. It seems that he does not like popular senators being reelected for "pandering to their constituents." That would be too *democratical!*

Beck's dislike of democracy is also apparent whenever he discusses the presidency of Franklin Delano Roosevelt.[38] He complains that it took the Twenty-second Amendment to make sure that a "popularist" such as FDR, who was elected with overwhelming majority support for a fourth term, would not happen again. His implication is that the Twenty-second Amendment (ratified in 1951) was in some way a congressional censure of FDR for acting unconstitutionally. In addition to dismissing the significance of the fact that there was not any constitutional term limit for presidents at that time, Beck has ignored the fact that FDR was president during the Second World War, which started during his second term. It seems that there is a case for claiming that these were extraordinary times for which continuity of the presidency was understandable. Beck's implication that this was somehow unconstitutional simply does not make sense. It seems to me that Beck's complaint is based on nothing more than his sneering contempt for the electorate and his dislike of FDR. (See chapter 10 for further discussion.)

CONSTITUTIONAL POWERS AND LIMITS OF GOVERNMENT

What does Beck have to say about the powers of Congress? He is quite right to quip that Congress has never had any difficulty following the constitutional clause empowering it to borrow money, but he does take an interestingly narrow interpretation of the Commerce Clause: "To regulate Commerce with foreign Nations, and among the several States, and with the Indian Tribes."

For Beck, the significance of this clause comes down to states' rights and Congress having no authority to regulate commerce within states. We shall come back to this when discussing the Tenth Amendment. However, what I find interesting is what he does not say. Beck tells us that the Founders intended government to keep its hands off private business. He argues that government regulation of business is an infringement upon the "free market." Yet in this clause we see that the Framers intended unequivocally for Congress to regulate all interstate and international commerce, and this section of the Constitution gives Congress the right to levy taxes and duties as well. It seems that the Framers intended for Congress to have a great deal of regulatory oversight over and raise revenue from commerce. And with the ratification of the Sixteenth Amendment in 1913, Congress also has the power to levy income tax (which Beck blames President Woodrow Wilson and progressives for; see chapters 10 and 11 for further discussion).

Article I, Section 8, contains an extensive list of the powers and duties of Congress. The first clause states, "The Congress should have Power To lay and collect Taxes, Duties, Imposts and Excises, to pay the Debts and provide for the common Defense and general Welfare of the United States; but all Duties, Imposts, and Excises shall be uniform throughout the United States." Beck has nothing to say about this clause, apart from what is not in it. His complaint is with a recent law proposed by Congress that taxes heavily the bonuses received by AIG executives after they received a federal bailout. He complains that this tax amounts to a "redistribution of wealth." Odd choice of phrase, I know, to describe the *taking back* of 90 percent of bonuses provided by taxpayers' money in the first place. It seems particularly perverse of him to interpret this as Congress "imposing extraordinary taxes on successful people … to 'redistribute wealth' to the less fortunate."[39] One might suggest that if these people were so "successful" then they would have not have needed federal bailout money in the first place. One might also suggest that it is reasonable for the representatives of "less fortunate" people to object to taxpayers' money going toward executive bonuses for bailed out companies—at least not until those companies have paid back the bailout. In my view, the only extraordinary thing about this whole affair is that Congress bailed out AIG at all!

With some amusement, one can understand why Beck neglects to even mention that the Constitution explicitly gives Congress the right and duty to "establish Post Offices and post Roads," given that he tells us repeatedly that the Framers did not intend for government to run such things as the postal service, to build highways or railroads, or to have anything whatsoever to do with methods of communication throughout America. Similarly, it is interesting to see how Beck leaps to denounce President Obama's promises to "restore science to its rightful place" on the basis of the clause "To promote the Progress of Science and useful Arts, by securing for limited Times to Authors and Inventors the exclusive Rights to their respective Inventions and Discoveries."

Oddly enough, rather than criticize the vagueness of Obama's pledge, Beck psychically channels the Framers to have only intended this to mean twenty-first-century patent and copyright protection laws. However, what this clause does is impose on Congress the duty to protect the exclusive rights of authors and inventors to their writings and inventions for unspecified "limited Times." It does not protect their right to sell patents to corporations so the latter can sit on them in order to prevent competition and maintain a monopoly in the market. It does not protect the right of authors and inventors to sell these patents at all. It also implies that after this limited time has passed, such exclusive rights are not protected. What does this mean? Arguably, after this limited time, they become public domain. Again, the Constitution allows for interpretation and debate. Furthermore, given that the first clause in this section gives Congress the right to raise taxes and use them for the general welfare, it seems not too much of a stretch to suggest that to "promote the Progress of Science and useful Arts" might allow for some public funding of education, science, and technology.

In his discussion of Article I, Section 6, and the "Saxbe fix," which he considers to be "an abomination," Beck once again demonstrates his partisan reading of the Constitution.[40] But what is the "Saxbe fix"? Let's take a closer look. The "Saxbe fix" is the name given to a salary rollback mechanism that allows the president to appoint a sitting congressman to a Cabinet position and thereby avoid their ineligibility under Section 6 and Clause 2 of Article I:

> No Senator or Representative shall, during the Time for which he was elected, be appointed to any civil Office under the Authority of the United States, which shall have been created, or the Emoluments whereof shall have been increased during such time; and no Person holding an Office under the United States, shall be a Member of either House during his Continuance in Office.

In other words, senators and representatives cannot be appointed to any position that was either created or awarded greater salary or benefits during their elected term of office. The "Saxbe fix" involves rolling back the salary and benefits to the level they were at the time the congressman was elected to Congress. Beck claims that this clause was violated by President Jimmy Carter (who appointed Ed Muskie as secretary of state) and by President Bill Clinton (who appointed Lloyd Bensten). However, his real target is Hillary Clinton's appointment as secretary of state, which he claims was unconstitutional. He accuses Congress of shredding the Constitution by using the "Saxbe fix" to confirm her appointment. However, although this "fix" is named after Senator William Saxbe (who, as Beck rightly points out, was nominated by President Nixon, a Republican, in 1973 to the office of attorney general), this rollback mechanism was first implemented by Congress in 1909 to confirm Republican president William Taft's appointment of Philander Knox as secretary of state. Beck would like to blame Democrats for this "abomination," but it was established by Republican appointments long before it became a commonly used mechanism by presidents from both parties. Even President Reagan considered using it to get Senator Orrin Hatch confirmed as a Supreme Court Justice, but in the end, Anthony Kennedy was appointed and confirmed. Now, while there are legitimate questions regarding its constitutionality, is it reasonable to call this fix "an abomination"?

The purpose of this clause in the Constitution was to prevent individuals from holding more than one position in two branches of government simultaneously, and to prevent congressmen from creating new federal offices or increasing salaries for themselves. The "Saxbe fix" does not allow either of these proscriptions to be violated. Furthermore, since 1992, when the Twenty-seventh Amendment was ratified, congressmen are unable to award themselves a pay rise until an election of representatives has intervened. It is also the case that the "Saxbe fix," since 1980, has been used only as a temporary measure, extending only until the congressman's term of office has expired. Obviously, if we take the wording of the Constitution literally, this is a fudge, but it also has to be pointed out that if we do take the wording literally, this clause does not apply to Hillary Clinton anyway, given that she is a woman and the Framers had no expectation of a woman ever being elected to Congress or being appointed as secretary of state. Of course, we would think this literal interpretation to be ridiculous. Obviously this clause should apply to a female senator as it does to her male colleagues. As I have already said, the Constitution cannot be treated as a sacred, static text, and the interpretation and significance of various clauses change as society changes. Yes, perhaps Beck is right and Congress should amend this clause, but if its purpose is to maintain the separation of powers and prevent corruption, then the "Saxbe fix" suffices to respect the spirit of the clause, even if it does not follow its exact wording. Maybe Congress is right to consider this problem solved and move on to more pressing concerns of government.

For example, if Congress has the time to consider an amendment to the Constitution, it should consider the presidential use of "signing statements." In my opinion, Beck is quite right to question the constitutionality of presidential signing statements. According to the Constitution (Article I, Section 7; Article II, Section 3), the president has the choice to either send the law unsigned back to Congress or "take care that the laws be faithfully executed." As they stand, signing statements, wherein the president either declares provisions within the law as unconstitutional or informs federal agencies how the law should be interpreted, threaten the separation of powers. However, while Beck is right to point out that these statements have been used by presidents since James Monroe, what he does not mention is that, until Ronald Reagan, only seventy-five signing statements had been issued in total. These were mostly political and rhetorical statements that a president attached to his signing of a bill for the sake of posterity. Between President Reagan, President George H. W. Bush, and President Clinton, 247 signing statements had been issued raising either constitutional queries or giving executive interpretation. Since Bush Junior took office, 157 signing statements have been issued, either taking issue with over one thousand provisions of federal law or stating how these provisions should be interpreted by federal agencies. President Obama has followed in his predecessor's footsteps.

However, the problem is that the Constitution does require interpretation and it periodically requires amendments to clarify the procedures and rules of the presidency, Congress, and elections (the Twentieth, Twenty-second, Twenty-third, and Twenty-fifth Amendments all being examples of this). Given the complexities involved in taking "care that the laws be faithfully executed," it may well be the case that presidential signing statements are a political fact of life in the executive branch of government and the numerous federal agencies that it directs. Beck avoids the reality that the Constitution needs to be interpreted and, as American society and government have changed and become increasingly complicated, signing statements perhaps represent genuine attempts by the executive branch to state and clarify how legislation should be executed in the light of these complexities.

How does Beck view the federal obligation to protect the rights of citizens? Perhaps, most shockingly, he seems to view the constitutional clause allowing the suspension of habeas corpus "when in Cases of Rebellion or Invasion the public Safety may require it" as something to celebrate. Although he does not elaborate upon his source of glee, he implies that he objects to the idiotic view that habeas corpus is an absolute right under the Constitution. However, this contradicts his argument in the chapter on the "Nanny State" in *Arguing with Idiots*, in which he objects to freedom being curtailed in the name of public safety. (I shall discuss this notion of the "Nanny State," as well as Prohibition and the Eighteenth and Twenty-first Amendments, in chapter 7.) But he is right. Habeas corpus is not an absolute right under the Constitution. It was suspended by George W. Bush during cases of "extraordinary rendition" and holding "enemy combatants" in the Guantánamo Bay prison without affording them the rights of either POWs or accused criminals. It also was suspended by President Roosevelt after the Pearl Harbor attack, when Japanese Americans were interned, without charge or accusation. And it was suspended by President Lincoln during the Civil War. Actually, in 1861, the Supreme Court overruled Lincoln.[41] Chief Justice Roger Taney ruled that Lincoln's suspension of habeas corpus was unconstitutional. Lincoln ignored the verdict. However, what Beck does not ask is, who has the right to suspend habeas corpus? Who decides when public safety is sufficiently threatened? Given that this section of the Constitution falls under Article I, it would suggest that this authority belonged to Congress rather than the president.

What does Beck have to say about the executive powers of the presidency? Apart from noting that Article II does not give the president the authority to run private companies, Beck does not really have anything to say about the limits and powers of the executive branch. He is much more concerned with Article III and the power of the Supreme Court. The problem is that he can't quite make up his mind whether he is for or against it. He is against any notion of judicial activism or judicial review, except when the Supreme Court rules in favor of states' rights, in which case he considers the Supreme Court to be the champion of freedom. He is against judges interpreting the Constitution, except when they so happen to interpret it in a way that he agrees with. But what is judicial review?

Even though judicial review was discussed by Hamilton in the *Federalist Papers* before the Constitution was even ratified, as mentioned at the opening of this chapter, the Supreme Court power of judicial review dates back to the case of *Marbury v. Madison* in 1803. This case was the result of Adams' election defeat by Jefferson. After his defeat, the day before his first and only term was to end, Adams appointed Federalist judges (sixteen circuit judges and forty-two justices of the peace), thus making sure that a Federalist judiciary continued after his presidency. Jefferson, of course, was a Democratic-Republican who advocated states' rights. Adams managed to push these appointments through the Senate, but the letters of appointment had yet to be delivered. Upon taking office the next day, President Jefferson ordered Madison, the new secretary of state, to withhold any undelivered judicial commissions. One of the withheld commissions was that of William Marbury, who appealed to the Supreme Court to order that his letter of appointment as justice of the peace be delivered to him. Chief Justice Marshall presided over this case (despite the fact that he was Madison's predecessor as secretary of state, in charge of delivering the commissions under former President Adams!). He ruled against Secretary of State Madison as having acted unconstitutionally, and, by doing so, he claimed for the Supreme Court the power of judicial review.

However, this power is not specifically mentioned in the Constitution. Jefferson was so outraged by this decision that he not only needed to invent a new word—twistification—for Justice Marshall's opinion, but also said, "The opinion which gives to the judges the right to decide what laws are constitutional and what not, not only for themselves in their own sphere of action but for the Legislature and Executive also in their spheres, would make the Judiciary a despotic branch."[42]

Yet despite the fact that the Supreme Court is unable to enforce its judgments without the consent of the other two branches of government, it has maintained its power to decide whether the actions of the executive branch or the laws passed by the legislative branch are indeed constitutional. Despite having over two centuries to do so, Congress has not attempted to challenge this notion that the power of judicial review belongs to the Supreme Court. Furthermore, Marshall's opinion did not come out of thin air. Arguably, judicial review is implied by the Constitution, in Article III, Section 2, which states that "the Supreme Court shall have appellate Jurisdiction, both as to Law and Fact, with such Exceptions and under such Regulations as Congress shall make." And, after all, if the Supreme Court is independent of the executive and legislative branches of government, and all other courts are inferior, then should the Supreme Court find a law to be unconstitutional, on what basis could the executive or legislative branch *compel* the judiciary to apply the law to the letter? And without judicial review, in what way could the Supreme Court act as a "check and balance" on the president and Congress? It can be argued that it is anti-democratic to allow nine judges to decide laws (or even one judge if he or she so happens to be a swing vote on the bench), and at present there is nothing that can prevent judicial activism (writing laws from the bench) apart from the conscience of the judges. However, this argument fails to acknowledge that there is an important "check and balance" on the Judiciary called *impeachment*, which allows a judge to be removed from office should she or he undermine the Constitution.[43]

For now, while we are on the subject of impeachment, I should like to bring up the topic of "good behavior," which is constitutionally demanded of Supreme Court judges. Beck seems to have a particular problem with Supreme Court Justice Ruth Bader Ginsburg. Why? He is irked at her because she expressed an opinion in a speech at Ohio State University that U.S. judges would be well advised to look toward international law and the rulings of judges from other countries to help them rule on cases. He questions whether this counts as "good behavior" (i.e., whether it qualifies as "during good behavior") and whether Justice Ginsburg should be impeached and removed from the Supreme Court. Apparently, according to Beck, even the suggestion that judges look toward international law or foreign court precedents for advice counts as "Treason, Bribery, or other high Crimes and Misdemeanors." Is Beck accusing Justice Ginsburg of "misconduct," which would imply an attempt to subvert the Constitution? But why should he take such an extreme view? Apparently, he implies that making such a suggestion is in breach of her oath of office.

It is not to Beck's liking that Justice Ginsburg is not looking exclusively enough to "the Constitution and laws of the United States." But let's take a look at Article III, Section 2 of the Constitution:

> The judicial Power shall extend to all Cases, in Law and Equity, arising under this Constitution, the Laws of the United States, and Treaties made, or which shall be made, under their Authority;—to all Cases affecting Ambassadors, other public Ministers and Consuls;—to all Cases of admiralty or maritime Jurisdiction;—to Controversies to which the United States shall be a Party;—to Controversies between two or more States;—between a State and Citizens of another State;—between Citizens of different States;—between Citizens of the same State claiming Lands under Grants of different States, and between a State, or the Citizens thereof, and foreign States, Citizens, or Subjects.

If we take a look at the phrase "and Treaties made, or which shall be made, under their Authority," it would seem that the Supreme Court has the authority to consider treaties entered into by the United States alongside the laws of the United States. But wait! There's more. In fact, under Article II, Section 2 of the Constitution, the president has the power to make treaties "with the Advice and Consent of the Senate." Wouldn't it be in breach of the separation of powers for the Supreme Court to ignore treaties signed by the president "with the Advice and Consent of the Senate"? Actually, Article VI of the Constitution answers this question for us: "This Constitution, and the Laws of the United States which shall be made in Pursuance thereof; *and of all Treaties made, or which shall be made, under the Authority of the United States, shall be the supreme Law of the Land; and the judge of every State shall be bound thereby, any Thing in the Constitution or Laws of any State to the Contrary notwithstanding.*"

So it turns out that the Supreme Court has an obligation to treat treaties as the laws of the United States. Given that international law is based on treaties between the United States and other nations, it would seem that not only would the Supreme Court be well advised to look toward international law, but it has a constitutional obligation to do so and to treat international law as the law of the United States. We can hardly consider it treasonous for Justice Ginsburg to obey the law and her oath to do so. Clearly, Beck must be thinking of some other kind of "high crime and misdemeanor." But what of her heinous suggestion that judges could look to foreign courts for precedents? Surely, Justice Ginsburg has gone too far. Well, no. She did not say that judges should obey foreign powers over and above the laws of the United States. What she said was that the decisions of foreign judges could help Supreme Court judges in the same way as a law review article written by a professor could. It seems that, once again, Beck has been indulging in the not so subtle art of twistification!

In the mode typical of the media pundit and propagandist, Beck tries to slip between discussing the meaning of "good behavior" in relation to Justice Ginsburg's liberal jurisprudence to complain about how Americans have become too tolerant of traitors. He complains that "it is now impossible to rise to the level of 'treason' in this country" and that the "penalty for treason is no longer death, it is state-sponsored therapy."[44] Of course, this assertion is false. Americans captured in Afghanistan and Iraq while fighting against U.S. Armed Forces have been arrested, held as "enemy combatants," and charged with treason. I suspect that Beck is sulking about the 2004 Supreme Court case of *Yaser Esam Hamdi v. Donald Rumsfeld*.[45] In 2001, Hamdi was captured in Afghanistan and held as an "enemy combatant," first in Guantánamo Bay and later in South Carolina. He was held in solitary confinement without charge and not permitted to communicate with anyone, including legal counsel. In 2002 his father filed an appeal for habeas corpus. Although opinion was divided on the legal principles involved, the Supreme Court overruled the lower court dismissal of the appeal for habeas corpus. While the Court ruled that the president did have the authority to hold American citizens as "enemy combatants," the Court also ruled that either they must be afforded due process or Congress should pass an act and suspend habeas corpus. As a result, Hamdi regained his right as a citizen to have the evidence against him presented and reviewed in a court. Or, perhaps, Beck is upset with the Supreme Court for ruling that the military commissions set up in Guantánamo Bay violated both the Uniform Code of Military Justice and the Geneva Conventions.[46] It is possibly the mention of these foreign Geneva Conventions that has upset Beck's sense of patriotism (although the U.S. government did sign these conventions in 1949 and thereby agreed to abide by them). Although, the final straw might be the Supreme Court ruling that all constitutional rights extend to all prisoners (including foreigners!) at Guantánamo.[47] This meant that all detainees should be afforded due process.

What I suspect lies at the heart of Beck's complaint is that the Supreme Court and American liberals do not share his nationalistic and conservative understanding of patriotism, which would allow the government the power to arrest and detain anyone at all, without having to give any reasons or afford that person any rights whatsoever, for as long as the government deemed fit, providing that the government classified that person as an "enemy combatant." It seems that, far from advocating small government based on the Constitution, Beck is twisting how the Constitution should be read in order to legitimate an all-powerful militaristic police state. It seems that even affording prisoners the right to due process is tantamount to "giving Aid and Comfort to the Enemy." However, regardless of what the person is accused of, in a republic based on equality under constitutional law, all persons are equal under the law. Trial by military commissions, admitting evidence obtained by torture, coercion, suspicion, hearsay, and secret evidence and witnesses, should not be acceptable, especially when the accused could be convicted of treason and executed, if Beck has his way.

Of course, it goes without saying that Beck is entitled to his opinion. We all are. This brings us nicely to the Bill of Rights and the First Amendment: "Congress shall make no law respecting an establishment of religion, or prohibiting the free exercise thereof; or abridging the freedom of speech, or of the press; or the right of the people peacefully to assemble, and to petition the Government for the redress of grievances."

Surprisingly, Beck does not have much to say about the First Amendment. He only discusses religion—primarily to make the claim that this amendment does not secure "the separation of Church and State"—and ignores the other provisions: freedom of speech, freedom of the press, freedom of peaceable assembly and association, and the freedom to petition the government. Instead of discussing these very important provisions, Beck informs us that the term "separation of Church and State" does not appear in the Constitution. Indeed, it does not. He also informs us that it first appeared in a letter written by Jefferson to the Danbury Baptists Association in 1802 (fifteen years after the Constitution was written), while Jefferson was president.[48] On this, Beck adopts a strict constructionist line—arguing that we should stick to the literal wording—and claims that religions were protected from the government, not the other way around, and, therefore, apparently, this means that there can be religious displays on public property, which, one may presume, also includes things such as prayer in public schools. He is right to point out that "the establishment clause" simply means that Congress cannot make any law that establishes a religion; this clause prohibits any official or national religion (such as the Church of England). As he also points out, "the free exercise clause" protects beliefs and opinions, but not all actions. As the Supreme Court has ruled, although not always consistently, a person cannot commit illegal actions (such as polygamy, human sacrifice, smoking marijuana, or eating hallucinogenic mushrooms) on the grounds of religious practice.

However, what Beck does not inform us is that Jefferson first discussed the notion of the separation of Church and State in his *Notes on the State of Virginia*, which discusses this as an essential concept for a free society and already written into the Virginia constitution. Jefferson's description of the First Amendment as "building a wall of separation between Church and State" (in his 1802 letter to the Danbury Baptists) was taken from the book titled *The Bloody Tenent of Persecution* written by Roger Williams, Baptist theologian and founder of the Rhode Island colony, in 1644. The concept of the importance of secular government for religious freedom can be seen also in the 1777 *Virginia Statute for Religious Freedom* (authored by Jefferson), which declares that civil government should be separate from religion. While the phrase "separation of Church and State" does not appear in the Constitution, neither does the phrase "separation of powers," and this is taken to be basic to the nature of the Republic. Neither does the word "federal" or "democracy" appear in the Constitution, yet these words have all been used to interpret the Constitution. Arguably, the separation of Church and State is implied by "the nonestablishment clause." While this was intended to protect religions from persecution by the state, and to protect the already existent religions within the various states from interference from Congress, it needs to be recognized that, in order to do that, the state cannot endorse or support any one religion over the others. In other words, in order to protect the religious freedom of anyone, the state cannot have anything to do with any religion at all. The state must remain a secular arrangement of institutions. This means that public funds cannot be used to support or promote any religion or religious practice, which is why prayer is not permitted in public schools, and religious displays should be kept off government buildings (although the Supreme Court has not been consistent about this either).

The Second Amendment is the only amendment that Beck considers worthy of a chapter in its own right in *Arguing with Idiots*. I shall discuss this in detail in chapter 2. Beck does not have a great deal to say about the Third and the Fourth Amendments. I shall discuss these amendments further in chapter 8. However, Beck does briefly indulge in a bit of twistification when discussing the phrase "unreasonable searches and seizures" in the Fourth Amendment, which states: "The right of the people to be secure in their persons, houses, papers, and effects, against unreasonable searches and seizures, shall not be violated, and no Warrants shall issue, but upon probable cause, supported by Oath or affirmation, and particularly describing the place to be searched, and the persons or things to be seized."

Unsurprisingly, Beck does not consider it necessary for this amendment to be taken literally, and he ignores the phrase "shall not be violated, and no Warrants shall issue, but upon probable cause." Although, as we have already seen, Beck denounces the "Saxbe fix" as "an abomination," he had this to say about "warrantless wiretapping": "At this point, your idiot friend is likely screaming, 'George Bush's warrantless wiretapping program!' I don't know of a single American citizen (who's never had a conversation with an Osama wannabe in some musty cave in Pakistan) that is actually affected by this program ... and neither does your idiot friend."[49]

Here we see another example of Beck cherry-picking from the Constitution. When it suits his argument, he does not have any problem with governmental violation of the Constitution. Putting aside my hunch that I doubt that Beck is privy to classified documents and he does not in fact know whether anyone he knows is affected by this program, one of the reasons there is the need for a warrant before wiretapping is to leave a paper trail among various government agencies, which prevents police or federal agents from using wiretaps for personal gain, to obtain business secrets, or to pry into otherwise personal conversations for personal reasons. It is also the case that the need for a warrant provides a "check and balance" (again by leaving a paper trail) to prevent the executive branch from using wiretaps to spy on political opponents (anyone remember Nixon?). There is also a First Amendment issue to consider. After all, how can the freedom of the press, or the freedom of association, or privileged speech (say, between a lawyer and client, a doctor and patient, or even spouses) be protected if government agents can pry into these conversations any time they wish, without having to justify that intrusion to a judge and leave a record of having done so? The Fourth Amendment secures a very important "check and balance" between the three branches of government. After all, who is to decide whether or not a search and seizure is "unreasonable"? According to Beck, this is pretty much the decision of the executive branch and the federal agents doing the searching and seizing. But isn't that a police-state principle of jurisprudence? I would say so.

It is not difficult for federal agents to obtain a warrant to set up a wiretap. The 1978 Foreign Intelligence Surveillance Act (FISA) allows for a secret court (FISC) to issue warrants and even for a review (FISCR) if FISC does not issue a warrant for some reason. If any American citizen is suspected of communicating with a suspected spy or terrorist, FISA even provides everything federal agents need to obtain a warrant retrospectively (the wiretap can be set up in advance if the agent has a reasonable expectation of obtaining a warrant). So, what is Beck's issue about warrantless wiretaps and the Fourth Amendment? He is not at all clear on this point. All of a sudden, when it comes to warrantless wiretapping, we should just trust the government.

But why isn't FISA sufficient? In my opinion, what Beck is defending is the 2007 Protect America Act (PAA) which allowed the federal government the right to wiretap, without needing a warrant, any phone call that began or ended in a foreign country (this is also provided for in FISA, but providing that American citizens are not involved). It is this law that could have been challenged as a violation of the Fourth Amendment, and given that FISA provided the means to obtain a warrant retrospectively and in secret, it makes me wonder why PAA was needed at all. Of course, arguably, the reason why it was needed was that under PAA the executive could classify all or any aspect of the wiretapping program and conceal it from Congress and the Supreme Court. It means that federal agents could wiretap anyone without leaving a paper trail available to all three branches of government. Given that federal agents would have no trouble whatsoever in obtaining an FISC warrant for wiretapping suspected spies or terrorists (or drug dealers, for that matter), it makes me wonder who the federal government was really spying on. Could it have been their political opponents? Perhaps we will never know, but the PAA had a "sunset clause" that expired in 2008. However, as Beck points out, the Obama administration has expanded the legal basis of the executive branch's authority to conduct warrantless wiretapping. It would seem that, finally, Beck can be proud of something done by President Obama!

Beck goes into more detail when discussing the Fifth Amendment. He discusses the phrases "twice put in jeopardy," "witness against himself," and "public use." Given his views on habeas corpus and the Fourth Amendment, however, it should come as little surprise to note that he omitted discussing the phrase "nor be deprived of life, liberty, or property, without due process of law." The concept of "due process" is a fundamental principle of law, which is also made applicable to the states by the Fourteenth Amendment. Warrantless wiretapping, extraordinary rendition, and being held as an "enemy combatant" without charge all violate the notion of "due process." By doing so, the constitutional notion of "equality under the law" is undermined, which turns citizens back to being subjects and undermines the very principle upon which the republican form of government is founded. In fact, the principle of "due process" dates back to the English common law principles of "the presumption of innocence until proven guilty" and a "fair trial." These principles place the burden of proof on the accuser rather than the accused, and they form the basis for the notion of "probable cause" as a condition for obtaining a warrant and performing a search or arrest. They also form the basis for the right to remain silent when questioned by the police. The idea that a citizen has a right not to "be deprived of life, liberty, or property, without due process of law" seems to get in the way of Beck's apparent faith that only a guilty person would be subject to arrest, held indefinitely, and executed as a traitor if the government declares them to be an "enemy combatant" or a "terrorist." But, if the government cannot be trusted to run the post office, how can it be trusted to run wiretapping   grams and secret courts?

Regarding "eminent domain," Beck does mention that the recent Supreme Court decision that allowed a Connecticut city to seize private property so it could make money by selling it to a developer ran contrary to the original intent of the term "public use."[50] Beck is referring to the 2005 *Kelo v. City of New London* case.[51] The city condemned Susette Kelo's house and fourteen other properties in a working-class neighborhood, seized them under eminent domain, citing "economic development," and then sold these properties to a private corporation. The Supreme Court voted 5–4 that this was constitutional. While Beck does disapprove of the court's decision, he does not discuss how this is yet another example of how Big Business is interfering with government—how the institution of local government and the Supreme Court have become instruments of corporations and private developers. It is interesting to note that, throughout its history, the Supreme Court has struck down local, state, and federal laws protecting workers' rights; laws banning child labor; laws setting minimum wages; banking and insurance regulations; and the regulation of transportation companies—all on the grounds that these laws and regulations unconstitutionally violated private contracts, which the Supreme Court construed as private property. Yet the Supreme Court upheld the violation of private property rights, even when it was clearly for the benefit of a private corporation rather than "public use."

The notion of "eminent domain" dates back to Roman and English law. The expression was coined by Hugo Grotius in 1625, when he wrote that "the property of subjects is under the eminent domain of the State."[52] Herein lies the rub. The Fifth Amendment only allows limited protection of private property, giving the state absolute power to seize private property for whatever "public use" it deems fit (while also providing for "just compensation"). As such, as I shall explain in chapter 8, Americans remain *subjects* rather than citizens. This is further reinforced by the recent Supreme Court decision to allow corporations to spend unlimited amounts on political campaigns.[53] Henceforth, it should come as little surprise that elected politicians will serve the interests of corporations, rather than their constituents, and when "public use" and "economic development" come hand in hand, further interlocking the "public good" with the interests of corporations, the republican form of government envisioned in the Constitution is transformed into a corporate state.

The Sixth Amendment guarantees the right to a fair, speedy, and public trial by jury, along with the right to hear and dispute the charges, to face accusers and witnesses, to compel the testimony of witnesses, and to have access to legal counsel. Beck does not discuss any of this. All of these rights were denied the detainees at Guantánamo Bay, until the Supreme Court stepped in. Of course, Beck does not mention this, either. The only two things that seem to concern him are how frivolous lawsuits are jamming up the system and how the media (like Fox News, perhaps?) are not allowed in courts as a matter of routine. We only need to reflect on the O. J. Simpson trial to understand the reluctance of courts to admit television cameras. However, Beck's complaint about frivolous lawsuits seems somewhat bizarre, given that the Sixth Amendment covers criminal trials, not civil trials, which are covered by the Seventh Amendment. Yet if we consider the burden that civil trials place on the legal system, which are private suits with privately hired lawyers to resolve civil matters, we can see that this is a consequence of the privatization of the legal system and its transformation into a for-profit business. On what basis can Beck, as an advocate of the "free market" and "individual freedom," object to this? This is a direct consequence of the very same principles he endorses, when it suits his argument to do so.

However, when it comes to the Eighth Amendment—"Excessive bail shall not be required, nor excessive fines imposed, nor cruel and unusual punishment inflicted"—Beck's response is to apologize to "the idiots," but this right does not apply to "battlefield terrorists."[54] Once again, he unquestioningly surrenders the authority to determine guilt and punishment to the military and the government in times of war. Far from taking a strict constructionist line, Beck adopts his usual tactic of twistification when it suits him to do so. He demands that those parts of the Constitution that he likes are adhered to by the courts to the letter but considers those parts that he does not like to be irrelevant. Unfortunately for Beck, but fortunately for those who care about preserving the Constitution, the Supreme Court does not agree with him. Until Congress suspends habeas corpus, "enemy combatants" should either be treated as prisoners of war (in which case the Geneva Conventions apply) or tried in civilian courts (with their Sixth Amendment rights intact). The suspension of habeas corpus allows "enemy combatants" to be held without trial, as prisoners of war, until the end of the war, but it does not empower military courts, summary executions, and the use of torture. Nowhere in the Constitution are the military and the government granted the power to dispense "justice" as they deem fit in times of war. Respect for habeas corpus is one of the crucial distinctions between a republic and a police state. It places the burden of proof on the government to prove whether a person being detained is in fact a "battlefield terrorist" or not.

In passing, Beck noted that the Ninth Amendment—"The enumeration in the Constitution, of certain rights, shall not be construed to deny or disparage others retained by the people"—was agreed upon by the Framers in order to prevent the Bill of Rights from being treated as an exhaustive list of specified rights. He is correct to point this out, but the Ninth Amendment is much more important than this. It *affirms* that the people *retain* rights that preexist both the Constitution and the United States of America. These are the rights derived from English common law and the rights considered to be natural rights, from which many of the rights enumerated in the Constitution were derived. The legislature or court cannot deny or disparage these rights on the basis that they are not explicitly mentioned in the Constitution. For example, one cannot deny a right to privacy because it is not mentioned in the Constitution, and this right can be even seen to be derivable from it (see chapter 8 for further discussion of the right to privacy). In other words, people have a right to do anything that is not explicitly denied by statute, and, furthermore, people can appeal to natural rights and common law in order to argue that any new statute is unconstitutional.

This places limits on the possibilities for amending the Constitution and passing future statutes. It not only acknowledges that the Constitution is incomplete and open to interpretation regarding its limits and those of new statutes but also declares that human freedom preexists and transcends the Constitution rather than being defined by it. My argument is that this implies that the Constitution must be treated as a living text, as belonging to the people, as a guide for civic life, for jurisprudence, for governance, not some static, sacred Scripture on the basis of which the rights and liberties of people can be unquestioningly and unthinkingly defined or denied. The Ninth Amendment implies that the Constitution should aid and express civic and political life and, as such, should be deliberated and interpreted by the citizenry, not only by the legislature and judiciary.

The Tenth Amendment, which Beck considers "a profound and critical amendment" and claims is "widely ignored by the federal government," states that the "powers not delegated to the United States by the Constitution, nor prohibited by it to the States, are reserved to the States respectively, or to the people." He interprets this to mean that anything that is not specified in the Constitution (such as abortion) must be left to the states to decide, but the federal government has ignored this and "unconstitutionally overstepped its boundaries in almost every way conceivable."[55] However, Beck has failed to take into account the Fourteenth Amendment, Section 1, which reads,

> All persons born or naturalized in the United States, subject to the jurisdiction thereof, are citizens of the United States and of the State wherein they reside. No State shall make or enforce any law which shall abridge the privileges or immunities of citizens of the United States; nor shall any State deprive any person of life, liberty, or property, without due process of law; nor deny to any person within its jurisdiction the equal protection of the law.

His only comment about this section is to complain that it allows the children of illegal immigrants to become citizens if those children are born in the United States. He resents how these "anchor babies," as he terms them, have access to emergency rooms in hospitals, public schools, and welfare, all at taxpayers' expense. But apart from his rant against illegal immigrants, he has nothing further to say about the first section of the Fourteenth Amendment. He ignores completely that this amendment compels the states to respect the "due process" of law for all citizens (which does make anti-abortion law a federal issue) and makes the Constitution applicable to the states, as well as to federal government. As I have already pointed out, Beck is not a big fan of "due process," so it is quite possible that he wants to pretend that this modification of the Tenth Amendment by the Fourteenth Amendment simply does not exist.

However, if we take the Constitution as a whole, we see that sections 1 and 4 of Article VI of the Constitution already place federal law above state law. By modifying the Tenth Amendment, what the Fourteenth Amendment does is prohibit the states from passing laws that violate the rights of citizens, as defined by the Constitution, and place an obligation upon each and every state to grant all citizens within its jurisdiction equal protection under federal and state law. This simply has passed Beck by. But what Beck has also ignored is how the Fourteenth Amendment (ratified in 1868 after the Civil War) fundamentally transformed the relationship between the states and the federal government. In other words, far from having "overstepped its boundaries in almost every way possible," the Constitution grants the federal government the authority to impose and enforce the Constitution over the states. After 1868, the states lost a great deal of their power to decide everything not spelled out in the articles and the Bill of Rights. Once again, this shows that the Constitution is not written in stone as an unchanging doctrine but is subject to change in accordance with the changing needs and circumstances of the United States of America. States' rights are not absolutes.

Beck's concern with states' rights is pretty much limited to the conservative issues of abortion and guns. This is another example of cherry-picking. For example, what I find to be interesting is that, despite his claim to be concerned with states' rights and taking the wording of the Constitution literally, he says nothing whatsoever about how the 1996 Defense of Marriage Act undermines Article IV, Section 1, of the Constitution: "Full Force and Credit shall be given in each State to the Public Acts, Records and judicial proceedings of every other state." In other words, any marriage recognized in one state must be recognized in all states. This is a fundamental states' right. If any one state recognizes a same-sex marriage, then all states must recognize that same-sex marriage. But what DOMA does is allow the states to choose whether or not they recognize same-sex marriages recognized by other states. The states get to choose whether to abide by Article IV, Section 1 for this and only this. The Constitution does not define what marriage is, either. Yet this federal law defines "marriage" to mean only the legal union between a man and a woman. Beck is silent about this. However, while it is arguably the case that the English word "marriage" commonly and historically refers to a union between a man and a woman, surely, on the basis of the Ninth and Tenth Amendments, the meaning and usage of English words should be retained and reserved for the people, rather than a matter for the federal government to decide. Or should the federal government be in the business of writing English dictionaries?

It is also disturbing how the Supreme Court can consider that civil suits for sexual assault and harassment fall under the jurisdiction of the state courts, and thereby that part of the 1994 Violence Against Women Act was struck down in 2000 as being unconstitutional, given their interpretation of the Commerce Clause; yet the Supreme Court upheld the federal prohibition on states deciding their own laws on growing, possessing, and distributing cannabis for medical use within the state, even though, on a strict interpretation of the Commerce Clause, this should fall within state jurisdiction.[56] Beck is aware of this, but he largely considers this only in relation to future efforts by the states to challenge federal registration and regulation of firearms within the states. If his claim to be a libertarian in favor of states' rights is to be taken seriously, Beck should come out unequivocally in favor of the states' right to decide on the laws dealing with the growth, possession, distribution, and use of cannabis within the jurisdiction of the states. But, also on this issue, it seems that his conservative side trumps his libertarian pretensions, and he remains on the fence, even though he admits that the legalization of cannabis in the state of California would obtain revenue and reduce the power of Mexican drug cartels.[57] For Beck, the Supreme Court's dismissal of the right of the state of California to legalize and regulate the medical or recreational use of cannabis is only significant in the context of aiding the efforts of the states of Montana, Texas, and Alaska to prepare their own challenges to federal jurisdiction over the regulation of the right to bear arms. This leads us to the Second Amendment, which is the subject of the next chapter.

2

THE MILITIA CLAUSE

The militia is our ultimate safety. We can have no security without it. The great object is that every man be armed.

—*Patrick Henry*[1]

Before a standing army can rule, the people must be disarmed; as they are in almost every kingdom in Europe.

—*Noah Webster*[2]

The Second Amendment, as ratified by Congress in 1791, reads as follows: "A well-regulated militia being necessary to the security of a free State, the right of the people to keep and bear arms shall not be infringed." Glenn Beck claims that he interprets the Second Amendment strictly in accordance with its wording, which he says means that all American citizens have the right to buy and possess firearms for self-defense, sport, and any other lawful purpose.[3] He declares that "normal people understand the natural existence of the right to bear arms, the plain language guaranteeing us that right, and the clearly documented history that led to its enshrinement in the Bill of Rights. But those who distrust individual freedoms in favor of an all-powerful government are horrified by the idea that one person can possess enough power to lawfully resist, with force, unacceptable intrusions into his or her life."[4]

Beck interprets the (subordinate) militia clause—"A well regulated militia being necessary to the security of a free State"—as being a preamble and an antiquated clause that does not restrict the meaning or scope of the main clause: "the right of the people to keep and bear arms shall not be infringed."

It should be noted that the Second Amendment, as written on the original Bill of Rights (which hangs in the National Archives in Washington, D.C.) by congressional clerk William Lambert in 1789, states: "A well-regulated Militia, being necessary to the security of a free State, the right of the people to keep and bear arms, shall not be infringed." Does this second comma change the meaning? Perhaps it does. Or perhaps it is just an old-fashioned way of writing that represents a pause without significance or perhaps it is just a smudge.

Broadly speaking, Beck adopts the same interpretation of the Second Amendment as did Justice Antonin Scalia in the Supreme Court case of the *District of Columbia v. Heller*, 2008.[5] Scalia took the "individual right to self-defense" as the basic meaning of the Second Amendment, which won a 5–4 majority in declaring the Washington, D.C., law to be unconstitutional because, by banning handguns and requiring trigger locks on all firearms in the home, it unreasonably infringed on the individual right to self-defense. Scalia added that this right is not absolute, in the sense that it is not a right to keep and carry any weapon in any manner for any purpose, and it is reasonable for the state to regulate the carrying of concealed weapons, prohibit felons and mentally ill people from possessing firearms, prohibit the carrying of firearms in schools and government buildings, regulate the sale of firearms, and prohibit the possession and carrying of "dangerous and unusual weapons." This ruling can be generally taken to be the *individualist interpretation* of the Second Amendment.

Beck considers the debate over the Second Amendment as being not only a debate about whether citizens should have the right to protect themselves or whether this is the exclusive responsibility of the state but also a debate about the balance of power between the citizenry (the people) and the government (the state). He opposes the view that the right to bear arms should be limited to the police, the military, and state organized militias (such as the National Guard) while individual citizens should either have no right to buy and own firearms or only have a strictly limited right (i.e., subject to background checks or only able to buy and own a limited number of firearms of a limited caliber, type, rate of fire, etc.). This view is known as the *statist interpretation* of the Second Amendment, taking the militia clause as the main clause rather than as a preamble or subordinate clause. This largely underwrote the majority decision in the *United States v. Miller* (1939) and upheld the National Firearms Act, which banned civilians from possessing automatic weapons.[6] Broadly speaking, this interpretation presupposes that the citizenry cannot be trusted with modern firearms and that the state should strictly control or have a monopoly over the means to inflict violence. Against it, Beck argues the following:

- Gun control does not reduce gun-related crime. It simply disarms the citizens of the ability to defend themselves against armed criminals.
- Relying on the police to defend the citizens against violent criminals is naïve. There are too many examples of cases in which the police were

not available: they did not arrive on time, they refused to help (say, in instances of domestic abuse or violence), or there was a communication breakdown and the police were not properly informed of the seriousness of the situation.

- The individual citizen's right to self-defense was taken for granted by the Founders. Thomas Paine, Thomas Jefferson, and George Mason all argued in favor of the individual citizen's right to self-defense.

However, Beck's claim that the statist interpretation of the Second Amendment is part of a larger conspiracy to erode the Constitution is far-fetched, to say the least. In general, the statist interpretation is based on the following premises:

- Violence is morally wrong;
- Firearms make violence easier;
- Legally available firearms make it easier for criminals to obtain them.

Hence, the statist interpretation is based on the belief that strict gun control reduces the level of gun crime in society. But is this true? Beck argues that the 40 percent increase in gun crime in the United Kingdom since handguns were banned in 1997 shows that evidence does not support this conclusion. Let's take a look at this claim. He cites a report from BBC news that reported a 40 percent increase in handgun crime.[7] However, this is misleading. What the BBC news report failed to take into account was that the increase in handgun crime was largely due to a change in how the police categorized handgun crime in the UK after the 1997 Firearms Act. This act included the use of imitation guns and starting pistols during a crime under the category "handgun crime." According to an official Home Office study published in 2007, the number of homicides committed with firearms has remained constant since 1997, but the number of handgun crimes has increased, largely due to changes in police reporting rules and an increase in gang-related crime, without any significant rise in firearm related deaths or serious injuries.[8]

If we compare the United Kingdom with the United States in 2005–6, we find that police in England and Wales reported less than 1 firearms-related death per 100,000 people, whereas, in the same period, there were over 4 firearms-related deaths per 100,000 people in the United States. Yet the reported crime rate in the UK and U.S. is approximately the same (at about 800 per 10,000 people). Furthermore, since the 2006 Violent Crimes Reduction Act, crimes involving the use of air pistols are also included under the category "handgun crime," and this has resulted in a dramatic increase in police reporting of handgun crimes. Hence Beck's claim that a handgun ban in 1997 led to a rise in gun crime in the UK is misleading. He also has failed to take into account that prior to 1996 there were fewer than sixty thousand firearm certificates (permits) issued for the possession of a handgun (which is less than 0.1 percent of the population). Most British citizens did not even notice that handguns had been banned!

Let's take a brief look at the history of firearm control laws in the United Kingdom. The right to bear arms in England was written into common law in 1181, known as the Assize of Arms, as decreed by King Henry II. Gun control in Britain began in the sixteenth century, after the English Civil War, when Parliament announced parliamentary sovereignty to write laws and abolished all prior pronouncements by monarchs. The 1689 Bill of Rights gave only Protestants a conditional right to bear arms: "That the subjects which are Protestants may have Arms for their defense suitable to their conditions, and as allowed by law." This was largely considered to be a natural right to resist oppression and for self-defense.

This continued until the 1824 Vagrancy Act allowed constables and watchmen (the police were not formed until 1829) to arrest any armed person if they were deemed to be intent on committing a "felonious act" and the 1870 Gun License Act required the purchase of a license (for twelve shillings from a post office) to bear a firearm outside one's own house. It was only in 1903, after the Pistols Act had been passed, that it became a legal requirement to obtain a license before purchasing a pistol. Licenses could be bought from the post office, and it was an offense to sell pistols to children and drunkards.

After the 1920 Firearms Act, a certificate was required to possess any firearm in the home. The local chief constable decided whether the applicant had given "good reasons" for possessing a firearm, and applications were denied if the chief constable decided that the applicant was "of unsound mind," "intemperate," or "unfit to be trusted with firearms." This law was passed largely to disarm the working class after the First World War. In 1933, the Firearms and Imitation Firearms (Criminal Use) Act increased the punishments for the use or a firearm (or imitation) in the commission of a crime. It also imposed a mandatory sentence of fourteen years for anyone using a firearm (or an imitation) to resist arrest. (Remember that police officers in the UK are not issued with firearms as standard equipment.)

The 1937 Firearms Act gave chief constables increased discretionary powers when granting certificates. This law also regulated arms dealers and strictly controlled the sale and possession of machine guns. The 1934 U.S. National Firearms Act provided the model for this law and the control of automatic weapons, but under the British law, self-defense was no longer considered to be a "good reason" to possess a firearm. English, Scottish, and Welsh legislation were reconciled under the 1968 Firearms Act, which became the basis for British firearms regulation for twenty years.

Since 1968, UK subjects have largely been restricted to double-barreled shotguns, requiring a firearms certificate and police approval that the applicant has "good reason" to own a shotgun and can be trusted to use it "without danger to the public safety or peace." Anyone who has served more than three years in prison or shown mental health issues is denied a certificate. Firearms certificates for other types of firearms have to be applied for separately, each application stating type and purpose, such as for sport or work. The procedure for vetting applications requires positive verification of identity: two referees of "veritable good character" (who could be interviewed and/or investigated) who knew the applicant for at least two years, a good report from a family doctor, a police inspection of premises and storage facilities where the firearm was to be kept, and a national police background check. In addition, the applicant is interviewed by a Home Office Firearms Inquiry Officer. Penalties for the illegal possession of a firearm were set at between five and ten years' imprisonment and an unlimited fine.

It was after the 1987 Hungerford massacre, when Michael Ryan went on a shooting spree in the town of Hungerford and killed sixteen people before shooting himself, that the conservative government effectively banned semiautomatic rifles, pump-action shotguns, and explosive ammunition in the 1988 Firearms Act. Stricter controls on shotguns were imposed, but semiautomatic pistols and .22 rifles were unaffected. This remained the legal basis for gun control in the UK until the 1997 Firearms Act. This law was a response to the 1996 Dunblane massacre, when Thomas Hamilton, a licensed gun owner and former scout master (dismissed from the Scout Association five years earlier) shot dead sixteen children and their teacher, Gwyneth Mayor, in the gymnasium of Dunblane Primary School. The act banned all handguns for private ownership (with the exception of muzzleloading black-powder guns and pistols made before 1917 or of historical interest). Even the Olympic shooting team is not exempt from this law and has to train outside of the UK. Now the UK firearms laws are among the strictest in the world.

Thankfully, instances of legally licensed gunmen going on shooting sprees are extremely rare. Violent crimes with firearms involving otherwise law-abiding citizens are also rare. The UK's example shows that removing firearms from the general population reduces the likelihood that petty (unorganized, opportunist) criminals, curious or alienated children, or mentally ill people will gain access to firearms, and if they do, they are limited to air pistols, imitation firearms, or starting pistols. This cannot be reasonably denied. Of course, we can agree that the existence of a legal firearms market means that criminals, children, and mentally ill people will find it easier to find firearms. Simple probability and logic shows that there will be a greater number of accidents and crimes that will happen if more firearms exist in society. Accidental shootings are much, much lower in the UK than in the U.S. simply because there are far fewer firearms in the UK. Most accidental shootings are the result of hunting accidents. While some evidence suggests that the presence of a firearm in the home increases the chance of suicide or a crime of passion, often in conjunction with drug or alcohol use, this evidence is far from conclusive and incontrovertible.[9]

However, what we do see from the UK's example is that strict gun controls do not significantly lower the levels of homicides and serious injuries from firearms. The number remains fairly constant. This is largely due to the fact that organized criminals obtain their firearms, including military hardware, illegally, and will do so regardless of the law. Banning the legal possession and use of any weapon will not have an impact on organized criminals. In fact, if anything, it extends the black market to sell the newly banned weapons and affords profitable opportunities to smugglers and corrupt officials. Police and FBI reports consistently show that the vast majority of shootings and crimes involving firearms are committed by people using illegally obtained firearms. It can be reasonably surmised that, even if there was a worldwide ban on all firearms, criminal organizations would be able to make and distribute their own guns. It is also the case that people intent on murder will choose a different kind of weapon if a firearm is not available. However, it is clearly a fact that firearms make it easier to kill people, intentionally or otherwise. Beck points out that the use of toasters, coffins, video games, and nitrous oxide have resulted in deaths, but I would argue that firearms are better weapons than toasters; otherwise we would be discussing whether toasters should be banned or whether citizens have a right to possess them for self-defense. Smith & Wesson would be lobbying Congress to keep their latest model of the two-slice toaster off the banned list, even if the heavier muffin toaster was to be strictly controlled.

Having said that, we also need to look at how the legal possession of firearms has prevented crimes. American citizens' media watch organizations show that there are numerous cases in which armed citizens have prevented armed criminals or mentally ill people from committing crimes or acts of violence, without a shot being fired.[10] Each year, there are millions of incidents of citizens using firearms for self-defense. In most cases, the firearms are not fired and no one is injured. These cases are too boring to make the national media. The media are not interested in reporting that an armed assailant was successfully disarmed and handed over to the police without any shots being fired or anyone being injured. It is arguable that, in the UK, the Hungerford massacre would have involved fewer deaths if the local citizens had possessed firearms for self-defense. It is arguable that the Dunblane massacre, too, could have been prevented if the school had armed security, just as it is arguable that the massacre would not have happened if people like Thomas Hamilton were unable to obtain firearms. It seems that both sides of the argument have merit. There is a strong argument that law-abiding citizens can possess firearms responsibly and effectively use them for self-defense. There is also a strong argument for the need for some kind of gun control to prevent wanted criminals, children, and mentally ill people from gaining access to firearms.

Bringing both sides of the argument on the Second Amendment together allows us to argue that the citizenry has "the right to bear arms" for self-defense, sport, and any other purpose allowed by law, but on condition that they do not belong to any of the following groups of people: wanted criminals or convicted felons, children, or people suffering from serious mental health problems. Clearly, some kind of permit and background check is required. Citizens who own firearms should have a legal responsibility to prevent members of these groups of people from gaining access to firearms and should be held accountable for the irresponsible care and storage of firearms. However, legal requirements should not unduly hinder law-abiding citizens from gaining permits, nor should any storage regulations prevent citizens from effectively using firearms for any lawful purpose, including as a means of self-defense.

But should gun controls limit the kinds of firearms that permit-holding, law-abiding citizens should be allowed to possess? In order to answer this question, we need to reexamine the militia clause and bring together both clauses of the Second Amendment. What does the word "militia" mean in the Constitution? As well as appearing in the Second Amendment, the word appears in three other parts of the Constitution:

- Article I, Section 8: This section empowers Congress to "raise and support armies, but no appropriation of money to that use shall be for a longer term than two years"; to "provide for calling forth the Militia to execute the laws of the Union, suppress insurrections and repel invasions"; and to "provide for organizing, arming, and disciplining, the Militia, and for governing such part of them as may be employed in the service of the United States, reserving to the States respectively, the appointment of officers, and the authority of training the Militia according to the discipline prescribed by Congress."
- Article II, Section 2: "The President shall be Commander in Chief of the Army and Navy of the United States, and of the Militia of the several States, when called into the actual service of the United States."
- The Fifth Amendment: "No person shall be held to answer for a capital, or otherwise infamous crime, unless on a presentment or indictment of a grand jury, except in cases arising in land or naval forces, or in the militia, when in actual service in time of war or public danger."

Beck says that "gun-grabbers like to fantasize that the Founders used 'militia' to mean a government organized military unit—but, as usual, they couldn't be more wrong."[11] Actually, Beck is wrong on this point and the "gun-grabbers" are right. The Constitution is very clear on this. Article I, Section 8 and Article II, Section 2 explicitly empower Congress and the president, respective, to organize, discipline, and command the militias of the several states when called into service. This clearly gives two branches of government responsibility for organizing the militia as a military unit during times of invasion or insurrection. When he was president, even Thomas Jefferson was also quite clear that during peacetime the militias should be under the command of their respective state governor, giving state government the responsibility for organizing the militia.

Jefferson wrote in 1776: "No free man shall ever be debarred the use of arms."[12] Why? According to Jefferson, the possibility of freedom is dependent upon the ability of the people to thwart those who would enslave them. It is a condition of being a free man that one has the means to defend one's freedom from tyrants and invaders. However, he limited the right to use arms to free men; women, slaves, and convicts were excluded. As George Mason wrote in 1788, disarming the people is the best means to enslave them, and in "a free state," the militia and the people are one and the same.[13] The term "militia" refers, in the fullest reading of the Second Amendment, to the right of the people to defend themselves—as the people—and this right is necessary for the existence of a "free state." Hence, according to George Mason, the Second Amendment is a right granted to all the people, by which he meant the citizenry, which, of course, initially meant the white male population. It was only during Andrew Jackson's presidency that the right to bear arms was extended to male freed slaves; women, slaves, and Native Americans were still excluded. Women did not have full citizens' rights until 1920. These rights were extended to Native Americans after 1924 (when they were considered taxable).

This idea of the militia as the people is distinct from militias like the Minutemen, who are private citizens formed into a small group, and also distinct from paramilitary organizations or mercenaries. The organized militia was created by the 1903 Militia Act and consists of the state-based and organized National Guard (distinct from the National Guard of the United States, which is a federally controlled reserve military force) and the Naval Militia. U.S. Code Title 10, Sec. 311–313 defines the militia of the United States as consisting of all able-bodied males at least seventeen years old and under forty-five years old who are or intend to become citizens of the United States, and all female citizens of the United States who are members of the National Guard. This unorganized militia is basically able-bodied male adults who are eligible for the draft and females who have already volunteered to serve in the National Guard.

The Constitution clearly empowers Congress to raise an army and navy, and to organize the militia. But is the existence of a standing army during peacetime compatible with the spirit of individual liberty envisioned by some of the Founders? Jefferson and Paine, for example, considered a standing army to be a threat to the liberty of the people because it secures an imbalance of power in favor of the government over the people. On their argument, the "common defense" of the union should be the responsibility of the militias, trained and organized by the several states, until such time as they are called into service by Congress upon declaring war. Only thereafter should an army be raised by Congress and placed under the command of the president, acting as commander in chief. Even the 1973 War Power Act allows the president to deploy the armed forces for only up to sixty days in the event of "a national emergency due to an attack upon U.S. territory" before seeking the approval of

Congress, which still retains the right to demand that the president withdraw the troops before the sixty-day limit.

Briefly, I would like to raise the question of whether the draft is constitutional. The Second Amendment defines a right, not an obligation, to bear arms. Isn't the draft prohibited by the Thirteenth Amendment—"Neither slavery nor involuntary service, except as a punishment for a crime whereof the party shall have been duly convicted, shall exist within the United States, or any other place subject to their jurisdiction"—as a form of involuntary service?

However, the Supreme Court declared that U.S. citizens had a "supreme and noble duty" to contribute "to the defense of the rights and honor of the nation, as the result of a war declared by the great representative body of the people."[14] Yet the Constitution does not mention any such "supreme and noble duty." Was this an example of the Supreme Court legislating from the bench? Furthermore, this ruling only legitimates the draft once Congress had declared war. Congress has not declared war since 1941. Does this mean that the drafts during the Korean and Vietnam wars were unconstitutional?

This is an important question. The draft after the Second World War was ended in 1946 (and the Selective Training and Service Act passed in 1940 prior to declaring war!) was allowed to expire in 1947. However, in 1948, Congress passed the Selective Service Act, which made all males between the ages of nineteen and twenty-six subject to the draft for twenty-one months, followed by a commitment to service for either twelve months of active duty or thirty-six months in the reserves. Despite not formally declaring war, in 1951, to raise an army for the Korean War, Congress passed the Universal Military Training and Service Act. This lowered the draft age to eighteen and increased active duty from twenty-one to twenty-four months, but it granted exemptions to students. Where did Congress draw the authority to pass these acts? Not from the Constitution.

This is further complicated by President Johnson's signing of an executive order (Executive Order 11241, August 26, 1965) that rescinded the exemption for married men without children granted by President Kennedy (Executive Order 11119, September 10, 1963). These executive orders bypassed Congress altogether. They were revoked by President Reagan (Executive Order 12553, February 25, 1986).

In 1967, Congress passed the Military Selective Service Act, which expanded draft eligibility to the ages of eighteen to thirty-five. Student exemptions were limited to the completion of a four-year degree or their twenty-fourth birthday, whichever came first. Again, Congress had not declared war against Vietnam, so from where in the Constitution did it draw the authority to pass this act? In 1971, this act was amended to base selection on a lottery, and all eligible male citizens were compelled to register for the lottery. Student deferments were ended (except for divinity school students!), and conscientious objectors could elect for non-combative military service or alternate community service. It seems that compulsory service did not equate to "involuntary service" in the minds of the congressmen who voted for this act, nor did it do so in the mind of President Nixon, who signed it into law. On January 27, 1973, Secretary of Defense Melvin Laird announced the end of the draft and the creation of an all-volunteer armed forces. The registration requirements were ended by President Ford on March 29, 1973 (Proclamation 4360, Terminating Registration Procedures Under Military Selective Service Act).

While the draft may well seem unconstitutional, to date, the constitutionality of these acts and executive orders has not been ruled on by the Supreme Court—not since the 1918 Selective Draft Law Cases. However, we can raise the question of whether the Selective Draft Law Cases apply when Congress has not declared war.

The downplaying of the militia clause has been part of the process by which the balance of power has shifted from the people to the government. The result of the statist interpretation is that it delegates responsibility for the protection of liberty from the citizenry to the agents of the government, such as law enforcement officers and the military. The result of the individualist interpretation is that the right to bear arms is treated as an individual right to bear arms for self-defense, sport, and any other lawful purpose rather than a right of the people, as a militia, to protect the freedom of the people from tyrannical government. As a result, on one side, the protection of the people is no longer the responsibility of the people but that of their representatives and agents of the state, supposedly acting on behalf of the people, while, on the other side, it is every man and woman for themselves. For both sides, at most, the individual is to be allowed the choice to possess a limited kind of firearm for personal protection against intruders in one's home or for personal amusement at a target range or when shooting animals (once the requisite permit has been obtained and during the allotted season), but the formation into a militia has been downplayed or limited to meaning joining the National Guard. The statist interpretation of the Second Amendment is made by conservatives and liberals alike. However, criticism of this position is not the monopoly of libertarians. Any genuinely democratic person will be concerned with the extent that this statist interpretation leaves the people largely defenseless against tyrannical government.

It is a myth and falsehood, largely spread by media pundits and propagandists on the conservative right, that progressives, liberals, and Democrats are all "gun grabbers" who claim that only agents of the state should possess firearms. Democrats, liberals, and progressives can adopt a Jeffersonian interpretation of the Second Amendment. In a genuine democracy, the responsibility for the protection of that society must be divided throughout that society to be a property of society—it must be a responsibility of the people in practice as well as principle. If the existence of a standing army threatens the very possibility of a democracy by providing the government with an imbalance of power over the people, then in a free society it would be the responsibility of the people to arm, train, and organize themselves so as to defend themselves and society effectively. In a democracy, the principle of a right to self-defense extends into a principle of a right to defend the people, as being a condition for the possibility of the existence of a genuine democracy. The responsibility for the protection of liberty and the people are both the responsibility of the people; to delegate this responsibility to agents of the government is to surrender liberty because it gives the government the monopoly over violence, which gives it a monopoly over power.

The balance of power between government and the people cannot be maintained if the government possesses a monopoly over the means of violence. In part, I agree with Beck's individualist interpretation. If violence is absolutely wrong, it is absolutely wrong for governments as well as for people. If people cannot be trusted with weapons, then governments cannot be trusted with weapons. The statist belief that government employees are somehow morally superior and more capable of restraint than everyone else is not only naïve but also opposed to the spirit of the Constitution and the form of the Republic. Agents of the government must be considered as part of the people and cannot possess any rights or privileges that the people do not possess. However, in my view, the individualist interpretation does not go far enough in understanding the scope of the Second Amendment and its implications for democracy. We need to note that the word "individual" is not used in the Second Amendment. It does not discuss the right of the individual citizen to bear arms and how this right should be "well regulated." What it says is that "the right to bear arms" belongs to "the people," which is a collective term, not the sum of individuals. This highlights that in a democracy "the people" and a "free state" are one and the same thing. The militia being "the people," once armed, organized, and trained to defend themselves from invaders, insurrection, and tyrannical government. The statist interpretation is anti-democratic because it assumes that agents of the government are more responsible than any other citizen and thereby can be trusted with weapons that cannot be trusted to the citizenry in general, and the individualist interpretation is anti-democratic because it assumes that self-defense is only an individual right rather than a collective responsibility of the people.

A broader, democratic interpretation of the Second Amendment needs to bring the individualist and statist interpretations together by properly incorporating the militia clause into how the Second Amendment is interpreted. The purpose of the Second Amendment is to state the conditions needed to secure a free state, not just free individuals acting as if in isolation from each other. It describes the necessity of the right of the people to defend themselves collectively, as the people, not as a sum total of individuals, but as a free people—as the safeguard of their freedom as a free society—acting through self-governance, which is the foundation of a free state. The Second Amendment is a statement of the conditions for the possibility of the existence of a free state, through the right of the people to bear arms. Of course, in a free state, whether and how any individual citizen fulfills this responsibility must be voluntary in order to respect pacifism, individual liberty, and various religious beliefs that prohibit violence, even in self-defense. Hence the Second Amendment must be understood as a right, not an obligation, to bear arms. And hence, in a free state, the draft must be considered by the people as being strictly unconstitutional.

Beck treats the militia clause as if it is an antiquated preamble that should not be taken as limiting individual citizens' rights to possess firearms. On this point, he is shortsighted. However, the militia clause in its fullest sense places responsibility for the defense of the free state upon "the people," acting collectively, in virtue of being a "well-regulated militia." Arguably, this interpretation better grasps the original meaning of the Second Amendment than Beck's individualist interpretation. The Framers had just survived the War of Independence, which made them all too aware of the importance of possessing the means to fight for one's freedom from tyrannical government and an invading army. The Bill of Rights shows how the Framers recognized that limits on governmental power were necessary to preserve the liberty of the people but that these rights could only be preserved if the people had the means to preserve the security of a free state from tyrannical government by acting collectively as a well-regulated militia. As Jefferson wrote in the Declaration of Independence,

> That whenever any Form of Government becomes destructive of these ends [the right to Life, Liberty, and the Pursuit of Happiness], it is the Right of the People to alter it or abolish it, and to institute new Government, laying its foundations on such principles and organizing its powers in such form, as to them shall seem most likely to effect their Safety and Happiness. . . . When a long train of abuses and usurpations, pursuing invariably the same Object evinces a design to reduce them under absolute Despotism, it is their right, it is their duty, to throw off such Government, and to provide new Guards for their future security.[15]

If only words were required to secure liberty, then it would have been secured the moment John Hancock signed the Declaration of Independence on the 4th of July 1776. But, alas, as the following war showed, sometimes securing liberty comes only through the successful armed struggle of a people against the armed forces of a violent and determined oppressor. Hence Jefferson was profoundly distrustful of standing armies. He considered them to be opposed to a free state as they were capable of being placed at the disposal of tyrants. During his presidency he made it clear that during peacetime, the governor of each state is constitutionally the commander of the state militia. In his 1808 state of the union speech, he said, "For a people who are free, and who mean to remain so, a well organized and armed militia is their best security. It is, therefore, incumbent on us, at every meeting to revise the conditions of the militia, and to ask ourselves if it is prepared to repel a powerful enemy at every point of our territories exposed to invasion."[16]

Could the United States be defended by the people acting as a militia? History provides us with numerous examples of militias being able to defend their national territory against technologically superior armed forces. Consider the examples of the American Revolution and the War of Independence, the French Revolution, the Haitian slave revolt, the Boer War in South Africa, Nestor Makhno and the Ukrainian peasant militias against the German army and then the Bolsheviks, the Russian workers and peasant militias against the invading foreign and "white armies" during the Russian Civil War, the CNT-FAI militias during the Spanish Civil War, the French Resistance against the German Occupation, Tito and the Yugoslav partisans against the Nazi German army, Mao and the Chinese Red Army against the Japanese army and the Nationalist forces, the Cuban revolutionaries, the peasant resistance during the Vietnam War, and the militias in Iraq and Afghanistan. If the people were organized into a "well-regulated militia" in America, with the citizenry of every state, city, and town armed and prepared to fight an invading army, it would be impossible for any invader to invade and occupy the United States. Even the largest army in the world, even if equipped with better weapons, would not be able to achieve this. The vastness of this country, combined with a well-armed and determined citizenry, would make the campaign doomed from the outset. Just imagine the problems facing a military force when invading a country the size of the United States of America, populated by nearly three hundred million armed and organized citizens.

The key to understanding the militia clause is the term "well regulated." What does this mean? Contrary to Beck's assertions, the term "well regulated" does imply some level of gun control (such as keeping firearms out of the hands of criminals, mentally ill people, and children). However, as Beck observed, in the eighteenth century, the term "well regulated" meant trained and properly disciplined. This is indeed the case. According to the *Oxford English Dictionary*, in the eighteenth century, the word "regulated" meant "properly maintained and working" when used to describe the condition of a watch or instrument. In the context of a "well-regulated militia," it meant properly trained and disciplined, capable of fighting effectively. However, Beck makes this point only to hurl scorn at the statist interpretation that "well regulated" means having a comprehensive set of rules to control the possession of firearms. But he retains the individualist interpretation, which only treats the right to bear arms as an individual right to possession of firearms, and, as a result, he does not think it through. My argument is that if we take the militia clause seriously, we can go much further than this and understand how the eighteenth-century meaning of "well regulated" has implications for the meaning of gun control in a way that brings together the individualist and statist interpretations.

Taking this older meaning of "well regulated" into account, we can see that the militia clause makes it a condition for the right to keep and bear arms that "the people" are properly trained and disciplined in how to bear arms. It should be a condition of the right to possess firearms that the possessor has learned how to properly use, care for, and store them. This brings the connotations of skill and knowledge to the idea of gun control, rather than merely imposing limits upon the categories of people permitted to possess firearms. In this respect, the right to bear arms would require that citizens learn how to bear arms responsibly and safely, demonstrating skill and knowledge and proving that they are capable of being a responsible member of a "well regulated militia." Despite Beck's assertions to the contrary, firearms are inherently dangerous. The problem is that without proper training, gun users are a threat to bystanders as well as themselves. It is therefore in the public interest that gun users are properly trained in how to use firearms as a condition for ownership. It is reasonable for society to prohibit untrained, ill-disciplined, and inexperienced people from owning and using dangerous weaponry. This is not much different than the restriction that a person must be able to pass a test to demonstrate that they know how to drive a car before they are given a license to do so. But what of the question of limits to the kind of firearms the people have the right to bear?

Beck is right to point out that it is ridiculous to claim that the Framers, when writing the Second Amendment, had in mind muskets and single-shot pistols and therefore these are the only kinds of firearms the people should have a right to bear. If the purpose of the Second Amendment is to protect the right of the people to possess the means to protect themselves from invaders, tyrants, and criminals, then technological innovation in the means of violence requires that the people have a right to keep and bear the firearms of their day. Does this mean there should not be any restrictions on the kind of firearms the people should keep and bear? Again, Beck hit on a very important point but did not go far enough with it. Once we take the broader understanding of "well regulated militia" into account, we can argue that, while it would be reckless and irresponsible to allow unregulated (i.e., unrestricted, untrained, and undisciplined) possession and use of automatic handguns, assault rifles, and machine guns, it would also be unconstitutional to prohibit citizens from possessing automatic handguns, assault rifles, and machine guns while allowing the police and military to use these, if citizens were capable of demonstrating that they were sufficiently skilled, knowledgeable, and responsible to bear them. If the only things that qualify a police officer or soldier to use automatic weapons are training and discipline, then any citizen who can demonstrate the same level of training and discipline should be able to possess the same kind of automatic weapon as their professional counterparts. Providing that a citizen is a law-abiding adult who has no record of serious mental illness, adequate training should be the only restriction upon firearm possession.

If one's neighbors constituted a well-regulated militia, skilled in the proper use of their firearms and trained in rapid response, and could be called upon by using communications or panic buttons, then there is good reason to believe that crime would be reduced. It is reasonable to believe that such a militia would be able to defend the country from an invading army, an insurrection, or a tyrannical government. But, you may ask, what of heavier weaponry? The same argument applies. Providing that citizens are properly trained and disciplined in their use, care, and storage, there is not any good reason to prevent law-abiding adults, without serious mental health problems, from possessing weapons such as bazookas, grenade launchers, antitank rocket launchers, flamethrowers, and so on. Such weapons would be very useful in the event of having to defend against an invading army or prevent a coup d'état. It is also reasonable for trained and disciplined citizens to possess high explosives and be skilled in sabotage and guerrilla warfare fighting. But what about the possession of weapons such as tanks or fighter aircraft? Surely the citizenry should be banned from owning these? Again, the same argument applies. However, clearly there is a greater level of training and discipline required to use, properly care for, and store such armaments. In all practical likelihood, given this requirement for a higher level of training and discipline, as well as the expense of tanks and fighter aircraft and the need for proper storage, these would be used within the state organized militia and owned by the militia in general, such as the National Guard, rather than by individuals. Ultimately, in a democracy, all the defensive functions of the military would be performed by a well-regulated militia. The current standing army would be gradually demobilized, as and when the people are trained and equipped as a well-regulated militia capable of taking over the common defense of the union.

But surely there are limits? We cannot let a militia, no matter how well regulated, have access to nuclear, biological, and chemical weapons, right? That would be madness, right? Yes, it would. But the implications of this run deeper than we might initially think. It is ridiculous to assume that military training conveys a deeper moral character than militia training would. All other things being equal, there is not any difference between well-trained and -disciplined military personnel and well-trained and -disciplined citizen militia. If any weapon is too dangerous to be possessed by a well-trained and -disciplined citizenry, then it is also too dangerous to be possessed by the military. Given that the government is supposedly a civilian government, representative of the people and answerable to the people, if the people cannot be trusted with any weapon, neither can the government. If we consider it madness to have the nuclear arsenal under the watch of a well-trained and -disciplined volunteer militia, even with all the checks and safeguards, including oversight and control by Congress and the president of the United States, then in what way is it sane to have such weapons under the control of the military? It is not. Such weapons should be banned outright! No government should be permitted any weapons denied to the people, and all nuclear, chemical, and biological weapons should be internationally outlawed and destroyed.[17]

However, many people will be horrified at the idea of allowing citizens access to military weaponry, even if they are properly trained in their use, care, and storage. For many people, this idea will invoke images of thugs driving around in trucks, terrorizing their town with machine guns, or drunken young men taking their militia-issued stinger missile launchers down to the freeway to play with the traffic. Many people will have concerns about the possibility of vigilantism, mob rule, street gangs, and civil war. People may recall the Kent State University massacre, May 4, 1970, when the Ohio National Guard opened fire on unarmed students, killing four and wounding many others. Even though these actions are hardly the behavior one would expect from a well-regulated militia, these concerns are legitimate. People also would be reasonably concerned with the prospect of criminals being able to steal heavy weapons from the citizenry. Most people, liberals and conservatives alike, adopt some kind of statist interpretation of the Second Amendment because they hold that society is safer if citizens are not permitted military weapons, such as machine guns and rocket launchers, and the dissemination of such weapons are strictly controlled. Many people think that the national defense is best secured by professional armed forces.

If you think that individual citizens should not have the right to own and use an Apache helicopter gunship, then you advocate some level of gun control. If you think it reasonable for the armed forces to have such weapons, then you hold to a statist interpretation. After that, it is a matter of degrees. Where the line should be drawn is a matter of debate and opinion. One person may think that the line should be drawn at rocket and grenade launchers, another at automatic weapons and assault rifles. Most people would agree that some level of gun control and regulation (in the sense of rules and laws) are necessary to prevent irresponsible and violent individuals from gaining access to powerful weapons. These people are not "gun grabbers" and "idiots," as Beck calls them. They are citizens with genuine desires to live in a "well regulated" society without fear of being gunned down in the street. People are not idiots for wanting to regulate the right to keep and bear machine guns, assault rifles, and even handguns, especially in a society for which the very idea of collective responsibility is an anathema. The right to bear arms is not an absolute right. In a democratic society, people have a right to debate regulations and laws, and they are not idiots for disagreeing with Beck's interpretation of the Second Amendment, which itself admits of some degree of gun control.

As I argued in chapter 1, the Constitution is not a sacred text to be blindly followed as doctrine. It was written by human beings and is interpreted by human beings. It is open to differences of interpretation. This is not only unavoidable, but it is desirable in a democracy. In a complex society like the United States of America, the meaning of the Second Amendment must be debated and agreed upon by the people. Differences of interpretation show that negotiation and compromise are required to not only interpret the Second Amendment but also to apply it to the changing circumstances of America. Like it or not, the Constitution is a living document. Debates over the original meaning of the words written in the eighteenth century are helpful for interpreting the Second Amendment, but they are not binding absolutes. In a real sense, it does not matter what the Framers intended. Their circumstances were different from those of today. What matters is how the Constitution helps and guides the people to better understand the nature of the Republic and how to build and live in a democracy in relation to a complex and changing world. The Constitution is there to guide the public debate into how freedoms and rights—such as the right to bear arms—should be exercised and applied or, if need be, amended. This comes down to an ongoing experiment in self-governance. What is needed is a better public debate about what it means to be a good citizen and how this relates to good government.

3

PUBLIC EDUCATION

Glenn Beck wants the Department of Education to be closed down, an end to teacher tenure, and all teachers' unions to be dissolved.[1] He states that *"the federal government has no constitutional authority to be in the education business. . . . Education is not a federal issue, it's a local and state one—which is* exactly how it was treated for over two hundred years. Then Jimmy Carter came along and, by the slimmest of margins (we're talking about four votes in the House), won approval to create a new ginormous government bureaucracy: the Department of Education (DOE)."[2] He wants an end to public education, or, more to the point, apart from allowing a state-funded voucher system for private schools, he wants an end to taxpayer-funded public education. He wants education to be privatized—with children from poor families relying on receiving financial aid from schools or charities: "I will never agree with the premise that because someone can't afford something, it's not good or fair. Frankly that sounds a little socialist. A lot of people can't afford a Mercedes S Class sedan—but does that mean that Mercedes should be forced to stop making them? No—people generally accept the fact that in order to buy a car like that, they will need to have more money. That gives them a little something we capitalists call 'incentive.'"[3]

Putting aside the weakness of this analogy (given that an education is not a luxury comparable to an expensive foreign car), I agree with his claim that a good education, even though we need to debate what this means, is the key to success in life. My problem is that I do not agree with Beck's vision for the future of education. His vision is a for-profit private education system in which the best education is available to those children either fortunate enough to be born into a wealthy family or able to receive some kind of charity. This means that education will become a for-profit service industry, no different from beauty salons or dry cleaners. Whether or not children from middle-class families receive an education will depend on whether their parents are capable of finding a beneficent charity, using savings, or borrowing the money. If parents are unable to pay for the private education of their children, and they do not receive charity or borrow the money, then that is just their hard luck. It seems that Beck believes that children from poor families don't really need an education. After all, they will be needed by corporations in the future, as part of a low-paid workforce that can be hired or fired at will.

His argument against public education is largely based on a tirade against educational progressivism and the teachers' unions. But as I shall explain, his opinion is not based on facts or reasoned argument but on Beck's conservative right-wing ideology, which he wraps in the cloak of free-market libertarianism. His criticisms of the teachers' unions are that (1) they support teacher tenure and therefore support bad teachers, and (2) they are unions and therefore bad by definition. His criticisms of educational progressivism lack any substance and are based on either a misunderstanding or misrepresentation of what it actually is or should be. Instead, he appeals to the need for a traditional education, but this largely comes down to his authoritarian view that American children should learn what he (and other right-wing conservatives) think is best for them to learn.

Beck asserts that public education is a failure and a colossal waste of taxpayers' money. He blames governmental waste and mismanagement, teacher tenure and unmotivated teachers, classroom overcrowding, and unmotivated and undisciplined students. However, in my opinion, while all these factors are serious concerns, it seems to me to be rather simplistic to put the blame on the government and teachers' unions for a failed education system. We need to examine which goals, norms, and standards are being used to evaluate the success or failure of public education. His assertions strike me as being motivated by ideology rather than facts or reasoned argument, and therefore they are nothing more than anti-government and anti-union propaganda and sloganeering. Furthermore, it is not evident that public education is a failure, and certainly not to the extent that Beck claims it is. However, even if we agree that public education is failing, we need to discover why this is the case. We also need to look at whether this state of affairs is national or varies between different regions, cities, and states, or among different socioeconomic classes or ethnic groups. Broad and sweeping declarations of failure are not helpful for the purpose of working out how to improve the situation. Before we can make the claim that public education is failing, we need to be clear what we think public education is for. It is not at all evident that there is any national consensus on this. America needs to raise the level of public debate and ask these two questions: What is education for? What is a good education?

Even if we take Beck's shocking claims at face value, such as his claims that thirty-two million Americans cannot read or write and that 63 percent of those aged eighteen to twenty-four could not find Iraq on a map, we still have to ask ourselves why the federal government is to blame for this.[4] After all, most American children have access to television, public libraries, books, magazines, and the Internet. An atlas costs less than the price of a computer game. Public school is not their only source of information. Is the inability of young adults to find Iraq on a map really the fault of the Department of Education and the public school system? Surely, some responsibility for the education of children must fall to their parents and to the children themselves. How is it the federal government's fault that thirty-two million Americans cannot read or write? Why didn't their parents teach them? After all, in the United States of America, parents do have the option to homeschool their children. Of course, in many families both parents have to work, and pretty much every single parent has to work, so homeschooling is not an option for these parents. But surely even the hardest working parents could find one hour per day to make sure that their children know how to read and write. However, to be fair, public schools must take a share of the responsibility, but is the failure of public schools to teach these thirty-two million Americans to read and write really the fault of the *federal* government?

Republicans have been complaining since the Department of Education was formed in May 1980 that federal influence in education is unconstitutional and that education should be a state and local issue. Indeed, the Constitution does not grant the federal government any authority over education, so they argue that, in accordance with the Tenth Amendment, education must be left to the states and the people. The problem with their argument is that the Department of Education does not control the content of education. It leaves this to the states and local districts. There is no constitutional prohibition on the federal government funding state and local education, or offering federal educational projects, and states can refuse federal funds if they so decide. It is as simple as that. Any state can refuse federal funding, and there is nothing the Department of Education can do about it. The problem for Beck and Republicans is that the states want federal funds. The Department of Education was formed to provide federal funding to overcome poor levels of funding for public education in some states and districts.[5]

These poor levels of funding were due to the inability or reluctance of state governments to raise state taxes to pay for education. Still, public school education remained under the jurisdiction of state governments and state boards of education. Until the passing of the No Child Left Behind Act (NCLB) in 2001 (which I shall discuss later), curricula and testing were left to state boards of education and local school districts. State and local authorities have had considerable autonomy over the content of public education, while being additionally funded by the Department of Education (which has a budget of slightly under $70 billion), which does not even have any direct jurisdictional control over accreditation agencies (the Council for Higher Education Accreditors and the Association of Professional and Specialized Accreditors are both non-governmental organizations). However, the Republican claim that the federal funding of education is unconstitutional is yet another example of cherry picking. More often than not, the same Republicans who object to the constitutionality of federal funding of public school education want federal bans of same-sex marriage, flag burning, abortion, or the recreational use of narcotics, even though the federal government has no constitutional authority to ban any of these.

Even taking NCLB into account, public education is largely determined by the states and the people. State legislatures and the residents of the state (via school boards and the ballot box) can have enormous say in how public schools are run and funded. How is it the fault of the Department of Education if a state accepts federal funds for public education yet the public schools in that state perform poorly? Since 1980, the Department of Education has provided public schools across the United States with hundreds of billions of dollars. What have the states been doing with these additional funds? Even if we agree that there has not been any significant improvement in public school education as a result, how could we claim that the federal government has made the public education system worse by providing the states with more money? We can't. Federal funding for public education is not responsible for millions of Americans not being able to read or write, or being unable to find Iraq on a map. The blame must lie elsewhere. Are the states and the people to blame? Could there be a social or cultural problem involved? Could it be possible that some Americans are to blame for neglecting the education of their own children? Dare we suggest that the lack of motivation for learning among students is the fault of their parents and the students themselves?

At this point, Beck would interrupt to point his finger at another possible culprit: the teachers' unions! The National Education Association is the largest teachers' union in the United States, with over three million members. The second largest is the American Federation of Teachers, with over 850,000 members (it is affiliated with the American Federation of Labor and Congress of Industrial Organizations, which is the largest federation of unions in the United States). How are these teachers' unions to blame? Well, according to right-wing conservatives and media pundits like Beck, there are four ways that the teachers' unions are to blame:

(1) They are to blame by being powerful and because they are successful in lobbying the Department of Education, and, by doing so, they have managed to secure tenure and have allowed bad teachers to keep their jobs.

(2) They are to blame by pushing left-wing political agendas and progressive ideologies in the classroom.

(3) They have prevented parents from having any control over the content of their children's education.

(4) They are unions and are bad, by definition, so somehow they must be to blame.

Let's start by looking at tenure. The reason why tenure is a bad idea seems quite obvious if it prevents teachers from being fired for not doing their job properly. It seems reasonable for a school to be able to fire a bad teacher. Why would anyone want to keep bad teachers in schools? Well, it is not so simple. The problem is: Who decides what good teaching is? The Department of Education? The state boards of education? The school boards? The parents? The students? Other teachers? If Beck had his way, anyone who taught anything he disagreed with or did not like would be fired as a bad teacher. The purpose of tenure should be to protect intellectual freedom and freedom of speech. A teacher should be able to dissent from mainstream opinion, explore sensitive topics, or openly disagree with the authorities. Tenure should allow teachers to disagree with parents or administrators without fear of losing their job. It should afford teachers the same protection as afforded university professors or judges with lifetime appointments.

Without tenure, the tendency would be for schools to teach prevailing opinion and orthodoxy. In addition, tenure does not require good grades as a condition of continued employment and, therefore, there is no motivation for teachers to lower standards or falsify results in order to keep their jobs. This is the problem with so-called merit-based pay. Unfortunately, once teachers become financially motivated to secure good grades or results, corruption and deception will inevitably occur. Tenure secures impartiality. It increases the chance of problem areas and struggling students coming to public attention. The risk of lazy and unmotivated teachers is the price to pay for allowing good teachers the freedom to teach as they think best and to teach what they deem to be important. It is the way to keep educational standards high. (It is also the case that without tenure, without job security, teachers would want higher salaries.) Nobody wants children to be taught by bad teachers. However, the risk of bad teachers could be somewhat mitigated by having higher standards in teacher training and recruitment, and by making sure that children only have the same teacher for a single school year or subject, at most, thereby allowing children the experience of being taught by several or many teachers. This is largely what happens in most public schools. Tenure is not the reason why millions of Americans cannot read or write or find Iraq on a map.

Of course, it is also worth mentioning that a great deal has been made by Beck out of cases of teachers not being fired despite alleged sexual misconduct involving students. But, again, here tenure is important. Quite understandably, parents tend to be very concerned when there is even the suggestion of sexual misconduct by a teacher. Journalists are also attracted to such cases. There is the tendency that a teacher can be subjected to a witch hunt or lynch mob mentality based on accusation and rumor alone. Tenure protects a teacher from being unjustly forced from his or her job, due to false accusation. It also must be remembered that sexual misconduct involving a child is a crime and, as such, is a police matter. If a teacher is convicted of any kind of sexual misconduct with a child, he or she can be fired immediately. What we do not want is for teachers to be fired on the basis of a lower standard of evidence than that of a court. It is essential that firing a teacher requires either a criminal prosecution or a strictly observed procedure involving many people at many levels of oversight. Once again, we see Beck's total disregard for due process.

Beck's real problem with tenure is that teachers can teach ideas that contradict his ideology. His real objection to tenure is that teachers can teach ideas that those on the conservative right do not agree with or like, and there is nothing they can do about it. He wants schools to teach only what he thinks is right and best for children. He is against intellectual freedom and freedom of speech in public schools; if teachers teach something that he does not agree with or like, he wants them fired. What he wants is for teachers to reinforce his right-wing view of the world, and for conservative parents to have a mechanism by which they can pressure schools to fire teachers who do not teach the orthodoxy. To put it simply, those on the conservative right are concerned that leftist or liberal ideas might make their way into classrooms. (It may come as a shock to some people, I know, but it seems that many teachers who accept modest levels of pay and are motivated to spend their lives teaching children, rather than working in the private sector for more money, tend to have leftist or liberal ideas.) Well, here is Beck's real bugbear. In fact, he spends most of his chapter on education sneering at and ridiculing the ideas taught in public schools. He considers the real culprit for the failure—as he sees it—of public school education to be progressivism!

What does Beck consider a progressive education to be? He describes it as a "touchy-feely period of self-awareness and discovery" in which the focus is on the students, who have to "get in touch with their feelings" and have fun rather than learn facts. Apparently, this is achieved by teachers refusing to judge students' work and focusing on their experience instead. Whether students' answers are right or wrong is not important. There are no right or wrong answers! Beck claims that progressives are undermining public education by being nurturing and comforting rather than discouraging, by making children's experience of education friendlier, warmer, and happier. What fiends!

He complains that the progressive methodology emphasizes empathy over narrative. He asserts without any argument or evidence that a progressive education does not teach the facts about historical events but instead encourages students to explain how they feel about those events. He states that competition and grades are rejected in favor of freedom of expression and play. And he holds this to be responsible for poor literacy and mathematical ability. He complains that the aim of a progressive education is to make school fun, but at the expense of teaching children basic things like what a map of the United States looks like.[6] Of course, at this point you might well be asking whether there are any students in public schools who wouldn't recognize a map of the United States as just that. My guess is that if we scoured public schools across America, we might find one student who was unsure, but only because he or she thought it might be a trick question. But even if it is true that there were students who could not recognize a map of their own country, it would indicate a level of cultural ignorance and neglect far deeper than a failing of progressive teaching methods in schools.

Beck gives us four examples of schools teaching progressive methods. He mentions the Little Red School House in Manhattan. He wonders whether you would choose to send your child to a school that aimed at nurturing social consciousness and awareness, that drew upon the progressive tradition, and that considered education to be an organic process of growth of the all-around development of the child. He also asks whether you would choose to send your child to the Prairie Creek Community School in Northfield, Minnesota. Would you choose a school that believed in authentic and holistic assessment, for which there are no tests or letter grades and, instead, children write narratives about their educational experience and personal development? He also mentions the School in Rose Valley, Pennsylvania, and wonders whether any parent would choose to send their child to a school that believed in developing a balanced mind and body, through intensive study and play, and learning how to be better stewards of the natural world. And finally, he mentions the Wingra School in Madison, Wisconsin. He questions whether anyone would choose to send their child to a school that did not grade, test, or even believe in competition of any kind between students. We have to ask: Who would choose to send their children to any of these schools? Well, if Beck had done his homework (or, more to the point, his research staff had) and spent five minutes on the Internet, he would have learned that these are not public schools. Three of these schools are private, and one is a charter school. It turns out that all of the parents who send their children to these schools have chosen to, presumably because they value the kind of educational methods and ideas these schools offer. So either Beck is against parental choice or he is more concerned about how he *feels* about progressive education in public schools, rather than the *facts* about it.

Does Beck provide us with any examples of any public school in America teaching the kind of progressive methods he describes? Well, no. But he does assure us that progressive education has undermined public education in the United Kingdom, as well as America. What is his evidence for this claim? He says that an education secretary in the United Kingdom has "decried" progressive education as "a misplaced ideology" that has let down generations of children. He cites an article published in 2008 in *The Guardian*, a British newspaper.[7] If you were to read this article, however, you would see that the "education secretary" cited by Beck as the authority on the subject was in fact

Michael Gove, the shadow education secretary for the Conservative Party (which was in opposition to the government in 2008). At that time, Michael Gove had no experience at all in government as the education secretary and had only been the shadow education secretary for a year. Prior to issuing his comment, he was the shadow housing secretary. If you haven't guessed already, Gove is a right-wing conservative in favor of the privatization of education in the United Kingdom. The article also points out that the schools minister, Jim Knight, and the general secretary of the National Union of Teachers, Christine Blower, both said that Gove's remarks were "out of touch" and did not reflect the reality of the classroom.

In the UK, children are taught from a national curriculum and are frequently tested, from an early age, using national tests. (This national curriculum and testing regime were the result of the Conservative national government of the 1980s, which largely believed in local government autonomy only when it came to paying for schools.) Since the Conservative-Liberal coalition formed the government in 2010 and he became the education secretary for real, Gove has overseen the scrapping of plans to build over seven hundred new public school buildings and has started an experiment in "Free-Schools" (similar to charter schools), which can teach such things as etiquette and table manners, compulsory Latin, classical civilization, collapsing all the humanities (including history) into English, and music (ironically, the proposed teaching methods are based on Venezuela's El Sistema). And, of course, "Free-Schools" may have "faith affiliations" (i.e., be religious schools). Thank heavens, you may say! At last, there is liberation from a progressive education. With children well versed in Latin, good manners, the histories of ancient Greece and Rome, and a proper grasp of the Queen's English, these schools will be providing the education needed by British children in the twenty-first century. But sarcasm aside, hopefully common sense will prevail and teachers and parents will opt for a more balanced and practical curriculum.

Is there any other evidence supporting Beck's assertions? He has uncovered that a couple of teachers at two elementary schools and a physical education teacher at a middle school prefer to use purple ink for marking rather than red ink, due to the negative connotations that red ink has. Aha! Clearly this is the progressive rot he has been talking about. His research here is limited to a few newspaper articles. If we take a look at one of these articles, which was published in the *Boston Globe*, it describes how some teachers over the last few decades and a color specialist consider red to be an aggressive color.[8] Some students agree. Teachers have been using different colors, but due to its distinctiveness, using purple ink to mark work has become a trend since 2003. However, as the article also points out, other teachers do not agree and still prefer to use red ink. Allegedly, some teachers prefer different colors, even green or yellow. Shocking as this may be, it is hard to believe that teachers' refusal to use red ink to grade papers is the cause of illiteracy or poor map reading skills in America.

Beck does cite some facts from "The Nation's Report Card" (2008) to show how public education has not improved the levels of literacy in America. He tells us that the percentages of seventeen-year-olds at different levels of reading have not changed significantly in comparison with their average scores in 2008, 2004, or 1971. Of course, we might venture that one possible explanation for the lack of any significant improvement in reading skills for seventeen-year-olds over the last thirty-seven years is that, for every generation, schooling tends to take a backseat to the "extracurricular concerns" of seventeen-year-olds. However, these facts, according to Beck, show that federal funding has made little difference, if any. But what Beck does not tell us is that this same report also states that in "reading, average scores increased at all three ages since 2004. Average scores were 12 points higher than in 1971 for 9-year-olds and 4 points higher for 13-year-olds. The average reading score for 17-year-olds was not significantly different from that in 1971."[9] It seems that there have been some improvements for nine-year-olds and thirteen-year-olds.

Furthermore, in "mathematics, average scores for 9- and 13-year-olds increased since 2004, while the average score for 17-year-olds did not change significantly. Average scores were 24 points higher than in 1973 for 9-year-olds and 15 points higher for 13-year-olds. The average mathematics score for 17-year-olds was not significantly different from that in 1973." It turns out that for nine- and thirteen-year-olds, average mathematics scores have been improving since 1971 and are now significantly higher than they were then. And there have been significant improvements in average scores for both mathematics and reading since 1971 for Afro-American students, for all age groups, and since 1975 for Hispanic students for nine- and seventeen-year-olds. "While the reading score gaps between White and Black students at all three ages showed no significant change from 2004 to 2008," the report states, "the gaps did narrow in 2008 compared to 1971. White–Hispanic gaps in reading scores also showed no significant change from 2004 to 2008 but were smaller in 2008 than in 1975 at ages 9 and 17."

And in addition, it seems that more public school children are taking increasingly higher levels of mathematics classes:

Taking higher-level mathematics courses was generally associated with higher scores on the 2008 mathematics assessment at ages 13 and 17. For example, 13-year-olds who were enrolled in algebra classes scored higher on average than those enrolled in pre-algebra or regular mathematics. The percentages of 13-year-olds who reported taking pre-algebra or algebra in 2008 were higher than the percentages in 1986. The percentage of 17-year-olds who reported they had taken pre-calculus or calculus was higher in 2008 than in 1978, as was the percentage who had taken second-year algebra or trigonometry.

It seems that public education is not quite the unmitigated failure that Beck would have us believe. Perhaps all that federal money hasn't been wasted after all.

Of course, statistics can be manipulated to show what people want them to show. Different selection criteria or methods can give different answers. There is quite a ring of truth to the old slogan: lies, damned lies, and statistics! However, we all know that there is something deceptive using only those parts of the report that seem to support one's claims and ignoring those parts of the same report that contradict them. In plain English, that is called dishonesty.

Let's move on from facts and figures and look at the philosophy behind a progressive education. Here Beck identifies the villain of the story: the American philosopher John Dewey.

Beck provides us with two quotations from John Dewey.[10] The first: "Existing life is so complex that the child cannot be brought in contact with it without either confusion or distraction; he is either overwhelmed by a multiplicity of activities that are going on so that he loses his own power of orderly reaction, or he is so stimulated by these various activities that his powers are permanently called into play and he becomes either unduly specialized or else disintegrated."

Beck not only asserts that this quotation is sufficient to show the wrongness of Dewey's philosophy, hence he does not feel the need to supply us with his analysis, but he is puzzled that Dewey did not even try to hide his beliefs when he wrote it. But why should Dewey try to hide his beliefs? What Dewey said is that children need guidance in how to live in wider society, and it is essential that the school simplifies wider society by being a model of it—in other words, providing an environment within which the child can learn how to act effectively within wider society. What is so self-evidently terrible about that? Beck does not tell us. Instead, he plucks another quotation from the same essay: "I believe that the teacher's place and work in the school is to be interpreted from this same basis. The teacher is not in the school to impose certain ideas or to form certain habits in the child, but is there as a member of the community to select the influences which shall affect the child and to assist him in properly responding to these influences." Beck interprets this to mean that, according to Dewey, teachers should not tell a child whether "he or she is 'right or wrong'" (especially not in red ink); they're there to help the child through "a touchy-feely period of self-awareness and discovery."[11]

Given Beck's repeated insistence that teachers should correct students' mistakes or factual errors, I find myself wanting to write "WRONG!" in red ink next to his misunderstanding of Dewey's words. Dewey said nothing of the kind. What he said was that teachers are to be representatives of their community—the same community within which the child lives—and guide the child through the process of learning how to be a member of his or her community rather than force ideas upon the child or demand obedience. What is so self-evidently wrong about guiding children to grow up as well-adjusted members of their community? What is wrong with guiding children in learning how to think for themselves and be able to live well in their community? Apparently "self-awareness and discovery" are so self-evidently bad, according to Beck, that the ideas of Dewey need no further discussion or analysis.

Perhaps Beck (or his research staff) did not bother to read and take into account what Dewey actually said. It doesn't seem that he did. However, that is not the task of the media pundit and propagandist. His task is to distort and misrepresent what a progressive education actually is in order to reinforce the beliefs of people who also have no idea what a progressive education is but somehow know that it is bad because they have been repeatedly told it is.

Unfortunately, there is not sufficient space in this book to do justice to the richness and depth of John Dewey's philosophy of education. This philosophy can be found in the following writings: *My Pedagogic Creed* (1897); *The School and Society* (1900); *The Child and the Curriculum* (1902); *Democracy and Education* (1916); and *Experience and Education* (1938). The most I can do here is to give a summary of Dewey's philosophy of education.

Dewey considered education and learning to be social and interactive processes situated within a community. Schools are social institutions from within which children should be guided through the process of learning how to think for themselves and live well within their community. Teachers are to act as guides and representatives of that community, rather than instructors or obedience trainers. In this way, children learn to become well-adjusted members of their community and schools can act as places wherein social reform can take place. Schools should have a civilizing influence on children. Dewey did not say that children should be left to do whatever they wanted or whatever they found to be fun. What he said was that students learn better when they are able to interact with the school's curriculum and play a part in deciding the content of their own education. He believed that students should have opportunities to participate actively in the directions and content of their education while being guided by teachers in the process of doing this. His philosophy of education was not that of laissez-faire child-centric education, which he considered to be tantamount to neglect, but, instead, a carefully teacher guided process based on child participation in learning how to be a good learner and a well-adjusted member of the school and wider society. He considered this kind of education to be good for both the child and wider society, and he argued that this was essential for the development of democracy, civic virtue, and good citizenship.

Education is not only about gaining knowledge and technical skills; it is also about learning how to learn and live well, how to participate in a democratic society, how to be a good member of the community, and how to become a good citizen. Acquiring knowledge and technical skills is important, without doubt, but the traditional methods of instruction and discipline were thoroughly anti-democratic and damaging to the possibility of the emergence of well-adjusted, critical thinking, free, and democratic citizens (which is possibly why Beck is in favor of a return to traditional methods). It was for this reason that Dewey argued that education should not be focused on the acquisition of a predetermined curriculum but *instead* should be focused on helping students realize their full potential, how to think critically about how society could be better, and how to use their skills and knowledge to work toward improving society. The goal of education should be to help students prepare for the future by helping them fully develop their capacities as human beings and democratic citizens.

Education is the process by which children come to develop "social consciousness," and the adjustment of individual behavior in relation to this process is the best way to achieve social reform. This cannot be achieved using the traditional methods of instruction and discipline without turning education into a form of brainwashing and obedience training. Dewey rejected these traditional methods because they force students into a passive relationship with their own education. He argued that the content of education must be presented to children in terms of their own experiences, deepening their connection with the new knowledge. This kind of dialectical and dialogic education finds its roots in the ancient Greek philosopher Plato's dialogue entitled *Meno*. In this dialogue, Socrates shows how an uneducated slave boy could deduce the first principles of geometry by being guided dialectically, through questions and answers. It is interesting that in this dialogue the Greek word *mathesis* means both teaching and learning simultaneously. The role of teachers is to learn from students how to teach those students to be able to learn how to see the new knowledge for themselves. For example, a child cannot be taught the general concept of the number 3 by being passively shown 3 chairs, 3 apples, or 3 cats and being instructed to grasp the concept of 3. This must be done by children for themselves, and the role of the teacher is to guide children through the process by which they will come to realize that for themselves.

Dewey criticized "child-centric" approaches to education (often developed by people who considered themselves to be followers of Dewey) because *too much* reliance on the child was detrimental to learning and *neglected* their education. Education, he believed, should seek a balance between the student and the teacher, wherein the teacher has an important responsibility as a guide through which the student properly engages with his or her own education. Hence, Dewey believed that the best method of education is one of guided interaction with real objects in the world through active "hands-on" approaches, which place the focus on both the activity and the child's own experiences of the activity in question. Rather than being child-centric education, this is *experiential education*. This does not mean that children should "get in touch with their feelings" (as Beck claims) but that teachers and students should interact within a learning environment that allows the student, guided by the teacher, to learn actively from direct experience and reflection upon those activities.

Put simply, the idea is that children learn by thinking about what they are doing and why they are doing it. There are two basic aims to this approach: (1) to help the student learn in ways that are meaningful to the student, and (2) to promote freedom of thought (and critical thinking). Dewey believed students should be able to judge the meaning and quality of their experience for themselves, in their own terms. Hence, he was opposed to both authoritarian and laissez-faire forms of education insofar as both approaches stunt or distort the development of students' ability to learn and think.

What is a progressive education? It is not finger painting, being indoctrinated by Marxist propaganda, or reading lovely poems and discussing feelings, as Beck would have us believe. If I had to write a report card for Beck (and his research staff), I would write, "Glenn is an active and talkative student, with quite a lively imagination, but he needs to pay attention in class and to do his homework. Must try harder!" I would probably write this in black ink. However, a progressive education is an interactive, social, and practical educational approach that is influenced by Dewey's model of learning: (1) become aware of the problem, (2) define the problem, (3) propose hypotheses to solve it, (4) evaluate the consequences from one's past experiences, and (5) test to find the most plausible solution. This seems more like common sense than some radical doctrine.

Following this model, progressive education emphasizes the importance of active, hands-on learning by doing, with a strong emphasis on problem solving and critical thinking. Instead of testing the ability of children to memorize and recall rote knowledge, the progressive assessment of learning involves evaluation of project work in terms of participation and productivity. Hence, a progressive education tends to deemphasize the importance of textbooks (and reading, writing, and textual analysis) in favor of the social, practical, project-based, and experimental use of varied learning resources and media. It also focuses on the needs of the students' community, selecting subject content according to estimations of those needs, and also aims at anticipating the future of society. It hopes to achieve these goals through an integrated curriculum. The focus on group work and cooperation is to help children see for themselves the value of social skills—leading toward helping children gain social skills and capacities for lifelong learning, democratic participation, and adapting to changes in future society. In my opinion, only someone with a vested interest in preserving the status quo or promoting an anti-democratic agenda would have a problem with this approach to education.

But who decides which varied learning resources are selected? Who estimates the needs of society? Who anticipates the future of society? Who designs the curriculum? These decisions should not be based on the directives of the Department of Education, using strings attached to funded federal programs. Nor should they be based on dictates from the leadership of teachers' unions. Regardless of how well intended they might be, these kinds of authoritarian directives and dictates are based on political criteria and aims, rather than on educational criteria and aims, and are detrimental to teacher and student relationships to the extent of making any kind of progressive education quite impossible. Any imposition of a curriculum and methods upon teachers and students would unavoidably result in a return to the traditional and authoritarian model, even if the content of the curriculum was seemly progressive.

This kind of education is not progressive at all and is, in fact, damaging to teacher and student motivation. It not only fails to achieve the goals of a genuinely progressive education but also fails to teach children basic knowledge and skills through traditional methods. It is the worst of both worlds.

Insofar as a progressive education has been damaging to public school education, it is to the extent that it has been implemented and developed badly by politicians and bureaucrats and is not a progressive education at all. The imposition of a seemingly progressive education results in a lazy form of pedagogy in which an ad hoc and conflicting mash of educational methods and policies are imposed from above without any degree of feedback from below. However, a progressive education simply cannot be imposed from above—it cannot be properly implemented and developed through any centralized policy, agenda, or curriculum—without distorting and destroying it. A genuinely progressive education can only happen if schools have autonomy and the content and methods used in that school are developed by teachers in relation with the students.

However, this raises an important question: Should parents be involved in deciding the curricula and methods used in their children's schools? The U.S. Ninth Circuit Court of Appeals has ruled that parents' fundamental right to control the upbringing of their children "does not extend beyond the threshold of the school door," and that a public school has the right to provide its students with "whatever information it wishes to provide, sexual or otherwise."[12] I strongly disagree with this ruling. In my opinion, a progressive educational approach can only work in a decentralized education model, wherein schools have autonomy and different schools can try different approaches; some schools try experimental approaches, some traditional approaches, and others try mixed approaches, as each school deems best, in accordance with the hopes, experiences, and wishes of local teachers, students, *and parents*.

While parents should not have absolute control over public education, they should be equal participants in deciding both the approach and content of education at their children's school. After all, a progressive education involves teaching children how to live well within their community, which also includes their parents. To exclude parents is to exclude the wider community, which is itself not only an anti-democratic act but also an act that excludes a valuable pedagogic resource. After all, the vast majority of parents went to public schools, and their experiences are valuable for learning how to improve educational methods and content. Teachers must learn from parents how to educate children as well as guide parents toward understanding the methods and approaches being tried at the school. Students also need to participate in this. There should be public dialogues among parents, teachers, and students about what a good education should be and how to achieve it, but it is also important that parents should not be able to impose their views upon the schools either. If the teachers and students consider sex education or evolution theory, for example, to be important and they wish to discuss them, parents should not be able to prevent children from participating. Sometimes it is necessary for schools to teach children what their parents refuse to teach them.

It is very important that the content of a progressive education is shaped and developed within a local context; the application of its methods should be shaped in accordance with the experience and reflections of local students, teachers, and parents. It is also important that the practical, project-based aspects of the content of a genuinely progressive education are related to and integrated with community concerns, projects, and interests. In this way, a progressive education is an inherently democratic model of education, which can be evaluated critically in relation to other approaches in different schools and communities. Any national curriculum and standardized teaching methods destroy this possibility.

But what about the No Child Left Behind Act? Since passing NCLB in 2001, the federal government has mandated standardized testing in literacy, mathematics, and basic science. The Department of Education has also claimed that federal funding for public education in these areas has increased by almost 60 percent. It is left to the states to set their own standards, and there are not any national curricula or set of teaching methods imposed. NCLB is part of a nationwide drive to improve literacy, numeracy, and knowledge of basic science, which still leaves states and local districts with considerable control over public school education. Generally speaking, this is a good thing if it works and improves knowledge and skills in these areas, right? Well, yes, but there are problems associated with national standardized testing. Without necessarily doing it consciously, some teachers start "teaching the test" rather than genuinely improving children's understanding of the subject matter. And as I have already said, statistics can be manipulated in accordance with the desired result. Determining the impact of NCLB may well prove difficult, if not impossible. States that improved their standards may well suffer lower scores in the early years, while states that lowered their standards would likely show higher scores, and any threat of punitive measures for failure encourages the lowering of expectations.

It is also questionable whether standardized testing of students is really a valid way of measuring improvement. It is certainly the case that it is not a valid means of evaluating the quality of education. Furthermore, the funding for and focus on non-tested subjects (called "electives") has suffered as a result of NCLB. Another problem with NCLB is that by focusing on standardized testing, it imposes a "one size fits all" approach to education, ignoring cultural, economic, and individual differences. This not only suppresses individual creativity but also could result in the segregation of schools along ethnic and class lines. Disabled children are also tested to the same standards as all other children, which has resulted in a poorer quality of education for those children.

Since NCLB, there has been an increase in the number of charter schools, and many of these schools have begun to adopt progressive teaching methods. In my view, providing that they remain nonprofit and do not charge tuition, receiving public funding on a per student basis, charter schools offer a promising approach to public education. The rules for setting up a charter school vary between states. Some states allow only the state board of education to issue the charters, while in other states the charters are issued by the local school district. Some states allow state universities to issue charters. Some states allow any existing public school, by district petition and referendum among the parents of children attending that school, to be able to decide to convert that public school into a charter school. The advantage of charter schools is that they offer the possibility for further local accountability and control over public school education, allowing curricula and teaching methods to be developed in accordance with local community needs and circumstances. This promises to further democratize public education by increasing local accountability and control. In my opinion, state government imposed caps on the number of charter schools in the state should be lifted. The number of such schools should be determined by local demand.

Beck's arguments against public education are weak and do not stand up to scrutiny. He wants a private education system wherein parents pay fees for their children to attend the school of their choice. "Do families still have to make sacrifices?" he asks. "Absolutely—but what better way to have parents invested in the success of their children than to have parents literally *invested* in the success of their children?"[13] Well, parents who can afford that can do it. There is nothing stopping them. They have the choice whether to send their children to public or private school. As Beck puts it, "The point is that you vote with your wallet, and businesses compete for that vote. That's how the whole free-market capitalism thing is supposed to work: the best succeed; the worst fail."[14]

Beck also wants parents who cannot afford private school fees to beg or borrow the money to do so. Well, there is nothing stopping parents from doing that, if they can, but many parents seem happy to send their children to the local public school. An increasing number of parents can choose to send their children to a local charter school. Parents also have the choice to homeschool their children. While the exact rules vary between states, it is easy and straightforward to homeschool a child in most states. Parents seem to have lots of choice in the United States of America about how their children are educated.

States retain a great deal of autonomy regarding the content of public school education. If parents are unhappy with their children's education, they can hold the state government and board of education accountable through the ballot box. Citizens could make public education an election issue for national elections too. The quality of public school education reflects political choices. People should have a great deal of say about the content and level of funding of public education in their states and the whole country. If it is political suicide to suggest raising taxes to pay for better public education, then the electorate is to blame. If people want better teachers in public schools, then taxpayers must pay for higher standards of teacher training and higher levels of pay. If Americans are unsatisfied with the public education system, then they have political routes by which they can change it. Citizens need to ask deep questions about what they think the purpose of education is and come together in local and national debates about the nature of a good education. Americans need to take interest in local politics and make sure that their elected representatives are being held accountable for how state and federal funds are being spent. If politicians are not accountable to their constituents, this exposes a much deeper problem with the American political system than public education.

Most teachers are also parents who send their children to public schools. While the teachers' unions are there to protect their members' interests, the education of the members' children is an important interest. It is up to the members to make their voice heard through their union and make sure that their union delegates and leaders are accountable to them. If the unions are protecting the jobs of bad teachers, at the expense of the public school system and students, that reflects political choices of the membership. Teachers need to stand up and be counted. Their voices need to be heard. What do they think a good education is? How can it be achieved? Through the unions, teachers have an opportunity to contribute to a national debate about public education and make it a political priority during elections. There have been plenty of opportunities to put public education higher on the list of national priorities. This current situation is the result of negotiations and political choices. If public education is failing due to a conspiracy between the teachers' unions and the Department of Education, as Beck asserts, then the voters—as teachers, as parents, as citizens—have been complicit in this too. People need to come together—through school boards, town hall meetings, political parties, and unions—to make their voice known through the ballot box by making public education an election issue when electing their mayors, governors, representatives, senators, and union leaders. Again, if elected leaders are not accountable to their constituents, this represents a deeper failure of the political system than that of public education.

Bad teachers are betraying the trust bestowed upon them, but parents need to take personal responsibility for their own children's education and make sure they are learning what they need to learn. Students also need to take personal responsibility for their own education. With access to the Internet, libraries, cable television, radio, magazines, newspapers, and books, students have many opportunities for learning outside of public schools. They have a great deal of choice about how and what they learn, and they need to make their voices heard to teachers and parents. It has become a very convenient excuse to blame teachers, unions, or governments for the lack of student motivation and poor educational performance. The bottom line is that education is a Ninth Amendment issue. The people are responsible for public education in America. There is no excuse for millions of Americans being unable to read or find Iraq on a map.

Public education is the silver bullet to overcome ignorance and poverty. Only an informed and enlightened citizenry—capable of critical thinking and political participation—can provide the foundation for a genuine democracy in the United States of America. But this costs money. Beck's argument against public education comes down to his objection to it being paid for by taxation. He does not want poor parents to be able to send their children to public schools at the expense of wealthy people. He considers public education to be "a redistribution of wealth." Improvements to the public education system, such as better teacher training and higher pay, will need more taxes, and that is what he is opposed to. This is why his only positive suggestion is the school voucher scheme.[15] This is a means by which public funds can be rerouted into the for-profit private education system. It means that the best students can be siphoned off from the public education system, at taxpayers' expense, and go to private schools. Of course, this means less money for public schools and lower performance in comparison to private schools, which can add further fuel to the media pundit and propagandist's claim that the public school system is failing.

Beck's argument masquerades as being based on a concern for the quality of children's education, but if he had his way, most of these children would not have any education at all, of any kind, except perhaps what they learn from sitting at home, watching TV. At the heart of his "libertarian" vision is the aim of dismantling public education and leaving the majority of parents in America facing massive debts, begging for charity, or educating their children at home. His concern for the liberty of the wealthiest Americans would leave most working Americans facing a lifetime of drudgery and hardship, just to pay for their children to have a chance at a better life. Generations of uneducated Americans will be left facing either a lifetime of unemployment or low paid labor. They will lack the skills and confidence necessary to participate effectively in politics at any level.

Finally, it is also interesting to note that Beck thinks that college and university students have too much choice.[16] Despite the fact that students pay fees for their college education and choose their courses, Beck complains about colleges offering courses such as these:

- Star Trek & Religion (Indiana University)
- The American Vacation (University of Iowa)
- Learning from YouTube (Pitzer)
- Feminist Critique of Christianity (University of Pennsylvania)
- Blackness (Occidental College)
- Queer Musicology (UCLA)

Given that these are optional courses, I wonder in what way fee-paying students choosing their courses offends Beck's free-market libertarian sensibilities. The answer is obvious, of course. He objects to students making choices different from his. These courses clearly appear a bit lefty for his right-wing conservative tastes, and obviously anything outside of his worldview must be condemned. But we should not be so narrow-minded. Regardless of what any of us might think about the courses listed above, a college education is for many students their first real foray into the marketplace of ideas. It is essential that these students be allowed to experiment and explore freely from a wide range of options. Higher Education is clearly a path through which the next generation of scientists, leaders, artists, and entrepreneurs will emerge, and often the routes they take are not clearly marked and predictable.

However, the future and purpose of Higher Education in America is also something that needs to be raised in public debates. It is something that should be up for grabs for each generation to discover or rediscover for themselves. Is the future and purpose of Higher Education to be constrained to serving the needs of the market? Or does it have intrinsic value? What role does Higher Education have in the development of intellectual, moral, personal, and civic character? The public debate about these questions has wider and deeper implications than the benefits of public education for individuals. It also involves questions about the constitutional duty of government to promote "the Progress of Science and useful Arts" and the "general welfare." This is more than "a redistribution of wealth." It is a question of how to invest public funds and resources to improve society by empowering its citizens to not only better adapt to the changing circumstances and complexities of the world but also, more importantly, to improve the quality of public debate upon the public good and enhance the power of the citizenry to realize it through democratic action.

4

Beyond Petroleum

Glenn Beck admits that America's overdependence on oil is a big problem.[1] His only "solution" to this problem is to reduce American dependence on foreign oil by taxing American oil companies less to encourage them to extract more and to allow them to drill in the Arctic National Wildlife Refuge (ANWR). And that is it! As Beck notes in *Arguing with Idiots*:

> The effort by those who use green energy to further their real agenda is called "the Watermelon Effect." It's a green rind of "pro-environment" policies hiding a core of wealth-redistribution policies that are as red as Marx's blood. This charade only prolongs America's oil addiction and keeps us slaves to nasty foreign governments.[2]

> The tax on Gulf oil is essentially an oil sin tax that will lead companies to produce less oil from the region. That, in turn, will reduce supply.[3]

> Our green energy prospects depend on our ability to use more of our own oil—and the most obvious place to get it is from the Arctic National Wildlife Refuse (ANWR) in Alaska.[4]

It should be quite surprising that Beck is scathing about sustainable and alternative technologies for electricity production. However, as with so many of his arguments, he is inconsistent. When objecting to "green energy," he complains that it is expensive, untested, little more than a dream, and not commonly available enough to satisfy the needs of the market. Yet Beck sings the praises of the 1893 entrepreneurial spirit of Samuel Insull, who worked under Thomas Edison for twelve years and took out a loan to build the world's largest power plant.[5] He tells us that electricity was "like private jets are today" and available only to the rich, but Insull had a vision to provide affordable electricity to everyone and used "revolutionary ideas" and innovations to realize that vision. Of course, what Beck forgot to mention was that this did not happen by magic. People such as Thomas Edison, Nikolai Tesla, and George Westinghouse had thrown considerable personal fortune and a great deal of time and energy into developing the basic patents and technologies that Samuel Insull utilized. Even his idea for a variable rate and metered billing system was taken from the system used by an electricity company in Brighton, England. None of this detracts from what Insull achieved, but new technologies require the investment of personal fortunes and many trials (including failures and dead ends) long before they are ready to be utilized in the market commercially. The same is true of solar, wind, geo-thermal, and tidal energy. These technologies have moved beyond their infancy, but they are only beginning to come into their own.

Rather than recognizing the role of increased levels of consumption for increased reliance on foreign oil, Beck asserts that Americans are to blame for the "energy crisis" by not celebrating the success of U.S. oil companies enough. Instead, they have punished these successful companies by imposing windfall taxes on them. He complains that the Watermelon Effect has led Americans to believe that there is some shadowy cabal working behind the scenes to control the production and supply of oil in order to force the price of oil up and thereby make more profits. The green lobby, he insists, has led Americans to believe that there exists "some Oil Council of Doom, consisting of mustachioed tycoons, sat in a smoky boardroom" that decides to limit supply in the face of increasing demand in order to drive the prices up.[6] Wait a minute! Isn't he talking about the Organization of the Petroleum Exporting Countries (OPEC)? It seems that, according to Beck, OPEC is a figment of some Marxist-Green conspiracy. Does Beck really expect us to believe that OPEC is a figment of some fruity plot to hoodwink the American people into supporting windfall taxes? Apparently so, according to Beck's theory of economics, as only an idiot would think that the producers of oil would limit supply at a time of high demand in order to keep prices high. That would not be a "free market," he tells us, and therefore, in accordance with economic principles, we must surmise that no cartel—such as OPEC—could exist. At this point, you are no doubt shaking your head with utter disbelief.

OPEC is a cartel of twelve countries: Algeria, Angola, Ecuador, Iran, Iraq, Kuwait, Libya, Nigeria, Qatar, Saudi Arabia, the United Arab Emirates, and Venezuela. Its statutes state that one of the cartel's principal goals is the determination of the best means for promoting its interests by controlling the price of oil, controlling its rate of production, and controlling supply to the world's markets in order to ensure a return on the capital of the member nations. Even though the discovery of large reserves of oil in the Gulf of Mexico, Canada, and Russia have limited the ability of OPEC to control the price of oil, OPEC nations still possess two-thirds of the world's known oil reserves and they account for over a third of the world's production of oil and petroleum. OPEC still retains considerable power over the supply and price of oil.

Of course, Beck's ideology explains why he pretends OPEC does not exist. After all, it is hard to propagate propaganda about the myth of the free market when that market is controlled by a cartel. What Beck does not seem to grasp is that the problem for environmentalists is not that the oil companies make profits for their shareholders—they are no different to any other commercial enterprise in this respect. The problem is the extent to which they are an obstacle to further research and development by suppressing patents and having too much power over government policy, regulation, and oversight. The real problem is that they interfere with government and the free market by restricting market competition. This is what Beck's ideology prevents him from seeing. Of course, he is right in pointing out that in the United States it is rather hypocritical to vilify the oil industry when there is a cultural love of the automobile and massive levels of consumption, but what Beck neglects to take into account is how the oil industries and car industries have conspired to suppress alternative means of public transportation and electricity generation by influencing politicians and suppressing patents.[7] Oil companies also have influence over foreign policy.[8]

Beck's complaint that the American people are somehow in error for expecting oil companies to pay windfall taxes neglects to attend to the fact that the oil companies do not produce the oil—they extract it. It is a natural resource and it is reasonable for the people of the United States to consider the oil discovered in the territory of the United States to be their property. The oil companies should have to pay the American people to extract it, and in my view, it is reasonable for them to return an additional share of their profits to the U.S. Treasury when their profits are extraordinarily high. My view is that either there should be a "Separation of Oil and State"—keeping the American oil companies from having any influence on public policy—or the government should nationalize the oil industry, before it is too late, and after paying "just compensation" for the infrastructure, in accordance with the Fifth Amendment, use revenues from the extracted oil to fund development in alternative technologies.

Unabashed, Beck, again with an astounding twist of logic, argues that American dependency on foreign oil is a direct result of Americans not opposing the taxation of American oil companies. He claims that these taxes drive American oil companies to seek out foreign and cheaper sources or to just decide not to extract any more oil! Of course, these are possibilities that exist only in Beck's imagination. The oil companies will go to any available source of oil if they can make a profit on it. The reason why oil companies don't flock to cheaper foreign sources is because foreign companies already have access to those sources. As things stand, most U.S. imports of oil come from Canada, anyway.

Regardless of the arguments for or against the oil industry, oil is a finite resource and is running out. In the long term, Beck does not offer any solutions at all. The rise of developing countries is only hastening the inevitable outcome. Fossil fuels and uranium ore are limited. We either develop alternative sustainable technologies or we go back to the Stone Age. Beck reluctantly admits that we could develop these technologies over time, but he insists that drilling in ANWR is the only practical solution. It doesn't even occur to him that it might be strategically advantageous to keep an oil reserve under ANWR should there be future shortages in the world's oil supply before adequate alternatives have been developed. Arguably, this is because Beck is not really concerned with solving America's energy problems. He is only concerned with trying to sell his ideology of unrestrained capitalism—the American oil companies want the oil under ANWR and they should have it now. When it's all gone, it's all gone. The consequences for the natural ecologies and indigenous people of Alaska are irrelevant. The strategic advantage of keeping oil reserves is irrelevant too.

The main argument of the proponents of U.S. offshore drilling and drilling in ANWR is that it would make the United States less dependent on imported oil. The U.S. Energy Information Administration reports American dependence on imports grew from 24 percent in 1970 to 66 percent in 2008.[9] The United States is the third largest producer of oil in the world. Saudi Arabia is the highest, producing over 10 million barrels per day. The second highest is Russia, producing just under 10 million barrels per day. The United States produces 8.5 million barrels per day (offshore drilling in the Gulf of Mexico accounts for less than 24 percent of oil production in the United States). In 2008, the United States consumed 19.5 million barrels of oil per day. This leads to quite a shortfall.

The United States imports twice as much oil from Canada as it does from any other country, about two million barrels per day. Mexico, Nigeria, Saudi Arabia, and Venezuela each supply the United States with about a million barrels a day. The United States imports about the same amount of petroleum from these countries as well. These countries accounted for roughly 65 percent of U.S. imports. Including oil and petroleum imports from Iraq, Colombia, Angola, Russia, and Algeria as well accounts for 85 percent of the total. The remaining oil and petroleum imports come from Brazil, the United Kingdom, Ecuador, Kuwait, Azerbaijan, the Netherlands, and the Virgin Islands. Does Beck really think that drilling oil from under ANWR is going to put a dent in this?

The United States Geological Survey (USGS) has estimated that between five and sixteen billion barrels of oil is technically recoverable from ANWR (including federal lands, native-owned private lands, and state-regulated waters).[10] This gives a mean estimate of ten billion barrels, seven of which lie under federal lands. These estimates are based on comparing the amount of oil that has been found in surrounding areas with similar geology. In 2008, the Department of Energy reported that annual United States consumption of crude oil and petroleum products was 7.55 billion barrels in 2006 and the same again in 2007, totaling 15.1 billion barrels.[11] Even if the oil could be extracted immediately, without any accidents and waste, even if we take the upper USGS estimate as about right and the United States consumes at the current rate, then within two years it will all be gone, and the country will be in the same position as it is now, but without this reserve. Given that the practicalities of extraction will take years before drilling could begin, and the maximum rate of extraction will be probably be on the order of a million barrels per day, this will hardly solve the U.S. dependency on foreign oil. ANWR and further offshore drilling in the Gulf would have to match the total output of Saudi Arabia and Russia combined to do that. Drilling in ANWR is at best a short-term solution and at worst will destroy pristine wilderness, irreversibly damage the traditional lives of the indigenous peoples who live there, deplete oil reserves, and not provide any solution at all. Of course, in the short term, it will make a lot of money for U.S. oil companies, lots of revenue for the government, and provide some additional jobs, but it is not a solution to America's oil consumption, let alone its energy problems.

Taking the above in mind, is it really worth risking ANWR and squandering the oil reserve there simply for short-term profits and a temporary measure that will not solve the problem and leave America facing exactly the same problems in the very near future? Beck, of course, tries to mislead us into believing that the area affected by drilling in ANWR will only be two thousand acres of the nineteen million acres of wilderness.[12] This figure is largely plucked out of thin air but at best only includes the proposed drilling sites. It does not include the infrastructure, such as pipelines, airfields, roads, housing, and so on, and what he also fails to mention is that, according to the Department of Energy, given that area of actual drilling, it would yield less than three-quarters of a million barrels per day. This barely scratches the surface of America's dependency on foreign oil. And it would take almost a decade before the country saw any of these revenues coming in to the Treasury. Even if we accept that Beck's promised $38 billion per year of tax revenue is accurate, this is actually a drop in the ocean of government spending, and it is nothing compared to the costs of the damage that could be done to Alaska.

Nonchalantly, Beck makes light of oil pollution, citing the USGS report of 2003 that claims that 47 percent of oil seeped into marine environments comes from natural seepage.[13] If he had read further, though, he would have learned that the intensity of natural seepage is far less than spills. He also claims that only 4 percent of oil spills come from offshore oil platforms, the rest coming from tankers and barges. Indulging in a flight of fantasy, he asserts that disasters such as that involving the *Exxon Valdez* would not happen if a pipeline from the ANWR was built. Of course, he forgets to mention that there have been leaks from the Trans-Alaska Pipeline, which runs from Prudhoe Bay to Valdez.[14] In 1978 an unknown saboteur blew a hole in it at Steele Creek, east of Fairbanks. Approximately sixteen thousand barrels of oil leaked before the pipeline was shut down. In 2001, someone shot a hole into the pipeline near Livengood, causing approximately 6,144 barrels of oil to leak from the pipeline, which spilled over two acres of tundra. In 2006, corroded pipelines on the North Slope gave way and spilled over six thousand barrels of oil. In March, 2010, five thousand barrels of oil leaked from a pipeline on the North Slope into Prudhoe Bay. In May of this year, several thousand barrels of oil spilled from a pump station near Fort Greely during a scheduled shutdown, due to a failed relief valve control circuit during a test of the fire-control system. This oil poured into a tank, overflowed onto a containment area, and was recovered.

This eight-hundred-mile long pipeline took two years to build and cost about $8 billion, and thirty-two workers were killed during its construction. In comparison, a pipeline from ANWR, across Canada, to the United States would be an enormous project and require the consent of the Canadian government, which without doubt would want a share in revenues, as would each and any U.S. state the pipeline passed through. Inspections and maintenance would be an enormous task in itself, and if it had the same carrying capacity as the Trans-Alaska Pipeline, would provide up to two million barrels per day. But this is all fantasy. Canada is unlikely to agree to it, it would take years and unknown billions of dollars to build it and all the necessary pumping stations. It is more likely that the oil companies will transport the oil by tankers from Valdez. And when Beck wrote the following words— "There's a reason when you hear 'oil spill' you think of giant tanker disasters like the *Exxon Valdez* not offshore rigs"—that was before the Deepwater Horizon explosion in April 2010.[15]

The Deepwater Horizon drilling rig explosion resulted in the fifth worst oil spill on record and the worst maritime leak in U.S. history. It has been estimated that between April 20 and July 15, 2010, between 560,000 and 585,000 tons of oil spilled into the Gulf of Mexico. About five million barrels of oil spilled into the Gulf, the equivalent of an *Exxon Valdez* tanker spilling its cargo off the southern coast of the United States once every ten days for four months. Even though the *Exxon Valdez* ran aground off Prince William Sound eleven years ago, Alaska still hasn't completely recovered from the *Exxon Valdez* disaster. Despite Exxon's assurances that there is nothing to worry about, according to the University of North Carolina and the National Oceanic and Atmospheric Administration's National Response Team, it could take another twenty years for the ecology of the area to recover. The local economy was devastated by this spill, which covered thirteen hundred miles of coastline.[16]

As of yet we do not know the damage the Deepwater Horizon disaster has caused the ocean and coastline ecologies of the Gulf. We can only guess how long it will take the local fishing and tourist industries of the southern states to recover from the damage caused by this spill. Scientists from NOAA and elsewhere claimed that radar satellite images showed that by the end of April, the spill had covered almost six hundred square miles of the Gulf. By the beginning of June, oil began washing up along 125 miles of Louisiana coast and on to the Mississippi, Alabama, and Florida barrier islands. By the end of June, tar balls were found in the Mississippi River, and at the beginning of July, strings of oil were found in the Louisiana Rigolets and tar balls on the shores of Lake Pontchartrain. Even as late as September, waves of oil were washing up along the coastline and marshes west of the Mississippi River. Oil was still washing ashore in October 2010. The National Institute for Undersea Science and Technology reported massive underwater oil plumes in the Gulf, including one ten miles long, three miles wide, and three hundred feet thick.[17] The largest underwater plume recorded by scientists from the University of South Florida was over twenty-two miles long.[18] University of South Florida and University of Georgia scientists have found large amounts of oil sediment along the sea floor, stretching for miles in all directions around the capped well, indicating that a great deal of the oil sank rather than evaporated.

Many of the workers and volunteers involved in the initial efforts to disperse the oil have suffered health problems, probably from the chemical dispersants Corexit EC9500A and EC9527A (which contain propylene glycol, butoxyethanol, and dioctyl sodium sulfosuccinate).[19] These substances have been banned by the British government from use on any oil spills in the United Kingdom due to concerns over the detrimental effects on human health. It is not known what effects these dispersants have had on the birds, fish, crustaceans, and other wildlife of the Gulf. British Petroleum (BP) reported that by mid-July it had used over one million gallons of Corexit to disperse oil on the surface and it had injected over seven hundred thousand gallons directly into the oil leak. By the end of July, almost two million gallons of Corexit had been used. The use of dispersants underwater may reduce the oil density sufficiently that it helps microbes break down the oil while it is still below the surface, but dispersants do not make the oil disappear. They simply spread it around, hopefully speeding up the rate it biodegrades, but in the deep cold waters of the Gulf, the oil remained in plumes longer than expected, much of it still below the surface, and a great deal of it dropped onto the sea bed.

NOAA estimated that 25 percent of the leaked oil was removed from the waters of the gulf: 17 percent recovered from the well head, 3 percent skimmed off the surface, and 5 percent burned on the surface.[20] This means that 75 percent of the oil—an estimated 3.75 million barrels—remain in the waters or along the coast of the Gulf, even if it has been dispersed, dissolved, sedimented, or buried or is still floating around beneath the surface. In addition, there is considerable controversy about NOAA's estimates among scientists, and the percentage of the oil that has evaporated into the atmosphere is not known. However this controversy pans out, it does seem rather absurd to claim that because the oil has either dissolved or evaporated, it has disappeared, as if by magic. While bacteria may well break down some of this oil (as well as the natural gases that were also leaked), the proliferation of these bacteria may have an impact on the ecology and public health. Large amounts of oil, dispersant, and bacteria could poison and kill many forms of marine life around the waters and the coasts of the Gulf. Damage to the sea bed is almost completely unknown. We will probably not know for decades the extent of the damage and harm caused by this disaster, and the Gulf environment could take even longer to recover. We do not even know if it can.

Without doubt, this spill has had an enormous impact on the local economy and food supply. The U.S. Travel Association has estimated that the impact of this disaster on the tourism industry could be as high as $23 billion over the next three years (in an industry that nets $34 billion per year and employs over four hundred thousand people).[21] By the end of May 2010, the federal government had declared fisheries disasters for the states of Louisiana, Alabama, and Mississippi, and it has been estimated that loses for the fishing industry exceed $2.5 billion. The consequences this has for levels of toxicity in seafood or the recovery of fishing grounds can only be guessed at this stage, and again controversy abounds over the question of whether the dispersants have entered the food chain. We also should not be surprised to learn that the 1990 Oil Pollution Act (OPA) limits BP's liability to $175 million for noncleanup costs. The passing of the OPA is another example of how Big Oil has interfered with government to its own advantage.

And Deep Horizon was only the fifth worst spill on record. During the Gulf War in January 1991, an estimated 800,000 to 1 million tons of oil spilled into the Persian Gulf, and the Kuwaiti oil fires during 1991 sent between 140 and 200 million tons of oil into the atmosphere. In the United States, the largest spill on record was the Lakeview Gusher in the Midway-Sunset Oil Field in California, which between March 1910 and September 1911 spewed over one million tons of oil. While the spills and fires during the Gulf War were caused deliberately, as part of an Iraqi scorched earth policy during its retreat from Kuwait, the Lakeview Gusher was an accident. The oil business is a messy business, involving politics, profits, bloody conflicts, corruption, failures, greed, mismanagement, and deceit, and sometimes accidents just happen. Murphy's Law—"Anything that can go wrong, will go wrong"—applies to the oil business probably more than any other. Do we really believe that drilling in ANWR will not result in an accident and irreversible environmental damage?

Whatever the fate of ANWR, the unpleasant fact of the matter is that the current level of consumption is not sustainable. Oil will run out. There are not any quick fixes to the problem. Nuclear power is another proposed quick fix. But uranium is a finite resource. It will run out, too, and leave behind radioactive waste that will remain deadly for thousands of years. Nobody has any idea how to safely dispose of it. Nuclear leaks and accidents are devastating for generations. The inconvenient truth is that America and the rest of the industrialized world—with India and China rapidly catching up—simply have to change their patterns of consumption. There is no alternative. One cannot have one's cake and eat it. Economics and ecology converge on this fact: People have to consume and waste less of the world's precious resources.

Simply switching from oil to bio-fuels will not solve the problem either. Not only do they continue to pollute the atmosphere, but bio-fuels, such as ethanol, are causing more problems than they solve. Once storage and transportation are taken into account, they use as much oil as they save. They also have a serious impact on food production and supply. Billions of taxpayers' dollars are given to big agribusinesses to produce corn for ethanol instead of food (for humans and farm animals). This drives the price of food up and leads to a reduction of the available land for food production. If the United States switches from oil to bio-fuels, it could lead to a global food crisis. Subsidized ethanol production is not only another example of how Big Business interferes with government, in this instance by buying politicians with campaign funds, but it shows how Americans need to stop letting corporate-owned politicians use taxpayers' money to buy their votes with promises of jobs and quick-fix "solutions" that, quite frankly, are wasteful and disastrous for America and the rest of the world.

Without doubt, we will continue to need to use fossil fuels for the near future, but the fact that alternative and sustainable technologies are required cannot be denied. The world needs to transform how we produce and consume energy. There is the possibility that a sustainable plasma fusion reactor could be built in the future—more publicly funded research into this technology is required—but we should not rely on this. We should not put all our proverbial eggs in the same basket, especially when we do not even know if this basket can be made. From the current vantage point, it seems that our best bet involves improving and implementing technologies to extract energy from the sun, wind, tides, water, and the earth itself. We need to focus more efforts—using the precious resources we have—to provide as much of our energy as possible by using solar, wind, tidal, hydroelectric, and geo-thermal power. Imagine the possibilities if one of the trillions of dollars given to bail out Wall Street had been spent on sustainable energy technologies instead! However slowly, progress is being made. More people are using solar power and wind farms are springing up throughout the world.

Beck rightly condemns the "Not in My Back Yard" (NIMBY) attitude that some people have shown regarding solar-cell arrays and wind farms. I agree with Beck that it is ridiculous not to take advantage of local conditions when deciding the location of these energy sources. But it also would be unacceptable to override the objections of local residents and impose developments on them—along top-down Stalinist lines, Comrade Beck! In a democracy, local voices should be heard and people do have a right to oppose developments, no matter how misguided we might think they are. For some people, some places are sacred and they should be left alone, no matter how advantageous they might be for solar- or wind-power generation. We need to be sensitive to people's concerns. But people also need to learn that electricity does not appear by magic; it requires technology and, in the case of solar- and wind-power technologies, it needs to be located where local conditions favor it. Further efforts to persuade and educate the public are required.

Furthermore, these new technologies allow us to escape the "big project" paradigm for electricity generation. A great deal of energy can be gathered from domestic grid-tied solar electricity and heating systems, while small wind turbines can also be used to augment electricity supply. Solar- and wind-power technologies not only offer the possibility of sustainable electricity generation but also offer the opportunity to decentralize the control over electricity generation and place it directly under local and personal control by distributing it throughout the whole nation, house by house, apartment block by apartment block. Hydroelectric, geo-thermal, and tidal generators offer possibilities for locally owned and controlled electricity generation. Through domestic grid-tied systems, people can supply the statewide or even national grid with their surplus electricity and buy it when they need additional kilowatt hours. Household insulation and better building materials can reduce waste. Improvements in efficiency in design and materials can also reduce waste. Better recycling systems—encouraged with tax credits—would reduce waste. Better public transport systems and more efficient vehicles also reduce waste. Hydrogen-burning and solar-powered electric vehicles already exist. Solar and wind technology design is improving in leaps and bounds. Many different kinds of technology can be employed to augment each other, reduce waste and pollution, and maintain a healthier and cleaner environment.[22]

However, technology does not offer a quick fix solution either. It is the case that, regardless of whether people like it or not, we come back to the same point: The world cannot sustain unlimited consumption. We all need to develop sustainable patterns of consumption, stop squandering precious resources, and reduce waste. This is why I agree with Beck's scathing criticisms of the latest fad in hybrid cars and the "cash for clunkers" scheme. He considers hybrids like the Prius to be little more than trendy status symbols rather than a solution to the world's environmental problems. Natural resources and energy are used to make hybrids, which results in pollution and waste. Does the increased efficiency of a hybrid over the old car really offset these uses of natural resources and energy, with their associated pollution and waste? Beck argues that 28 percent of the total CO_2 emissions from a new car come from manufacturing and delivering it to the dealer. The best thing to do with an old car is to run it into the ground.

I would go even further than this. The "cash for clunkers" scheme should have rewarded people with a tax credit for each year that they keep their old car running. People should be rewarded for maintaining their cars rather than buying new ones. Of course new cars should be more efficient, but there needs to be a paradigm shift away from consumption and toward conservation. How's this for a suggestion? The government passes a law that requires all new cars to come with a lifetime guarantee. If the car breaks down, the manufacturer has to repair it or give you back your money. What if the government offered cheap or free courses in how to repair and modify cars to make them more efficient instead of subsidizing the car industry? How about giving tax breaks for buying used cars? The hybrids and the "cash for clunkers" scheme are themselves the result of the ideological faith in the market—that more consumption will save the economy and the planet along the way. The problem is that this ideology blinds us to the problem: Our current level of consumption cannot be sustained.

I also agree with Beck's opposition to Cap and Trade. The basic idea behind Cap and Trade is to provide a market-based solution to the problem of how to reduce industrial pollution, such as CO_2 emissions. The government sets a cap to how much CO_2 can be emitted in accordance with agreed targets. Companies are then allocated or must purchase credits to emit an amount of CO_2 up to the cap. If a company needs to emit more CO_2 than the cap, it must purchase credits from other companies that emitted a lower level and can sell their excess credits. In this way, credits can be traded, emissions can be regulated, violators can be fined, and the cap can be lowered over time in line with future targets. This provides a market mechanism by which companies can find "the least cost" solution to the problem of how to reduce pollution. So what's wrong with that idea? Well, the problem is not that it is part of some global conspiracy to tax and control Western industry, as Beck implores us to believe.[23] The problem is that CO_2 is a global pollutant. Emissions of a global pollutant have global consequences, although each country has different verification and enforcement policies. Corruption and problems with monitoring, reporting, and enforcement can penalize the industries of those countries that meet their targets to the advantage of those of countries that don't meet targets and simply lie about having done so.

Even if we overlook these problems, the trading in offsets may well reduce emissions from some sources of CO_2 and increase the cost of emitting CO_2 from others, but it does not reduce the total amount of CO_2 in the atmosphere. If it does not deal with this problem, we still face the possibility of a runaway greenhouse effect and all its devastating consequences for life on Earth. At best, Cap and Trade reduces the level of CO_2 increase, but it does not reduce the total amount. It merely delays the inevitable. The lowering of the total amount of CO_2 pumped into the atmosphere also requires international agreements, such as the 1997 Kyoto Protocol, and their ratification by all nations, including the United States. However, industrial countries such as the United States are concerned that they will be unfairly handicapped in economic competition with developing nations such as India and China. While this may well be a means of reducing the gap between developed and developing countries, effectively acting as a mechanism of "redistribution," it will still increase the total amount of CO_2 in the atmosphere. Cap and Trade only looks at the problem in terms of national production, and given the global nature of markets, this does not address the problem in terms of consumption.

What's the alternative? Instead of merely increasing the cost of doing business as usual, we need to change how we live on this planet and learn how to live in a sustainable way. This involves a radical change in the economic paradigm. We need to stop measuring growth and development in terms of easily quantified factors such as gross domestic product, and instead measure growth and development in terms of how people evaluate the *quality* of their lives in their local communities. We need to put people and the world before profits. There are straightforward changes we can all make. We can consume less. We can waste less. We can learn how to fix things rather than buy new replacements. But most importantly, we need to start asking fundamental questions regarding how we wish to live. We need to examine deep questions about values and quality in relation to the current economic system. We need a renewed use of public reason and debate to examine how we can transform our patterns of consumption in a way that is sustainable and improves our quality of life. There is nothing utopian about the idea of developing a sustainable economy. What is utopian is the belief that the current level of consumption can continue indefinitely.

If the people of the United States and the European Union reduced our level of consumption by reducing our imports, it would indirectly place a cap on the CO_2 emissions of China and India. We need to support our local economies. This not only would reduce the amount of oil required and CO_2 emitted just to transport products around the world but also keep wealth and jobs within our communities. We need to stop buying cheap and shoddy products that we throw away when they stop working and instead return to the local manufacture of high-quality products that last for years and can be repaired when they break or parts wear out. This would also provide more jobs for repairmen, tool makers, and parts manufacturers. We can also buy locally produced food, join cooperatives, and learn how to grow our own food. This does not require a return to the Stone Age—it requires the recognition that neoliberal globalization is a disastrous economic policy based on an ideological commitment to a flawed economic model. I shall discuss this further in chapter 11.

There are lots of things that could be done other than Cap and Trade. We need to put pressure on politicians to implement effective environmental policies. Local governments can fund better public transport and recycling facilities, and they can provide grants for loft insulation, better building materials, and solar power for grid-tied systems. Local governments can reduce the tax burden on local businesses to help them compete with multinational corporations.[24] They can reward recycling through tax credits and penalize wasteful consumption through increased sales taxes on targeted products. The current policy of promoting increased consumption through increased borrowing, as the means to improve the economy in order to escape an economic crisis caused by unrestrained capitalism, shows the insanity of this ideological commitment to consumption. People need to reject this flawed paradigm and become fiscally conservative. Throw away credit cards. Buy less and save your money!

While national government can help by increasing the public funding of research and development into new sustainable energy production technologies, this needs to be developed within the framework of a new economic paradigm that is geared toward a sustainable economy based on improving the quality of life rather than only on measuring growth in terms of quantity of consumption. Indeed, regulations can impose increased efficiency standards for new power plants, cars, and appliances while placing tariffs on imported goods from countries that fail to reduce their CO_2 emissions or to meet higher quality-control standards, but this will only help to solve the problems facing us if the world's natural resources are treated as precious and not squandered.

And Nature has already provided us with a means to remove CO_2 from the atmosphere. We call them trees. What are needed are international efforts to reforest the world and protect the remaining rain forests. But we don't have to wait for those efforts. Plant a tree today! It is simply insane to cut down hundreds of thousands of trees of virgin woodland on Long Island for BP to build a massive solar-power array, especially when these public funds could have been used to provide American homes with domestic solar power, putting local people in charge of their own electricity supply and consumption.[25]

Without doubt, Beck will consider all the above suggestions to be wacky. Questions of sustainability just do not have any place in his ideology. Anything that restricts the pursuit of profits opposes freedom, according to Beck. This pro-corporate ideology demands increased consumption, global markets, lower production costs, and unrestrained capitalism. Corporations guzzle oil transporting products from China rather than making them in America in order to exploit access to cheap labor. This allows corporations to avoid the costs of paying American workers high wages and benefits, and also allows them to avoid environmental and workers' safety protections. Capital flight has been the main method to break American unions and reduce labor costs. The irony of neoliberal globalization is that it has resulted in funding the industrialization of Communist China, which now owns a large share of America's massive national debt and is soon to surpass the United States in the consumption of energy and natural resources. How long can the Earth sustain this growing level of consumption?

5

Union Bashing

It should come as no surprise that Beck is anti-union. In his vision of America, unions have no place. They are an unnecessary obstacle to capitalism because, according to Beck, it is no longer 1930 and workers have rights, protections, and benefits. He admits that these rights, protections, and benefits were gained by unions, but now that they have been gained, unions are no longer needed, and workers can rely on legislation to protect them:[1] "Have you ever noticed how union groups talk like it's 1930 and their members are headed down into the coal mine without any water or flashlight? Guess what? It's not 1930. These days, workers have rights, protections, and benefits that those from the early twentieth century couldn't even fathom. . . . So, why are unions still around? Good question, easy answer: they've got lots of friends in very high places."[2]

Wait a minute! When discussing the Second Amendment, Beck tells us that people cannot rely on the police or trust the government and need their own arms to protect themselves from criminals and tyrants. When discussing education, he tells us that Americans cannot trust the government to fund public schools. When discussing energy, he tells us that the government cannot be trusted to solve the energy crisis and should get out of the way of the American oil companies. According to Beck, the government cannot even be trusted to run the postal service. But when it comes to labor relations, the government can be trusted to enforce legislation, and workers no longer need unions to collectively bargain and secure their rights, protections, and benefits.

Of course, the motive for this contradictory reversal is obvious. Beck is a propagandist. It is not that he trusts government to protect the rights and benefits of workers—he knows full well that state and federal governments will take the side of corporations. He makes this contradictory reversal simply because his ideology of unrestrained capitalism sees trade unions or any form of organized labor as a threat—just as he blames teachers' unions for failures in public education—regardless of the fact that freedom of association is considered to be a constitutional right (protected by the First Amendment). But before I discuss Beck's union bashing, it should be noted that he does say a few words of praise for unions in the past, just as long as unions are a thing of the past. Whether he is sincere in his praise, I do not know. He admits that he is aware that American unions gave mistreated workers the right to bargain collectively and overcame tremendous difficulties and hardships to achieve this right: "Brave men and women stood up and stared down politicians, special interests, monopolies, and robber barons and fought for fairness and a slice of the American Dream. They didn't demand special rights, they demanded *equal* rights."[3] So before moving on to discuss Beck's arguments against unions, let's take a brief look at the history of unions in the United States of America.

America at the turn of the twentieth century was a time of industrialization and unrestrained capitalism. Slums spread throughout the cities, and factory workers faced harsh working conditions and long hours for low pay, without any benefits or protections. Miners probably faced the worst conditions. Women were paid less than men, and child labor was commonplace. Congress and the federal government did little, if anything, to protect workers from even the worst kinds of exploitation. Poverty, illiteracy, crime, prostitution, and alcoholism were major problems in American cities, while infant mortality was high and life expectancy low. Workers could be fired at will, and if unable to work, through injury, illness, or old age, people were reliant on family or left to starve on the streets. Workers were forced to organize themselves into unions in order to fight and collectively bargain for the legislation and contracts that gave them better pay, fewer working hours, improved working conditions, and other rights, protections, and benefits. Unions were fiercely opposed by the owners of factories, mines, railroads, and shipyards, who were able to use hired thugs and gain the support of government to bust unions. Until it was repealed by the 1914 Clayton Antitrust Act, the 1890 Sherman Antitrust Act had even been used to prosecute unions as illegal organizations. Time and time again, the courts and state and federal government sided with private companies and sent state militia or federal troops in to use force to suppress strikes.

Perhaps one of the most well-known union busters was the Pinkerton National Security Agency, founded by Allan Pinkerton in 1850, which was also known as the Pinkerton Agency, Pinkerton Men, or Pinks.[4] This private company was involved in many efforts to infiltrate unions and break strikes, often by using violent methods, and was used as a private militia to intimidate workers and prevent unions from forming in factories. The Homestead Strike is perhaps the most infamous industrial dispute involving the Pinkerton Agency.[5] During the steel works strike at Homestead, Pennsylvania, in 1862, when three hundred armed Pinkerton men tried to break through picket lines, a fight broke out between them and townspeople supporting the Amalgamated Association of Iron and Steel Workers picketing a lockout after a contract dispute between the union and the Carnegie Steel Company. Sixteen men were killed (seven Pinkerton men and nine strikers), many men and women were injured, and the state militia was called in to restore order. The strike lasted more than three months—with the militia escorting replacement workers across the picket lines—before the bankrupted union members voted to end the strike and accept lower wages and longer hours.

The Great Railroad Strike of 1877 is arguably the most infamous example of strike busting in American history.[6] This strike, which began in West Virginia, started when Baltimore and Ohio Railroad workers protested their second wage cut within a year. At the request of the Baltimore and Ohio Railroad Company, the governor ordered the state militia to put down the strike using force. When state militiamen refused to obey this order, the governor called for federal troops. Meanwhile, the strike had spread to Maryland. When the governor ordered the National Guard to use force to put down the strike, skirmishes broke out between strikers and the militiamen, resulting in the deaths of ten strikers and the injury of many more, including both strikers and militiamen. Rioting spread throughout Baltimore. Federal troops and U.S. Marines were sent in by President Hayes to restore order and put down the strikers. When the strike spread to Pittsburgh and local police refused to open fire on the strikers, the state militia was called in. The militia fired into the picketing strikers, killing over forty and injuring many more. Riots again broke out, resulting in railroad buildings and rolling stock being burnt and the state militia being chased out of the city. After more than a month of rioting and fighting, federal troops were sent in to put down the strike.

Federal troops were also sent to suppress the strike in Reading, Pennsylvania. The Reading Railroad Massacre resulted in the deaths of sixteen strikers and the injury of many more. In Shamokin, Pennsylvania, the mayor, who also owned the mine, deputized vigilantes to put down striking coal miners. When the strike spread to Chicago and East St. Louis, Illinois, state militiamen and federal troops combined forces to suppress strikers. When Illinois coal miners came out on strike in sympathy and the Chicago Workingmen's Party organized mass protests in support of the railroad workers, Judge Thomas Drummond of the U.S. Court of Appeals for the Seventh Circuit declared strike action interfering with railroads to be "a violation of United States law" and ordered federal marshals to protect railroads and arrest striking workers for contempt of court. Monroe Heath, the mayor of Chicago, deputized five thousand vigilantes to put down strikers. After these vigilantes killed over twenty strikers and caused many more injuries, which resulted in a riot, federal marshals with the support of federal troops broke up the strikes. Due to the action of federal troops and the National Guard, and the use of force to suppress strikers, the Great Railroad Strike ended after forty-five days.

Similarly, federal troops were used to put down the Pullman Strike of 1894.[7] The Pullman Palace Car Company cut wages and increased the length of workdays to twelve hours, without decreasing rents in Pullman (a town outside Chicago owned by the company). The company refused to meet with a delegation of workers elected to discuss this problem. The American Railway Union, led by Eugene Debs, called for a boycott of trains containing Pullman cars, and over 125,000 railroad workers across America answered that call and refused to connect Pullman cars. This effectively shut down Pullman.[8] In response, the railroad companies hired replacement workers. The companies also succeeded in having a pro-company man, Richard Olney, appointed as a special federal attorney to deal with the strike. He immediately declared the strike illegal on the premise that it interfered with the U.S. mail, obtained a court injunction barring union leaders (including Debs) from supporting the strike, and he declared that any workers who continued to strike would be arrested. When the leaders ignored the injunction and the workers continued the strike, Olney called upon President Cleveland to send in federal troops. Cleveland ordered twelve thousand U.S. Army soldiers and U.S. marshals to bust the strike. As a result of clashes between federal troops and strikers, over a dozen workers were killed, scores were injured, and rioting broke out leading to extensive property damage.

After the strike was busted, the American Railway Union was destroyed; Debs was arrested, convicted of violating the court injunction, and imprisoned for six months. However, Governor Altgeld was highly critical of President Cleveland for so blatantly putting federal troops at the disposal of a private company rather than using the state militia to keep order. Altgeld managed to use his influence to prevent Cleveland from regaining the Democratic Party nomination to rerun for president in 1896. And in 1898, the Illinois Supreme Court forced the Pullman Palace Car Company to sell the town of Pullman to the City of Chicago.

After the Great Railway Strike, Congress passed the 1888 Arbitration Act, which authorized arbitration panels with the power to adjudicate labor disputes. However, the arbitration awards were nonbinding and therefore toothless. The only panel convened was in the case of the Pullman Strike, which came up with a compromise solution, but only after the strike had been suppressed using federal troops. The 1898 Erdman Act empowered arbitration panels to make awards that would be binding in federal courts for both sides in the labor dispute involving railroad companies and unions. This law only covered railroads involved in interstate commerce. Any contracts prohibiting union membership were banned. However, in 1908 the Supreme Court ruled this law to be unconstitutional on the basis that it violated private contracts and property rights.[9] In response, Congress passed the Newlands Act in 1913, which further empowered arbitration panels, and the 1916 Adamson Act, which guaranteed railroad workers an eight-hour day (for the same wages as their previous ten-hour day) and time-and-a-half pay for overtime. This act also empowered President Wilson to assume control of any part of the railroad needed to transport troops or materials required by the war effort. These laws became redundant when the railroads were nationalized in 1917.

After the First World War ended, Wilson returned the railroads to their prior owners and Congress passed the 1920 Transportation Act, which allowed for the creation of the Railroad Labor Board. The board was to oversee nonbinding arbitrations, but in the following year the board ruled that railway workers should take a 12 percent pay decrease and outlawed any strike action the union workers might take in response. When the union launched a national railroad strike in 1922, the Department of Justice obtained an injunction against the strikers, and once again, federal forces were placed at the disposal of the owners of the railroads.

A particularly violent episode in the history of American labor relations was that of the Colorado miners' strikes between 1903 and 1905.[10] During these strikes, the state government took the side of the mine owners, who were able to call on the support of the National Guard, the Pinkerton Agency, the Mine Owners' Association, and vigilante groups, such as the Citizens' Alliance, against the Western Federation of Miners (WFM). Since 1894, the "Waite Agreement" had established an eight-hour working day for Cripple Creek miners. In 1902, the union argued that underground conditions and smelter fumes were hazardous to workers' health, and that the eight-hour day should become state law for both mine and mill workers. Mine owners opposed the proposed state law and the Colorado Supreme Court declared that such a law would be unconstitutional, unless the Colorado Constitution was amended. The WFM successfully campaigned for this amendment, and the Republican, Democratic, and Popularist parties all supported the proposed law and the constitutional amendment, and the state legislature passed the amendment. A state referendum showed that over 72 percent of voters were in favor of this amendment. However, Republican governor James Peabody, under pressure from the mining companies, refused to sign this into law; the state legislature did not override him, and the amendment was not passed.

When miners in Idaho Springs and Telluride protested, they were rounded up at gunpoint and thrown out of town by vigilantes hired by the mine owners, while local law enforcement refused to intervene. District Judge Frank W. Owens issued an injunction against the vigilantes to prevent interference with the return of the miners and issued bench warrants for the arrest of 129 of the vigilantes, charging them with breach of the peace and assault. The district attorney supported the mine owners and vigilantes and would not prosecute the warrants. Governor Peabody refused to intervene and worked with the Mine Owners' Association to form the Citizens' Alliance organization for anti-union vigilantes. He also appointed Sherman Bell, an anti-union mine manager, as general adjunct over the National Guard, and John MacDonald, another anti-union mine manager, as secretary to the state military board. When the United States Reduction and Refining Company refused to negotiate with the seventeen-thousand-member WFM about working hours, the union called for strikes throughout the unionized mines and mills of Colorado.

Local law enforcement, private security, deputized vigilantes, and the National Guard were called in to suppress strikes in Telluride, Colorado City, Idaho Springs, Cripple Creek, and the southern coal fields. The Mine Owners' Association and Citizens' Alliance bullied local businesses to cut off credit to union members and demand that they pay in cash throughout the strikes. Union officials and anyone who condemned the near state of martial law imposed on Colorado or who supported the strikes were arrested and imprisoned without charge. Even children of the strikers were imprisoned. The *Daily Record*, a newspaper supporting the union, was closed down and the reporters thrown into the stockade. District Judge W. Seeds of Teller County, after hearing writs of habeas corpus, ordered their release. At first, Sherman Bell refused, declaring, "Habeas Corpus be damned, we'll give them post-mortems," but he was ordered by Governor Peabody to comply.

Workers were forced at gunpoint to return to work and any mill owners who refused to join the Mine Owners' Association were blacklisted. Pinkerton agents had infiltrated the union, spied upon and sabotaged union efforts, and acted as agent provocateurs. While strikers did resort to violence and sabotage, Pinkerton agents also conspired to commit such acts in order to frame and discredit the union. Union members were also forced to give up their firearms, while vigilantes were allowed to keep theirs. Vigilante groups paid for by mine owners acted as local militias, supported by local law enforcement and the National Guard. The WFM Union Hall was placed under siege and then occupied by vigilantes. Workers who refused to denounce the union were arrested and thrown out of the state by the National Guard. Public officials and local sheriffs sympathetic to the union were forced to resign. Local newspapers were heavily censored, and the *Daily Record* resumed operations as an anti-union newspaper. Intimidation and beatings of union members and their families were commonplace. C. Hamlin, the secretary of the Mine Owners' Association, was elected as district attorney. He refused to prosecute any case brought against members of the Mine Owners' Association, the Citizens' Alliance, the National Guard, or local law enforcement. Governor Peabody denounced the strikers as members of "the lawless classes"; he declared full martial law, suspending the right of assembly for strikers, and in 1905 the strike was busted. The WFM moved to Chicago (many of its leaders helped set up the Industrial Workers of the World) and changed its name to the International Union of Mine, Mill, and Smelter Workers. It has now merged with the United Steelworkers.

The 1926 Railway Labor Act proposed that a government-appointed board of mediation should be set up if and when agreement could not be reached between railway employers and unions. This act specified the negotiation procedures that must be adopted by unions and employers. It also specified the rules by which agreements should be interpreted and applied. Unions were only allowed to strike if these procedures had been properly followed and exhausted, without agreement being reached, and the courts could punish unions if these procedures were not properly followed. However, employers were allowed to hire replacement workers during a strike, even though they were not allowed to fire or discipline workers for striking. This law was modified in 1932 by the Norris–La Guardia Act, which banned contracts that prohibited employees from joining a union, prevented federal courts from issuing injunctions to prevent nonviolent strike action, and declared employees free to join or form a union without interference from employers. In 1934, the National Board of Mediation was formed as a permanent agency, which established rules of elections to determine whether unions had the support of their members, and in 1936 this law was extended to include airline employees.

In the 1930s, large numbers of workers across America began to organize into unions. The employers continued their tried-and-tested tactics of strike busting. However, citywide general strikes and factory occupations by workers threatened to become a serious national emergency leading to pitched battles between workers, strike breakers, private security agents, local police, and the National Guard. Congress responded by passing the 1935 National Labor Act. This law prevented employers from interfering with the right of employees to organize into unions and collectively bargain, or from discriminating against union members. It prohibited the infiltration of unions by hired agents in order to spy upon and sabotage them. It also compelled employers to negotiate "in good faith" with unions and established the National Labor Relations Board (NLRB) to arbitrate, oversee negotiations, ensure fair union elections, and adjudicate whether employers were engaging in unfair practices.

> The right to bargain collectively is at the bottom of social justice for the worker, as well as the sensible conduct of business affairs. The denial or observance of this right means the difference between despotism and democracy.
>
> *Franklin Delano Roosevelt*[11]

Of course, conservatives at that time denounced this law as "socialism." Many employers refused to cooperate with newly formed unions and the NLRB. Employers campaigned and lobbied to restrict or outlaw entirely union practices such as closed shops, sympathy strikes or secondary action, jurisdictional strikes, and mass picketing, as well as collective bargaining for pension and health benefits. The American Liberty League was formed to oppose the "threat to democracy" employers took this law to be.[12] They began a national campaign of filing court suits to obtain injunctions to hamper unions and the NLRB.

In 1947, the Republican-controlled Congress passed the Labor-Management Relations Act over the veto of President Truman, who declared it to be in opposition to the principles of a democratic society. This law answered the campaigns of employers and the American Liberty League. It prohibited closed shops, sympathy strikes or secondary action, jurisdictional strikes, and mass picketing, and imposed limits and rules on unions before they could use employer funds to provide pensions and health care benefit to union members. But it did not stop there. It also outlawed wildcat strikes and political strikes, limited the right of unions to collect dues, allowed states to pass the "right to work" laws that banned compulsory union dues, and allowed employers to fire at will. It also prevented unions from making donations to federal political campaigns, and even required union leaders to sign affidavits disassociating themselves from communism. It also gave the executive branch the power to obtain court injunctions against strikes if the president deemed them to imperil the national interest.

These restrictions on strike action were further tightened by the 1959 Labor Management Reporting and Disclosure Act. This law also regulated the internal procedures of unions, made secret balloting compulsory, placed elections and union finances under the jurisdiction of the Department of Labor, and barred members of the Communist Party and convicted felons from being union officers. It required a trade union to file a petition with the NLRB before it could strike more than thirty days in order to compel an employer to recognize the union. This law extended the National Labor Act and Labor-Management Relations Act to include railroad and airline unions, and the U.S. Postal Service, but not public sector workers, local or state government employees, agricultural workers, or domestic employees. Federal employees had to wait for the 1978 Federal Labor Relations Act before they had the right to form a union and collectively bargain. The rights of local or state government employees, agricultural workers, or domestic employees to form unions and collectively bargain were left to the states to legislate.

The 1938 Fair Labor Standards Act established minimum wage and overtime rights for most private sector workers, with a number of exemptions and exceptions. In 1974, this law was amended to cover governmental employees. Many states have passed laws to provide higher minimum wages than provided for by federal law. The 1970 Occupational Safety and Health Act set standards for workplace safety, protects "whistleblowers" who complain to government agencies about workplace safety violations, and allows workers the right to refuse to work under unsafe conditions. The 1974 Employee Retirement Income Security Act set standards for the funding and operation of pension and health care plans provided by employers to their employees. However, even though the 1964 Civil Rights Act, the 1967 Age Discrimination Act, the 1990 American Disabilities Act, and the 1993 Family and Medical Leave Act all prohibit discrimination and provide protections for employees, unless they are covered by either a collective bargaining agreement or an individual contractual provision, an employer can still fire an employee at will, for no reason or any reason. The 1986 Worker Adjustment and Retraining Notification Act only requires private sector employers to give notice (no less than sixty days) in event of mass layoffs and plant closures, and even then the law admits exceptions.

While laws and regulations do offer American workers some protections and benefits, they are also clearly heavily skewed in favor of employers. So why is Beck so opposed to American unions? He complains that unions have become powerful political organizations, monopolies, and bureaucracies— "the very thing[s] they once fought against"—and they oppose competition, capitalism, and freedom.[13] What I find particularly perverse is his implication that originally workers formed unions to fight against bureaucracies and monopolies rather than fight against the unrestrained capitalism that became so excessive that workers needed to form unions to protect themselves. It also seems to me to require a particularly twisted logic to assert that unions are un-American by not celebrating unrestrained capitalism. Of course, Beck ignores the fact that labor relations and laws in the United States have forced unions to become bureaucratic in order to be legal and protective of their own interests. Instead, he claims that unions "are basically an afterthought—only 7.6 percent of nongovernment workers belong to one."[14]

This is puzzling. If unions are only "an afterthought" and "most Americans aren't fooled" by them, what is the problem? Why does he need to be so vehement in his opposition to unions? Why spend so much time bashing this "afterthought"? He complains that unions lower profits by causing higher labor costs and more regulations. In other words, unions are able to bargain collectively for higher wages and benefits for workers, which reduce the profits for the owners of the company, and unions are able to protect their members by securing better working conditions and regulations, which of course increase the cost of doing business. Unions facilitate a greater distribution of profits and secure a safer and healthier working environment. This obviously reduces the profitability of a company in comparison to one that pays low wages, does not provide any benefits, and does not provide safe and healthy working conditions. Hence, with the passing of "free trade agreements," allowing companies to import cheap goods made in countries with cheap labor and little in the way of worker protections, "capital flight" has become one of the main mechanisms by which the private sector has become de-unionized in America. Clearly Beck's pro-corporate ideology means that he is against American workers gaining a greater share of profits and having a safe and healthy working environment, and he is in favor of the exploitation of workers as the means to be "competitive." However, if unions are on the decline, his continued union bashing still remains puzzling.

Let's take a look at this claim that only 7.6 percent of private sector workers belong to a union. He tells us that he took this figure from the U.S. Bureau of Labor Statistics' "Union Members Summary" (January 28, 2009).[15] This was a news statement dated January 22, and the actual figure is 7.2 percent of private sector workers belong to a union, but let's not quibble over details. This summary says 12.3 percent (15.3 million) of American workers belong to a union (slightly down from 12.4 percent in 2008, due to a slight increase in the level of unemployment). In 1983, when the Department of Labor started compiling such statistics, 20.1 percent (17.6 million) of American workers belonged to a union. In 2009, the report states, "more public sector employees (7.9 million) belonged to a union than did private sector employees (7.4 million), despite there being 5 times more wage and salary workers in the private sector."

The report tells us that unionization rates depend on occupation, industry, demographics, firm size, and the state in question. Workers in education, training, and library occupations had the highest rate of union membership (38.1 percent); protective services (like police and fire) had 34.1 percent union membership; more men than women are members of unions; more black workers are members of unions than white, Asian, or Hispanic workers; New York has the highest union membership (25.1 percent) and North Carolina the least (3.1 percent); and 37.4 percent of public sector workers belong to a union, with local government workers having the highest membership at 43.3 percent. Age is also a factor, with 16.6 percent of workers age fifty-five to sixty-four belonging to a union and only 4.7 percent of workers age sixteen to twenty-four having union representation. It also tells us that unionization rates in the private sector depend on the industry in question. Most unionized workers (38.2 percent) were in the transportation, utilities, and telecommunications industries. Only 14.5 percent of construction workers belong to a union. In sales and related businesses, 3.1 percent belonged to unions. Forestry and fishing industries had only 2.8 percent of its workers belonging to a union. But the lowest union membership is in the financial and agricultural sectors, with only 1.8 and 1.1 percent, respectively, belonging to a union. It also states that "in 2009, among full-time wage and salary workers, union members had median usual weekly earnings of $908, while those who were not represented by unions had median weekly earnings of $710."

Beck cites a 2009 Rasmussen Reports poll that states 9 percent of non-union workers want to join a union.[16] This is a surprisingly low percentage that seems to contradict other polls and studies. The 1994 Worker Representation and Participation Survey (Princeton Survey Research Associates) showed a large gap between the kind of representation that private sector workers had and the kind they desired.[17] This study showed that 32 percent of non-union workers in the private sector wanted union representation. It also showed that 90 percent of workers already represented by a union would prefer to keep union representation. Taking the sample as a whole, 44 percent of workers favored union representation. Even among those workers who did not favor trade union representation, there was huge support—between 85 and 90 percent—for greater say in the workplace and for some kind of collective workers' representation. Of course, since 1994, there has been a drop in union membership from 11.3 percent to 7.2 percent, according to the Department of Labor statistics, but this raises the question of whether workers do not want to join a union or whether market and institutional obstacles to union membership have arisen. In their follow up to this survey, Harvard economist Richard B. Freeman and University of Wisconsin sociologist Joel Rogers (no relation to the author) found that in 2005 there was a much higher demand for unionizations between 1994 and 2005, with 53 percent of non-union workers wanting trade union representation in the workplace.[18] Only a few workers, about 14 percent, were satisfied with their workplace.

A 2001 Hart and Associates poll found that the majority of workers did not feel satisfied with their workplace and did not feel that employers were respecting their rights to fair wages, opportunities, privacy, respect, security, and equal treatment regardless of age and gender. However, workers did tend to feel that their workplace was safe, that they received reasonable levels of overtime pay and sick leave, and that there were low levels of discrimination due to ethnicity and disability and fewer incidents of sexual harassment. It seems that even though a majority of private sector workers want union representation, legislative anti-discrimination protections are working. This might reflect that, although anti-discrimination legislation has been enforced and there are remedies through the courts, many workers since 1994—between 60 and 70 percent—feel that the real value of their wages has fallen, they are receiving inadequate levels of health care and retirement benefits, they have less job security, and they receive less respect from their employers. Gallup polls also have shown that the percentage of workers who approved of unions has ranged between 65 and 70 percent since 1947.

While union membership has been decreasing, it is clearly the case that the validity of the Rasmussen poll is questionable. However, even if we accept that it is accurate, it still is not self-evident that Beck's popularist interpretation is correct. It is not the only explanation of this poll that private sector workers are against unions. As the Department of Labor statistics show, there are demographic, market, and industry differences to take into account. Also, while illegal firings of workers for wanting to join a union did decrease during the Clinton administration, they rose again during the Bush administration (although not to the same level as during the Reagan administration). It is also the case that employers use consultancy services to prescreen employees and enact anti-union programs within companies. Furthermore, there is always the constant threat and use of capital flight to bust and discredit unions. And we must not forget the effects of constant propaganda and union bashing in the media, of the kind that Beck disseminates.

Beck denies all this, of course, but he contradicts himself when, in order to refute any claim of employer intimidation or manipulation of workers, he cites a report by the National Labor Relations Board that states 60 percent of all secret-ballot elections to form a union actually succeed.[19] Wait a minute! How does this square with the claim that only 9 percent of workers without a union want to join a union? It doesn't. It seems that the majority of workers want to join a union, which fits with the findings of Freeman and Rogers. It is another example of Beck cherry-picking statistics and polls to suit whatever point he is arguing at the time. Similarly, without irony, again citing an NLRB report (September 30, 2008), he claims that unfair labor practices complaints are "levied against both sides" and then he goes on to tell us that 16,179 were filed against the employer and 6,210 were filed against unions, which apparently shows that unions are just as bad as employers, despite the fact that there were less than half as many complaints made against the unions.

Even if we concede Beck's assertion that unionization is in decline because most Americans do not want to be a member of a union, we still have to return to the question of why he is bothered about unions. Beck complains that unions are too powerful and influential because "they have friends in high places." He is outraged that unions donate far more money to the campaign funds of the Democratic Party than to the Republican Party. He considers this to be evidence of bias and unfairness. He ignores the fact that the Republican Party has been consistently anti-union and pro-employer. With his usual twisted logic, he argues that it is unfair and biased of unions to ally themselves with those politicians that would help unions. He accuses the unions of trying to buy elections because they donate to candidates who support their own agenda. Beck is clearly making a naïve and ridiculous argument. He also ignores the fact that corporations and businesses donate to the campaign funds of politicians that promote their interests. How does this differ from corporations or any other groups that exchange campaign funding for political influence?

Beck does not mention these, but it turns out that the reason why he is vehemently anti-union and continues his campaign of union bashing is because unions are successful at playing the political game in order to gain further influence, keep their members in employment, secure their contracts, and maintain their wages, benefits, rights, and protections. Far from being an "afterthought," it seems that Beck's problem with unions is that they are very successful. With a twist of logic, he complains that by gaining political power and influence, unions are betraying their original mission of gaining rights, protections, and benefits for their workers. Apparently, according to Beck, the best way for unions to serve their members is for them to have no political influence or power whatsoever! But, of course, as he has told us already, unions are not necessary at all. After all, according to Beck, American workers have enough legal protections, rights, and benefits, so there is no need for unions and no need for workers to be able to influence further legislation through collective power. In other words, for Beck, workers should have no power whatsoever beyond acting as individuals in relation to their employer, and they should trust government to look after their best interests.

Having basically argued that unions use political donations to influence politicians to protect the jobs of their members, Beck has backed himself into a corner. To get out of the absurdity of his own argument, he attempts to twist and distort the argument by claiming that there is a paradox in the union support of the Democratic Party. He argues that the unions want high wages and job security (finally, he admits it) and so support the Democratic Party, which supports lax immigration policies and thereby allows illegal workers to take American jobs and force down wages. I shall discuss immigration in the next chapter. However, putting aside the fact that the Republican Party has done little about illegal immigration despite its jingoistic rhetoric, what Beck has forgotten or misunderstood is that illegal workers and union workers tend to work in different kinds of employment. Most illegal workers are employed in agriculture, construction, or domestic work, whereas most union workers are in the public sector, telecommunications, or industry. There is little competition here at all. The fact of the matter is that most traditional union jobs—in heavy industry—have been outsourced to other countries. It is not illegal immigrants who have forced wages down and taken jobs, but it is the corporations who have moved their production base out of America into the developing world, where they can exploit cheap and unprotected labor.

Again, Beck uses the typical pro-corporate rhetoric that "capital flight" and "outsourcing" are the fault of the unions and American workers who should have been willing to work for the same wages as their counterparts in developing countries in order for their employers to have made higher profits and been more competitive in attracting investors. Illegal immigration is the fault of American workers not being prepared to work for the same wages as Mexican workers, according to Beck's argument. We are supposed to believe that it has nothing to do with decades of pro-corporate "free trade" legislation that has allowed corporations to outsource American jobs and take advantage of cheap labor costs to flood the American markets with cheap imports.

When discussing union efforts to get the proposed Employee Free Choice Act (EFCA) passed, Beck misrepresents it. After pointing out that this act would do away with the secret ballot and replace it with a card check, he goes on to tell us that it would allow the government to impose binding arbitration after ninety days if the parties do not come to an agreement. He says that in another era, this would have been called communism. Of course, the EFCA says nothing of the kind. Already, under the existing system, as has been established since the 1935 National Labor Relations Act, a union can be certified if the majority of workers already have signed cards, and the petition is uncontested by the employer. If only 30 percent of workers have signed cards or the employer contests the petition then a secret ballot is called. Under the EFCA, the employer would not be able to contest the petition to form a union if the majority of workers have signed cards. This act means that an employer must begin negotiating with a certified union with a view to reaching a collective agreement within ninety days, and if not, *at the request of either side*, the two sides will be referred to compulsory mediation. If mediation fails to reach agreement within an additional thirty days, then arbitration will be made, the results of which are binding for two years (although the employer and union can agree to extend this). This act would also include tougher punitive measures against employers who discriminate against employees who attempt to form a union. Currently, employers only have to pay back pay to illegally fired workers, and federal court injunctions can only be made against unions for violations. There is not any such course of remedy for illegal acts committed by employers in violation of workers rights. This act would correct this imbalance.

Since 2007, this bill has passed committee and the House of Representatives, but although obtaining a majority in the Senate in favor of this act, it has been blocked by Republican threat of filibuster. Apparently, the main sticking point is whether to keep or remove the provision doing away with the need for a secret ballot. While my own view on this act is that it does remedy the current legislative imbalances and should be passed, I have yet to see a good reason not to maintain the secret ballot. This seems to me to be an essential mechanism to prevent the coercion of workers from either employers or overzealous union members. The provision to do away with the secret ballot should be dropped and the rest of the bill passed.

The bottom line is that Beck's argument against unions is that they are able to do exactly the same thing as corporations, and influence government to make deals and come to arrangements that benefit themselves. His argument lacks any merit beyond his ideological assertion that what is good for American corporations is good for America. Hence, if American workers can get a better deal, such as higher wages, benefits, and job security, that is bad for America, especially if it makes American corporations less competitive (i.e., less profitable) than companies exploiting the workers of Asia. Whose America does Beck defend? The answer is obvious: the owners of American corporations. He is not defending American workers. This is most evident in his argument that the growth of employment in states somehow indicates the economic development of those states. It is a weak argument at best. It says nothing of the kind of jobs that are being created. Yes, it might be the case that low-paid jobs multiply in states without unions and those states supportive of unions may have a lower rate of employment growth, but the jobs are better paid and have greater security. In any case, how does an increase in low-paid jobs improve the quality of life of American citizens? Is it really the case that in a developed country like the United States, trade union demands for better pay, benefits, rights, and protections have destroyed the economy, as pundits and propagandists such as Beck assert and repeat over and over again?

Arguably, what has irreversibly destroyed the American economy is the way American corporations—clearly unconcerned with patriotism—have shifted their productive base and capital by outsourcing to developing countries, putting Americans out of work in order to increase profits and competitiveness in an international investors' market. It is due to corporations engaging in "capital flight"—disguised as "globalization"—that the American economy is collapsing and the quality of products and services is growing worse. Meanwhile, the economy and industrialization of Communist China is growing by leaps and bounds. This is one of the great ironies of globalization. However, any attempt at opposing this trend is called "protectionism" and derided by media pundits like Beck. He argues that employers should have an absolute right to fire at will. Workers should not negotiate their own wages; they should rely on the generosity of their employers and the national minimum wage as set by the government, according to Beck, even though he is against the minimum wage because it increases labor costs.[20] Workers should not have benefits like healthcare and pensions; they should rely on charity instead. The ideal asymptote in his vision of labor relations is that labor costs and the national minimum wage would be as close to zero as is humanly possible. In another era, that was called "slavery."

I will discuss this point further in chapter 11. However, I do not deny that there are bad unions and bad union practices. That would be a foolish thing to deny. But a union is only as good as its members. Yet insofar as a union is corrupt or its leadership is unaccountable to its membership, it reflects the wider society within which the union exists. Unions do not exist in isolation. If they have become reactionary and bureaucratic institutions, it is up to the members to change the leadership or democratize unions they feel do not represent them. This requires grass-roots activism and debate within the union membership about the directions of their unions. This is symptomatic of the problems facing wider society. It is up to citizens to democratize society through grass-roots activism and public debate about society's directions. (I shall discuss this further in chapter 12.)

The question of whether workers need to organize into unions capable of defending their rights as human beings and collectively bargaining for a fair share of productivity produced by their labor is independent of the question of whether any particular union is corrupt and does not represent its members. Media pundits and propagandists like Beck want to ignore this distinction. If they can find one example of a bad union or bad union practice, this discredits the very idea of collective bargaining through a union, according to them, whereas bad businesses or corporate practices merely indicate that freedom is messy. This is exactly the same twisted logic that tries to claim that a law that prohibits the amount of lead in paint or plastic toys is the start of the slippery slope toward communism, and that any attempt to regulate the public effects of any industry is an infringement on personal liberty. However, we need to turn away from this kind of propaganda and illogical nonsense. When it comes to the question of the legitimacy of unions, there clearly are hard and important questions about what constitutes a good union between workers. This is not just a question of how to best represent the interests of workers in negotiations with both employers and government. This is a deep question about the nature of democracy. As such, it is a question of justice, equality, and mutual respect among human beings.

6

ILLEGAL IMMIGRATION

Glenn Beck tells us that although illegal immigration is a "national crisis," Americans aren't taking it seriously enough, "activists" are trying to cover it up, and politicians are ignoring the problem.[1] In *Arguing with Idiots* he states that "approximately two thousand people willfully ignore that statute [U.S. Code Title 8, Section 1325] every day, making illegal immigration a national crisis that you're apparently not supposed to notice. Official estimates of our illegal population range from 10 to 20 million, and, at least if we are to believe the politicians and activists, not a single one of those people is anything other than a hardworking, down-on-their-luck foreigner trying to provide for their family."[2] He tells us that illegal immigrants are placing a heavy burden on public services, such as welfare, schools, and hospitals. He warns Americans that these illegal immigrants are taking American jobs and that a porous border is a route for terrorists to enter the country. His solution is to build a double-layer fence across both the southern and northern borders, to punish employers for hiring illegal immigrants, and, once the borders have been secured to his satisfaction, for some kind of amnesty program to be implemented for those who come forward and pay a fine.

Beck wants the law enforced and for illegal immigrants to be arrested, punished, and deported: "I am more than willing to talk about a program for people who want to come out of the shadows, admit they are guilty of a crime, and pay an appropriate penalty. But, . . . I'm willing to talk about that only *after* we have secured both borders to my satisfaction. . . . The truth is that 'comprehensive' immigration reform should be 'comprehensive' in that it deals with how we will comprehensively shut down the border and turn off the job magnet first."[3] Does this sound reasonable? Let's take a look at these proposed solutions in a little more detail.

Would a double-layer fence really secure the U.S.-Mexico border? Beck puts a great deal of faith in this idea. He admits that it would be expensive and estimates that it might cost up to $40 billion. He considers this a price worth paying, however, and suggests that this money could be recouped by the savings to unemployment benefit payments if illegal immigrants are prevented from taking American jobs. Let's accept Beck's estimate of the cost of this state-of-the-art double-layer border fence. And for the sake of argument, let's not worry about maintenance and repair costs. Would it work? Let's assume that it would prevent many people from entering the country and cut down the level of immigration significantly. But would it make the border more secure as a consequence? Well, no. It would make crossing the border more difficult, but smugglers also use planes and boats to smuggle drugs, weapons, and people. Also, unless every single vehicle that crossed the border was searched and every person's documents were checked, smugglers would also be able to use border crossings, as they do now. Ingenious smugglers have used tunnels, and, obviously, this would be one of the ways that they would smuggle people, weapons, and drugs under the fence. I suspect that the fence might also be subjected to sabotage attempts, which would misdirect border security personnel and increase costs.

Just as the Great Wall of China failed to prevent invasions and the Berlin Wall failed to contain defectors, so Beck's Great Fence of America would not be impassable either. Such a fence might offer the illusion of securing the border, but it would not stop determined smugglers and terrorists from entering the United States from Mexico. Furthermore, as roughly 40 percent of illegal immigrants enter the United States legally and then overstay their visas, Beck's border fences would cost $40 billion ($120 billion if one was built along the U.S.-Canada border as well) and, at most, only halve the level of illegal immigration, without actually stopping determined and ingenious smugglers and terrorists.

While Beck dismisses the concerns of environmentalists, it is a fact that building a fence across the border will damage protected lands and nature reserves, prevent the seasonal migration of animals, block access to water, and endanger species. It is also the case that the border fence would divide the lands of Native Americans along the border. Their rights need to also be respected. Given that this expensive and controversial fence would not actually secure the border, it does not seem to me to be reasonable to cause ecological damage and impose a fence on Native Americans just to present the illusion of security. Rather than build this fence, perhaps it might be wiser to spend the money on training and equipping more border patrol agents, better integrating law enforcement and border protection operations, allowing the U.S. Armed Forces and National Guard to patrol the border, streamlining the legal processes by which people can apply to enter the United States (currently there is a backlog of one million green card applications, with delays of up to three years), and tackling the real causes of illegal immigration.

Before discussing these real causes of illegal immigration, let's take a look at Beck's second proposed solution: removing the incentives to enter America illegally to find employment and receive welfare benefits, education, and Medicaid. Citing the Center of Immigration Studies (CIS),[4] Beck claims that illegal immigrants use more welfare than citizens, and take advantage of public education, Medicaid, and food stamps.[5] Beck cites two CIS studies.[6] What do these studies tell us?

Nearly 60 percent of illegal immigrants are from Mexico and 80 percent are from Latin America. Fifty-one percent of all Mexican immigrant households use at least one major welfare program and 28 percent use more than one program, 40 percent use food assistance, 35 percent use Medicaid, and 6 percent use cash assistance. Forty-five percent of all Latin American immigrant households use at least one welfare program and 24 percent use more than one program, 32 percent use food assistance, 31 percent use Medicaid, and 6 percent use cash assistance. In comparison, 20 percent of citizens' households use at least one welfare program and 11 percent use more than one program. Eleven percent use food assistance, 15 percent use Medicaid, and 5 percent use cash assistance. Ninety percent of Latin American households have at least one worker. Their level of "welfare use" reflects their low incomes, not an unwillingness to work. Their low level of income is the direct result of low levels of education, with only 39 percent of Mexican immigrants and 52 percent of Latin American immigrants having graduated high school.

While illegal immigrants are barred from the majority of federal aid programs, they do have access to hospitals and some state welfare programs, and all children born in the United States are American citizens and eligible for all welfare programs and school education. It is estimated that there were 1.4 million households of illegal immigrants and four hundred thousand children born of illegal immigrant parents in 2006. The welfare system is geared toward helping low-income families, especially those with children. Of course, illegal immigrants pay taxes, but according to the 2004 study, illegal immigrant households used $2,700 more dollars of welfare on average than they paid in taxes per year. Among the largest cost was to Medicaid claims and treatment for the uninsured (costing $2.5 billion in 2003), followed by food assistance programs (almost $2 billion), and federal aid to schools ($1.4 billion). Both studies concluded that barring illegal immigrants from welfare does not achieve any significant change in welfare costs because the vast majority of welfare is claimed on behalf on their U.S.-born children, who are American citizens. This study also found that immigrant households with at least a high school graduate level of education provided more in taxes than they received in welfare. However, it concluded that any amnesty program would increase costs to the taxpayer considerably because it would allow low paid immigrants greater access to welfare benefits and programs. Both studies concluded that education level is the key factor in determining the costs of illegal immigration.

For the sake of argument, let's accept that these studies are accurate. What does Beck suggest? Is he proposing barring the families of American-born children of illegal immigrants from access to welfare, schools, and hospitals? Of course, Beck wants to end taxpayer-funded public education for Americans anyway. He basically wants to end all taxpayer-funded welfare and health care for Americans as well. Clearly, he is in favor of preventing illegal immigrants from gaining access to taxpayer-funded public services, such as food assistance, Medicaid, and cash assistance. It seems that he is also opposed to the children of illegal immigrants—whom he terms as "anchor babies"—from being granted citizenship status. As we can deduce, Beck's solution to illegal immigration is to build the fences across the southern and northern borders, bar all illegal immigrants and their American-born children (which would entail amending the Constitution to repeal the Fourteenth Amendment clause granting citizenship status to all persons born in the United States and under its jurisdiction), and enforce the laws that prevent employers from hiring illegal immigrants.

Before discussing how Beck would prevent employers from hiring illegal immigrants, let's take a brief look at the history of immigration laws. The 1790 Naturalization Act barred freed slaves and immigrant non-whites from becoming citizens. Freed slaves had to wait until the Fourteenth Amendment was ratified in 1868. Immigrant non-whites had to wait considerably longer to be eligible for citizenship. The 1798 Alien Enemies Act empowered the government to deport resident immigrants should their country of origin be at war with the United States. This law remains on the books. The 1882 Chinese Exclusion Act restricted the immigration of Chinese laborers for ten years, prohibited Chinese naturalization, provided the procedures for the deportation of Chinese immigrants, and excluded Chinese immigrants from citizenship. This law marked the birth of illegal immigration and was a response to racism in America directed toward Chinese immigrants due to fears that Chinese immigrant cheap labor was taking American jobs. How history repeats itself! It was passed after the California Gold Rush (1848–55) had ended and the Transcontinental Railroad had been built, after which Chinese miners and railroad construction workers moved to the cities. The law was repealed in 1943.

The 1882 Immigration Act taxed all immigrants fifty cents when arriving at U.S. ports of entry, which funded the newly created Bureau of Immigration and empowered the superintendent of immigration to enforce immigration laws. Drunks, lunatics, idiots, and convicts (except those people convicted of political offenses) were excluded from entry into the United States. The 1917 Immigration Act extended the exclusion to beggars, epileptics, "all persons mentally or physically defective," illiterate adults, homosexuals, polygamists, anarchists, and anyone from India, the Middle East, South East Asia, and the

Pacific Islands. This law was passed over the veto of Woodrow Wilson. The 1921 Emergency Quota Act limited the number of immigrants from any country to 3 percent of those already in the United States from that country as per the 1910 census. This resulted in a new wave of illegal immigration. People were able to immigrate into Canada and Mexico and then cross over the border into the United States. The 1924 Immigration Act set down further limits to immigration quotas; began a quota system based on country of origin, which unfairly discriminated against Jewish people; and excluded people of Japanese origin from becoming naturalized. It also introduced the law that those people ineligible for naturalization could not immigrate into the United States.

The 1952 Immigration and Nationality Act included Guam, Puerto Rico, the Virgin Isles, Western Samoa, and the Mariana Islands in the territory of the United States. Racial restrictions against non-whites were repealed in this law. Instead, it set down a quota system based on skills and profession. However, this law allowed members of the Communist Party and "fellow travelers" to be excluded or deported. It also excluded adulterers and gamblers. In 1965, the country of origin quotas were repealed, as were the zones of exclusion, and a program was established for the reunification of families. In 1982, the Supreme Court ruled that children of illegal immigrants should be allowed entry into public schools, and that all people—regardless of their immigration status—should be protected by the Constitution and the law if they are in the United States or its territories.[7]

The 1986 Immigration Reform and Control Act made it illegal to hire knowingly an illegal immigrant. This law introduced the I-9 form as proof of the legal right to work; over three million illegal immigrant workers either received amnesty or were placed under a temporary agricultural worker provision. However, under this law, subcontracting exempted liability and was used as a loophole by which illegal immigrants could be hired. The number of legal immigrants allowed into the United States was increased by the 1990 Immigration Act to seven hundred thousand annually. This law also removed homosexuals from the list of excluded persons, introduced the lottery system for assigning visas, and increased border security. The 1996 Illegal Immigration Reform and Immigrant Responsibility Act provided more resources for border patrols, created the category of "unlawfully present" persons, and barred any person who was unlawfully present in the United States from reentering the country for three years, if they stayed illegally for between 180 and 365 days, for ten years, if they stayed illegally for over 365 days, and permanently if they attempted to reenter the country while their bar was still in place.

Under this law, if an unlawfully present person is arrested for any crime, he or she can be immediately deported, and this provision was applied retroactively to all those convicted of criminal offenses. In 2001, the Supreme Court prevented this part of the law from being applied to those who pleaded guilty to a crime before the law was enacted, providing that they could not have been deported for that offense at that time. The 1997 Nicaraguan Adjustment and Central American Relief Act allowed asylum seekers from Nicaragua, El Salvador, Guatemala, Cuba, and nationals of former Soviet bloc countries to be granted permanent residence. The 2002 Enhanced Border Security and Visa Entry Form Act provided for more border patrol officers, required that schools report foreign students attending classes, and made it compulsory for foreign nationals to carry IDs.

The 2005 Real ID Act was attached to the "must-pass" 2005 Emergency Supplemental Appropriations Act for Defense, the Global War on Terror, and Tsunami Relief. It established federal standards for state-issued driving licenses and other forms of ID; updated the rules for asylum applications and deporting persons suspected of terrorism; changed visa limits for temporary workers, nurses, and Australian nationals; waived laws that would prevent the director of Homeland Security from constructing barriers on the border; and funded pilot programs related to border security. Even though states were expected to comply with this act by May 2008, the deadline has been extended to 2011. To date only Alabama, California, Illinois, North Carolina, and South Dakota have made any progress in implementing this act. Arkansas, Colorado, Georgia, Hawaii, Idaho, Louisiana, Maine, Michigan, Minnesota, Missouri, Montana, Nebraska, Nevada, New Hampshire, North Dakota, Oklahoma, South Carolina, Tennessee, Virginia, Washington, and Utah have passed legislation opposing the Real ID Act. Similar oppositional resolutions have been proposed in Alaska, Arizona, Kentucky, Louisiana, Maryland, Massachusetts, New Mexico, New York, Ohio, Oregon, Pennsylvania, Rhode Island, Texas, Vermont, West Virginia, Wisconsin, and Wyoming. Opponents claim that it is an unfunded mandate that states cannot afford, that it violates the First Amendment freedom of assembly and right to petition government (as citizens without a federal standard ID will not be able to enter Congress or any federal building), that it violates the Tenth Amendment states' rights, and that it makes identity theft more likely. This law is likely to be either repealed or amended in the near future.

Beck does not have anything to say about the Real ID Act, or whether a national ID card could be a solution to illegal immigration, but he does consider the E-Verify scheme—along with heavy fines for employers who hire illegal immigrants—to be the means of "switching off the jobs magnet." First started in 1997, E-Verify is an online service run by the federal government that compares the data in an employee's I-9 form to government records. If the information matches, that employee is eligible to work in the United States. If it does not match, E-Verify alerts the employer and the employee has eight days to resolve the problem. While all employers must complete an I-9 form for each employee, using E-Verify is voluntary (except in Arizona, Colorado, Mississippi, Rhode Island, and the City of Lancaster in California). Since October 2007, all federal agencies and their subcontractors must use E-Verify, and in Georgia and South Carolina all employers with public contracts with the state must use E-Verify for newly hired employees. While there is some controversy about its accuracy, the CIS claims (as does Beck) that it is 99.5 percent accurate. For the sake of argument, let's assume that this figure is accurate.

Beck complains that E-Verify is voluntary and that "constant lobbying by business groups" has undermined this "commonsense program."[8] He urges the federal government to do the right thing. Even though he admits that the government has provided an easy to use, accurate, and voluntary system, somehow, according to Beck, the government is to blame because many employers have not chosen to use it. Why is the government to blame? Putting aside his admission that the government has provided a working, accurate, and easy to use "commonsense program," which he often tells us the government can never do, the shocking twist in Beck's argument is that his complaint against the government is that it has not made the use of this system *compulsory* for all employers. Here we see another one of Beck's ideological reversals. Apparently, the same government that cannot be trusted to run the post office, should not regulate commerce, should not set national tests in mathematics or literacy for school children, and should not even regulate the ownership of firearms, should be trusted to operate a system that says who can or cannot work in the United States—and all employers should be forced to use this system. This is similar to his reversal when it came to the question of workers' rights, protections, and benefits, in which he claims that workers do not need to organize themselves into unions to bargain collectively but instead should rely on the federal government to protect them. Beck argues that employers should not be allowed to choose who they employ, but should only employ people the government allows them to employ.

Apparently, when it comes to the question of whether someone should be allowed to enter into a private contract to sell his or her labor, for a price agreed between employer and employee, Beck's libertarian mask vanishes and is replaced with his mask of nationalism. When Americans want minimum wages and a regulated working environment, he denounces this as "socialism" that is bad for the American economy because it increases costs and reduces profits, but when employers hire cheap migrant labor in order to decrease costs and increase profits, he demands that the police check their workers' papers to see if they are illegal. When unions call for tariffs or restrictions on products imported by corporations that exploit cheap labor in other countries, he decries this call as "protectionism" and insists upon the "free market" demand that employers take advantage of lower labor costs in order to increase profits and lower prices. Yet when employers want to do exactly the same thing in America, he decries this as "criminal" and "cheating." In Beck's vision of the free market, there is to be the free movement of products, but not the free movement of labor. Of course, this vision benefits those corporations that have the capital to set up their business abroad and exploit cheap labor in developing countries or to engage in contracts with foreign governments. But in America, smaller companies and businesses are unable to compete against these multinational corporations without access to migrant labor. I shall discuss Beck's free-market ideology in chapter 11, but here we can see that, when discussing illegal immigration, he does not adhere to a free-market ideology at all.

In accordance with a genuine free-market ideology, the labor market should determine wages, and if someone from Mexico is willing to work at the same job for less pay than someone from the United States, the American employer should be free to hire the Mexican worker. Market forces should determine wages, and once levels of wages stabilize between the United States and Mexico, the market will resolve the immigration problem. Of course, Beck can claim that he is concerned about the welfare burden this causes the American tax-payer. For now, I would like to put aside the humanitarian argument for pro-viding poor migrant worker households with aid. I shall return to this below. Instead, I want to discuss some of the points that Beck and the CIS reports do not raise regarding welfare.

First, welfare is used to subsidize cheap labor for employers at taxpayers' expense. What the CIS studies should have included was how much migrant workers increase employer profits and taxable revenues in comparison to how much additional welfare they require over and above their household tax contribution. If there is a net surplus, then, in a capitalist economy, migrant workers positively contribute to the overall wealth of the economy. Beck considers profitability of American companies to be the measure of their success, and he considers them to directly benefit the U.S. economy through taxes and "trickle-down economics." Yet all of a sudden, employers should ignore labor costs and act as part of the border patrol. Where has Beck's faith in the market gone? As we shall see in chapter 8, Beck advocates that Americans should be willing to migrate in search of jobs, but appar-ently, when Mexicans do it, they should be treated as criminals and a threat. According to Beck, Mexicans should stay where they belong, on the other side of the border, even if employers in the United States want to hire them. Taking his self-contradictory reversal into account, I can see why some peo-ple might consider his position to be racist. I do not know whether this is the case and so I shall not make any judgment one way or the other. In my view, his nationalistic position on illegal immigration is popularist. Once again, he is appealing to his audience demographic and playing his role as a media pundit and propagandist.

Let us assume that Beck and the CIS get their way. Imagine that the northern and southern borders were secured by two massive state-of-the-art fences, and that as a result the rate of illegal immigration were halved, with visa overstays being the only route of illegal immigration. Also imagine that the Fourteenth Amendment clause granting citizenship to everyone born in the United States were repealed—something that Beck seems to favor—and the children of illegal immigrants denied welfare, Medicaid, and schooling. All employers would be forced to use E-Verify, and those who did not comply would face heavy fines. Law enforcement would be allowed to check anyone's immigration status and promptly deport illegal immigrants. At this point, despite relying on the same facts and figures, Beck and the CIS differ. With the border secure to his satisfaction, Beck would accept some kind of amnesty program. The CIS is opposed to this.

The CIS argues that amnesty would allow migrant workers access to welfare, hospitals, and schools for their children, which, given their low level of education, would place a growing burden on the taxpayers. And this would encourage people to overstay their visas and add to the problem of illegal immigration. They call their policy a "strategy of attrition": cut all access to jobs and welfare and illegal immigrants will return to their country of origin. The idea is that by causing misery and suffering to illegal immigrants, they will have no choice but to leave. Of course, this strategy does not take into account that most of the immigrants from Latin America come from impoverished countries run by corrupt or brutal governments, and that gangs of violent criminals and paramilitaries operate in these countries with near impunity. Many of the illegal immigrants from Latin America are running for their lives, not for welfare and jobs. And should legal access to welfare and jobs be denied to people, they will survive by forming a subcultural economic network—a black market—and by working for criminal organizations. This is called *negative social capital*: when people rely on illegal organizations and the black market to survive. Neither Beck nor the CIS have taken this into account. Instead of having to deal with relatively minor problems of funding welfare, hospital access, and schooling for families of illegal immigrants, the problem would be transformed into one of massive levels of violent and organized crime, wherein the poorest of people will have to work for drug dealers, murderers, and pimps, if not become one of them, just to stay alive and feed their families. The strategy of attrition—or strategy of misery—would backfire and be disastrous for America.

Let's also assume that the CIS are right that the problems associated with illegal immigrants from Latin America are due to their low levels of education, in which case, the policy of denying their children access to schools is quite absurd. By raising their level of education, the children of illegal immigrants would be able to gain better jobs, higher income levels, and pay more taxes. Not only would this lead to greater integration of the migrant population within wider American society, but it also would reduce the level of crime associated with migrant communities. The CIS admits that in 2004 illegal immigrants cost the courts and prison system approximately $1.6 billion. Driving illegal immigrants into further poverty and misery would simply shift the taxpayers' burden from welfare, hospitals, and education into police, courts, prisons, and mortuaries. The CIS studies are far too narrow in their scope. If they are going to calculate the costs of illegal immigration, they also need to calculate the costs of their "solution." We might see this as being a good reason for Beck to disagree with the CIS, but it is not at all evident that he is really in favor of

Americans taxpayers paying for the education of immigrants' children, health care, and welfare.

Moreover, the strategy of attrition is so inhumane, by any moral or ethical standard, that many Americans would not support it. Not only would it carry high political risk for those politicians who supported it once the criminality, violence, and misery began to rise, but many Americans, through churches, charities, and personal efforts, would aid illegal immigrants rather than see them starving and homeless on the streets, or living in slums. This would counter the strategy of attrition to such an extent that the government would either have to abandon it or start imprisoning people for aiding illegal immigrants. The CIS strategy of attrition would cause far more problems than it would ever solve.

Beck claims that there is a conspiracy afoot to destroy America as an independent sovereign nation.[9] He believes that "profit-minded global corporations" (the same guys he usually worships) and the Council of Foreign Relations are plotting to create the North American Union. At the heart of this evil conspiracy is the desire to open the borders and allow the people of Canada, Mexico, and the United States to move, seek work, and sell their products freely. However, apart from being a convenient reversal of his free-market ideology, what Beck omits from his conspiracy theory is that many of the problems of illegal immigration started due to profit-minded American corporations lobbying the U.S. government to sign the North American Free Trade Agreement (NAFTA) with the Mexican and Canadian governments, in accordance with the free-market ideology pushed by the World Bank and the International Monetary Fund. This is a consequence of exactly the same kind of ideology of unrestrained capitalism that Beck supports when it suits his argument to do so.

The neoliberal propaganda is that globalization and free-trade agreements raise wages and standards of living around the world, reducing poverty and the need for economic migration. Of course, the reality is that this has resulted in the destruction of local economies, the exploitation of cheap and unprotected labor, mass migration, and a dramatic increase in profits for multinational corporations. The promises of NAFTA and the Central American Free Trade Agreement (CAFTA) were that they would increase the level of investment in Mexico and Central America and reduce the level of economic migration to the United States. However, the economists' theories did not take into account governmental corruption in Mexico and Central America. The Mexican government failed to invest the billions of dollars needed for the infrastructure for NAFTA-proposed factories. It did not build the roads, sanitation, housing, hospitals, and schools. North American companies found it difficult to do business in Mexico, given the systemic corruption at every level of government, and few of the proposed new factories were built. Meanwhile, China became dominant as the source of cheap labor to make cheap products for the markets of Canada and the United States. Millions of Mexican factory employees have become unemployed since NAFTA came into force in 1994.

The first effect of NAFTA was to devalue the peso and decrease the value of Mexican workers' wages, leading to the further impoverishment of Mexican people. Furthermore, the elimination of tariffs on corn and rice meant that Mexican farmers could not compete with the heavily subsidized American agribusinesses. Between 1994 and 2001, the price of Mexican corn fell by 70 percent, many Mexican farmers went bankrupt, and millions of Mexican farm workers lost their jobs. Is it any wonder that Mexicans come to the United States legally or illegally in search of employment? Many Mexican families depend on the money sent back from their relatives north of the border. For them, it is a matter of survival. Of course, President Felipe Calderón opposes any border fence. He wants the poor of Mexico to escape across the northern border. In this way, he can avoid dealing with the failure of the Mexican economy. The last thing Calderón wants is to have to deal with "huddled masses yearning to breathe free." After all, his 2006 "election victory" against his socialist opponent Andrés Manuel López was fiercely contested—with allegations of ballot tampering and intimidation— and if it were not for the federal court's decision to halt an investigation and recount and order the immediate destruction of all ballots, Mexico might have a very different leader today. Perhaps Mexico might have had a government that invested Mexican oil money in schools, hospitals, roads, factories, and farms.

Furthermore, due to the highly profitable illegal drug trade, Mexican drug cartels have grown in power and wealth. Local governments are either too corrupt or powerless to deal with them. The Mexican federal government has proven unable to counter these gangs, and the federal law enforcement agencies and courts have shown themselves to be in the pockets of the cartels. Local people are at the mercy of these violent and ruthless criminals. Ordinary Mexican people are caught in the middle of a drug war among rival cartels, corrupt local police forces and federal agents, and the army. As well as being a transit country for cocaine and other illegal drugs from Central and South America, Mexico has become the main supplier of cannabis to the United States. The U.S. State Department estimates that 70 percent of narcotics and 90 percent of cocaine entering the United States transits Mexico—with Colombia being the main cocaine producer—and that illegal drug sales to the United States could soon reach $50 billion annually. There is also a growing trade in firearms smuggled from the United States into Mexico. Is it any wonder that Mexicans are fleeing northward? Again, it is a matter of survival. The CIS strategy of attrition—should it ever be implemented—would only empower the Mexican drug traffickers' and dealers' black market network by motivating illegal immigrants to work for them out of economic necessity, selling or trafficking in narcotics, firearms, or sex slaves. If Americans are serious about stemming the tide of illegal immigration, it is necessary to rethink the prohibition of cannabis and cocaine.

By allowing Americans to grow cannabis—in accordance with a strict interpretation of the commerce clause and the Ninth and Tenth Amendments—without fear of arrest and imprisonment, not only would billions of dollars be retained in the American economy, rather than going across the border into Mexico, but the Mexican cartels would be seriously damaged, their capacity to expand their operations, bribe officials, and purchase weapons reduced. Once Americans realize that the "War on Drugs" has achieved nothing but to waste billions of dollars on enforcement, fill American prisons, and make drug cartels wealthy, it will become possible to rethink this failed policy. Instead of spending billions of dollars on funding the corrupt governments and paramilitaries of Colombia and Guatemala—countries with some of the worst records of human rights violations in the world, and with horrendous levels of poverty and violence—a legalized cocaine trade would provide American companies and the federal treasury with revenue. The American taxpayer would save billions of dollars now spent on police enforcement, courts, and prisons, and billions of dollars of revenue would be raised. This not only would absorb the expenditure on welfare, Medicaid, and schools for illegal immigrants, but by putting the drug cartels out of business, would increase the chances of Mexicans, Colombians, and Guatemalans wanting to return to their home countries.

Even though cannabis was introduced into North America in the seventeenth century by the English and grown in the Colony of Virginia, the word "marijuana" was adopted when Mexican migrant workers introduced new and more potent strains of cannabis into America at the turn of the twentieth century. In 1914, the City of El Paso passed an ordinance banning marijuana in the city as a measure designed to curb the flow of migrants from Mexico, giving the police new powers to stop, search, arrest, and deport Mexican migrant workers. Their strategy was that by harassing migrant workers, they would want to return to Mexico. If this shows anything at all, it is that the one lesson of history is that we do not learn the lessons of history!

Americans need to consider migration as a global phenomenon. Just as their ancestors strove to escape persecution, poverty, tyranny, and to build a better life for themselves and their descendants, so do immigrants today. Migration is a continuing part of the human story. It cannot be isolated from causal events and policies. As the history of America shows, each new wave of immigrants changed the country, for better and for worse, and immigration cannot be treated in isolation from all the other issues facing the United States of America and the wider world. Many of the problems caused by illegal immigration are the result of disastrous U.S. foreign policies. The dictatorships and juntas in Latin America—funded and supported by the U.S. government during the Cold War—were brutal and ruthless regimes, responsible for the torture and deaths of millions of people, leaving a legacy of guerrilla warfare, terrorism, and corruption. The War on Drugs has been a continuation of this foreign policy, funneling hundreds of billions of American taxpayers' dollars to support corrupt governments and paramilitaries, while the illegal drug cartels have flourished and now all but control the governments and law enforcement agencies of Latin America.

NAFTA and CAFTA have destroyed what little remained of the local econ-omies of Mexico and Central America. Is it any wonder why the wretched, hungry, and poor of Latin America flock northward? It is not an easy path. They leave behind all they know—often their families too—and face a dan-gerous border crossing, often at the mercy of ruthless human traffickers. Many of these people would never be allowed to enter the United States legally, even if they could afford the application fees, given their poor level of education and lack of technical skills. Is it really a morally acceptable solu-tion to hold back these desperate people with a fence? Or if they do make it into the country or overstay on their visa, to deny them work and to starve them back to their impoverished, corrupt, violent, or crime-ridden country?

Unveiled in 1903, the plaque inscribed with the poem "The New Colossus" by Emma Lazarus (written in 1883) has promised welcome to immigrants from around the world:

Not like the brazen giant of Greek fame,
With conquering limbs astride from land to land;
Here at our sea-washed, sunset gates shall stand
A mighty woman with a torch, whose flame
Is the imprisoned lightning, and her name
Mother of Exiles. From her beacon-hand
Glows world-wide welcome; her mild eyes command
The air-bridged harbor that twin cities frame.
"Keep, ancient lands, your storied pomp!" cries she
With silent lips. "Give me your tired, your poor,
Your huddled masses yearning to breathe free,
The wretched refuse of your teeming shore.
Send these, the homeless, tempest-tost to me,
I lift my lamp beside the golden door!"

It is often said that America is a nation of immigrants. Even Beck declares himself to be in favor of legal immigration. He says that he understands and cherishes that America is "a nation of immigrants" but denies that this has anything to do with the issue of "illegal immigration." He calls for a legiti-mate debate and claims to be opposed to "spinning an argument about the rule of law into one about hatred for immigrants."[10] I agree that there needs to be a legitimate debate about what it means for America to be "a nation of immigrants." Tough questions must be asked, and any answers must face intense scrutiny. Americans need to stop dithering—or allowing their politi-cians to dither—and they need to make up their minds whether they want a tough stance or amnesty, a strategy of attrition, or a workers' program. What is unacceptable is to allow the status quo to continue by using illegal immi-grants as cheap labor, vilifying—scapegoating—them and denying them any rights. Yes, the rule of law should be an important part of the debate, but it should be applied equally—not by criminalizing the workers but allowing their employers to continue with impunity or face minor fines at worse. Unfortunately, media pundits and propagandists have been tireless in their efforts to spin an argument about the rule of law into hatred for immigrants, obfuscating public debate by reinforcing prejudices and fears, using selective images and slogans, and twisting history to suit their agenda.

Once again appealing to a Founding Father for support, Beck quotes his hero Thomas Jefferson: "In proportion to their number [foreigners] will share with us the legislation. They will infuse it with their spirit, warp and bias its direction, and render it a heterogeneous, incoherent, distracted mass." This quotation comes from *Notes on the State of Virginia*. Indeed, Jefferson was concerned about the impact of further immigration on Virginia. However, if Beck had read a few sentences further, he would have gleaned: "If they come by themselves, they are entitled to all the rights of citizenship; but I doubt the expediency of inviting them by extraordinary encouragement." Of course, Jefferson would have been concerned with how millions of Latin American immigrants would change America, but he also would have considered the very idea of terming a person an "illegal immigrant" to be a heinous violation of human rights and liberty running counter to the foundational principles of America.

WE ARE A NATION OF IMMIGRANTS

The only people in the United States of America who *really* have the right to hold up a sign reading "Immigrants Go Home!" are from the following indigenous peoples: Apache, Arapaho, Blackfoot, Cherokee, Cheyenne, Comanche, Cree, Crow, Iroquois, Shoshone, Shawnee, Navajo, Pawnee, Sioux, Yaqui, Manahoac, Abenaki, Lakota, Achomawi, Ahwahnechee, Atsugewi, Cahuila, Chumash, Chilula, Chupeño, Lassik, Mattole, Nongatl, Sinkyone, Wailaki, Esselen, Hupa, Juaneño, Karok, Cahto, Kitanemuk, Konkow, Kumeyaay, Luiseño, Maidu, Miwok, Monache, Nisenan, Nomlaki, Ohlone, Patwin, Salinan, Serrano, Shasta, Tataviam, Tolowa, Tongva, Tubatulabal, Wappo, Whilkut, Wintu, Wiyot, Yana, Yokuts, Ukomno'm, Yurok, Cayuse, Klickitat, Ktunaxa, Wayampam, Chinookan, Klamath, Modoc, Molala, Okanagan, Palouse, Kalispel, Sahaptin, Sinixt, Sanpoli, Umatilla, Mishalpan, Walla Walla, Wanapum, Wasco, Yakama, Chemehuevi, Paiute, Kawaiisu, Timbisha, Ute, Washoe, Ak-Chin, Aranama, Coahuiltecan, Cochimi, Cocopa, Genizaro, Halchidhoma, Hualapai, Havasupai, Jumano, Karankawa, Manso, Uzita, Kaw, Mamulique, Maricopa, Pueblo, Mojave, Pima, Piro, Quechan, Papago, Iowa, Hidatsa, Arikara, Atsina, Escanjaques, Kiowa, Mandan, Mayami, Missouri, Osage, Otoe, Ponca, Quapaw, Erie, Wichita, Accohannock, Anishinaabe, Algonquian, Assateague, Choptank, Ais, Conoy, Meskwaki, Hatteras, Huron, Mahican, Secotan, Chickanee, Sissipahaw, Chippewa, Objibwe, or any of the many tribes, confederacies, or nations I have not mentioned.

7

The Nanny State

What media pundits and propagandists like Glenn Beck have done is wrap their "conspiracy discourse" in libertarian garb in order to represent any attempt to regulate and improve things like water quality, the environment, public health, utilities, transportation, agriculture, and education as being part of a global conspiracy and government power grab. Anything that resists corporate power and strategy is considered to be part of a Marxist or anarchist plot to destroy America. However, equating "resistance" to this conspiracy with "a return to the founding principles of America" (as construed by Beck), further alienates dissatisfied Americans from democratic participation, driving them even deeper into the private realm of family and a cathartic sense of "individualism," which actually leaves ordinary Americans even more powerless and incapable of democratic self-governance. The function of anti-government conspiracy discourse is to reinforce and deepen a growing resentment to the very idea that government could be a force for good and a means to provide high-quality public services paid for out of national economic growth. This results in the preservation of the status quo, which benefits the strategic corporate takeover of American political institutions, the media, and all aspects of life.

Meanwhile, Beck complains about how a "Nanny State" has been constructed in America.[1] He claims to be concerned with the way federal, state, and local laws, which are passed in order to improve community standards, keep citizens safe and healthy, and maintain public order are eroding the freedom of Americans and damaging future generations:

> From punitive "sin" taxes and laws dictating your house's paint color
> to rules and regulations aimed at smoking, drinking, dancing, eating,

washing your car in the driveway, keeping a cat in your store, smiling for your driver's license, or playing tag, you can rest assured that local, state, and federal governments are more ready, willing, and able than ever to make decisions for you. Laws and taxes are passed in the name of improving community standards, keeping you safe and healthy, maintaining order, spreading morality, or because somebody somewhere complained, died, or had their feelings hurt.[2]

Let's take a look at this Nanny State. Beck shares with us his libertarian view of the principle of liberty: It is up to each one of us to decide for ourselves how to live our life. Each of us can think and act however we wish, just as long as we do not harm anyone else by doing so. Seems fair enough, you might think. But then, in a somewhat bizarre fashion, he uses drunk driving to illustrate how the Nanny State infringes on our liberty.[3] Now you might think, as I do, that drunk driving is an act that does harm other people. Every day people are killed or maimed because irresponsible idiots get wasted and drive their cars into other cars, into school buses, or up onto sidewalks. Isn't it a good idea to ban drunk driving and punish people who do it? Beck is fairly clear that he is against drunk driving and that people should not do it. He even goes as far to suggest that the Nanny State should even take away the license of repeat offenders (see below). Then what is his problem? He objects to the enforcement of the law banning drunk driving. He argues that this impinges on everyone else. He sees police checks, regulating the strength and type of alcoholic drink, ignition-locking breathalyzers in cars, and so on, as being ways the Nanny State infringes upon everyone else's liberty.

Beck's objection comes down to the fact that, in order to prevent drunk driving, other people who do not drink and drive are also affected by the enforcement measures. He sees this as a form of collective punishment. He does think that drunk driving should he punished (implying that he agrees that there should be a law that should somehow ban driving under the influence), but he insists it is the responsibility of each and every one of us to police ourselves and take a cab home or get a friend to drive us if we have been drinking. "Now, if you make the really, really terrible decision to get liquored up and hit the road," Beck tells us, "you deserve to be *severely* punished. Choosing to call a friend or a cab is your personal responsibility, and until recently, each of us used to be personally responsible for it. But not anymore. Now the government, assisted by a wide assortment of legislation-happy enablers, has decided that it knows best for you."[4]

While I agree that it would be great if everyone could police themselves in this manner and take personal responsibility, I find myself thinking that the problem facing us is that not all people do this; hence drunk driving is a problem that still happens, despite being a really stupid and selfish thing to do as well as being against the law and punishable. What does Beck expect? That drunk drivers will hand themselves in or hand over their licenses to the police? Or should the police only be able to enforce the law when dragging a drunk driver out of a car that has piled into a bus stop and killed four people? We shall assume that he does not believe that the police are telepathic, so how does Beck expect them to find drunk drivers without bothering other people? He does not tell us.

While I agree with his point that we should take personal responsibility for our own actions, it seems to me to be quite reasonable for society to be intolerant of those who do not take personal responsibility and instead choose to drink alcohol and drive home afterward. Laws are there to impose limits on those who cannot limit themselves. Otherwise there would not be any need of laws at all. We do not need laws to prohibit things none of us would ever choose to do. It is one of the foundations of the concept of law that it expresses the limits we impose on one another in order to be protected from one another. As well as an equal right to liberty, we have an equal right to life. People are not at liberty to harm others, but some people do not respect this; hence the *need* for laws.

I see this as an extension of the right to self-defense. (And as we saw in chapter 2, Beck is all in favor of that.) People have a right to drive or walk home without being in fear of some drunk driver swerving across the road at high speed and hitting them. Liberty is not only about the freedom to decide for oneself what to think or do. It is also about the freedom from having other people imposing their ideas and actions on you. The act of deciding to get drunk and drive home, risking killing or harming others, threatens the liberty of other people. A law is useless unless it is enforced. Of course the police should show restraint and not harass law-abiding citizens, but it is reasonable for law enforcement to try to catch drunk drivers *before* they cause accidents. As a result, some police measures to catch those who have broken the law will inevitably inconvenience those who have not. The question is one of which measures the police should use. Beck has muddled together his objections about specific law enforcement measures with the question of whether a ban on driving under the influence should be enforced at all.

Hence Beck's position is confused. Although he does not tell us how the police may enforce a law against drunk driving, he does tell us that people who drive under the influence should be "severely punished." How? Apparently this involves taking away the license of a repeat offender. Fair enough, we might say. (People outside of the United States might not consider this to be a severe punishment, but it needs to be remembered that for Americans, losing the right to drive is tantamount to cruel and unusual punishment.) But what does he mean by "license"? It seems that Beck does accept some kind of regulation after all. It appears that he accepts that the Nanny State should decide who is qualified to drive and who is not. Is this consistent with his notion of taking personal responsibility? Surely individuals should decide for themselves whether they know how to drive a car, right?

Just as we saw in the last chapter when discussing E-Verify, Beck is not consistent. He is not consistent about whether government should regulate our behavior or whether we should take personal responsibility. Furthermore, what does he mean by "repeat offender"? You might think that this obviously is someone who has committed the same crime before. Quite right, but this leads us to ask the question: How do the police and courts *know* whether someone has committed an offense before? They would need to keep records and be able to access them in relation to specific individuals. Presumably, this would involve some obligation on the part of suspects to tell the police their names and show their licenses, and this clearly involves the obligation that citizens identify themselves to police and that there be standards for the production of state-issued driving licenses. Again, this is another example of regulation. If Beck were consistent, he would be opposed to this.

It is also the case that law enforcement methods do not require the police to harass law-abiding citizens. The Fourth Amendment notion of "probable cause" should limit the police to only stopping and breathalyzing drivers who show some evidence of driving under the influence, such as swerving or driving through a red light, or who were involved in an accident. But should the police be prohibited from setting up road blocks and conducting random testing? And why should drunk drivers have a second chance? If they have demonstrated that they lack personal responsibility and care nothing for the safety of others, shouldn't they lose their license after the first offense? If someone drives without a license, shouldn't they face heavy fines and have their car seized? And if someone steals a car, shouldn't they go to jail? Why show leniency? The answers to these questions all reflect political choices about the kind of laws we wish to live by and the kind of society we wish to live in.

However, Beck does make an important point about "mission creep." This happens when a law or regulation is passed to prevent a specific act but then gradually becomes extended to encompass broader acts. To use his example, after passing a law banning driving under the influence, a regulation is passed requiring a convicted drunk driver to install an ignition-lock breathalyzer in their car. Mission creep sets in by soon requiring all cars to have these locks installed, supposedly as a preventative measure, while the campaigns against drunk driving start to become campaigns against drunkenness, then against drinking alcohol. I agree with Beck that this is a very troubling tendency and we should resist it.

What Beck overlooks, however, is that mission creep is often the result of special interest groups using a law or regulation as a means to promote their already existing agenda or an opportunity to make some money. For example, the campaign against drunk driving becomes a campaign against alcohol when the former campaign becomes hijacked by people who already were in favor of prohibition. The law becomes an opportunity to push their agenda further. Similarly, the installation of ignition-lock breathalyzers in all cars, rather than only those belonging to offenders, as a preventative measure, usually follows considerable lobbying on the part of the manufacturers of these devices. The law becomes an opportunity to extend the market and even have a monopoly. A recent example of this would be the 2010 Food Safety Modernization Act. Under the guise of protecting people from contaminated food by improving methods of tracking and controlling food, the law requires record keeping and licensing that proves very expensive for small producers and farmers while being trivial for agribusinesses and corporations. This law makes it very difficult for small producers to compete and effectively places food production in the hands of major corporations.

Beck also makes a good point when he argues that the assumption of the Nanny State ethos is that laws and regulations prevent crime. He argues that prohibitive legislation is premised on the assumption that it acts as a deterrent. Yet even in a totalitarian and authoritarian regime like China, which has many crimes that are punishable by death, people still commit these crimes, despite terrible prisons and mobile execution vans. Punishment does not have a guaranteed deterrent effect. Even the death penalty does not deter everyone from committing capital crimes. Even the cruel and unusual punishments invented by Roman emperors did not deter criminals from risking being boiled or skinned alive, fed to wild animals, or even nailed to a cross. There is probably a psychological explanation. Maybe criminals tend to think that they will get away with it, so the punishment for getting caught doesn't matter, whatever it is. If this is true, then the assumption that human behavior can be controlled or shaped through laws and regulations is probably nothing more than wishful thinking. Punishment does not guarantee contrition and rehabilitation either. Only capital punishment can prevent repeat offenses (assuming the guilty party was the person who was arrested, convicted, and executed).

But the point that Beck's argument misses is that laws and regulations are not just about controlling and shaping human behavior. They are not only supposed to be a deterrent. They are also about providing the legal basis for law enforcement, itself acting within limits, to enforce the limits placed on all citizens for the protection of all other citizens, including those citizens who are charged with enforcing the law. In a republic, everyone is equal under the law. In a democracy, these laws are imposed with the consent of the majority for the protection of the majority, and good legislation should express the consensus of the vast majority. (The problem arises when increasingly these laws are imposed by a minority on the majority for the protection of the interests of that minority. This is an oligopoly, not a democracy.) Laws and regulations define the relationship between individuals, as well as the relationship between the individual and the state. Good laws and regulations act as guidelines in how to exercise one's liberty and to live without harming other people. They provide a guide to acceptable behavior rather than an absolute guarantee of deterrence. It is true that often laws and regulations are knee-jerk reactions to terrible tragedies or horrendous acts, but this is not necessarily the result of a conspiracy to take away people's liberties gradually rather than en masse, as Beck's paranoia leads him to fear. Rather, it is the result of conflicts between positive and negative liberties.

A positive liberty is the freedom to do something. It is the liberty to go out to a bar on a Saturday night and drink alcoholic drinks if that is what one chooses to do. A negative liberty is the freedom from something. It is the liberty to enjoy sitting in that bar without being harmed or harassed by someone else. One's negative liberty places limits on the positive liberty of others. Laws are often the attempt to find a balance between these two kinds of liberty. A good law gets that balance right. A law banning drunk driving does limit the positive liberty to drink and drive, but by doing so, it preserves the negative liberty to drive home without fear of being injured or killed by a drunk driver. However, a law banning alcohol consumption, due to it being causal in cases of drunk driving, or banning driving, given that it provides the means, would be a bad law because it would arbitrarily and excessively limit positive liberty in order to protect negative liberty. Laws that demand that a car has certain safety features, such as working brakes, which are checked periodically, find a balance between positive and negative liberty, but, arguably, one that makes seat belts or crash helmets compulsory goes too far in limiting positive liberty, without really preserving negative liberty (except, perhaps, that of the person who has to clean up the mess after an accident!).

The point of balance is decided by this question: Who does the action risk? If an action only puts the person committing the action at risk, then a law would be an unnecessary constraint on positive liberty. The decision whether to commit risky acts has to come down to the personal judgment and responsibility of those at risk. Even if there is a possibility of risking another person, the likelihood and level of risk must be considered to avoid passing laws and regulations that unduly constrain everyone's positive liberty. Hence it is excessive to ban parachuting over sparsely populated areas (even if there is a non-zero possibility that the chute might fail to open and the parachutist might fall on someone else), but it is reasonable to ban or carefully regulate it over densely populated urban areas.

Some legislators think that the task of a law is to protect people from their own ignorance; to prohibit something that is bad for people but that large numbers of people enjoy. Well meaning though this may be, it is a case of overreach. In a democracy, laws must reflect a consensus rather than impose values. It may well be bad for people to drink alcohol, smoke tobacco, or eat fatty foods, but this should be left to people to decide for themselves. At most, the law should regulate quality-control standards and product labeling so people know what they are eating, drinking, or smoking, but it is a case of legislative overreach to prohibit people from deciding to consume things that are bad for them. Providing the public with knowledge, so people can be better informed about the consequences of their actions, is an important balance between positive and negative liberty. But, of course, in the short term it is cheaper to ban something rather than go to the lengths required to educate people and let them make up their own minds.

Arguably, following the principle of finding a balance between positive and negative liberty, it is reasonable for a law to ban smoking tobacco in public places if it can be shown that this pollutes the air and risks the health of others. It is reasonable to prohibit the sale of alcohol or tobacco products to children, given the serious health risks, if we can show that children are incapable of making an informed decision for themselves. This prohibition could be also extended to selling children fatty foods or refined sugar products! There is not any formula for working out the balance, and hence there needs to be public debate and representation in the legislature in order to make these kinds of decisions through consensus. Beck argues that it is wrong for legislators to treat adults like children. However, this reveals a deeper problem of representation and accountability in the political sphere. Ironically, when legislators treat adults like children, these legislators do not respect the judgment of the same people who voted for them! Mind you, if we take a look at some of the politicians who have been elected to public office, then perhaps they have a point.

Let's take a brief look at the history of the prohibition of alcohol in the United States. Prohibition in the United States (1920–33) imposed a federal ban on the sale, manufacture, and transportation of alcohol for consumption. This was mandated in the Eighteenth Amendment, which was ratified 1919. Several states, starting with Kansas in 1881, had already enacted statewide prohibition before the amendment came into effect with the passage of the 1919 National Prohibition Act (overriding the veto of President Woodrow Wilson).

Prohibition was largely the result of efforts of the Temperance Movement (which included various temperance groups and societies, largely comprised of Baptists and Methodists), with the support of tea importers and soda drink manufacturers. These people pressured legislators to ban the consumption of alcohol due to its effects on health and the various social problems associated with drunkenness and alcoholism. Saloons were associated with other vices as well, such as gambling and prostitution, and alcohol was seen to cause violence and mental disorders. It was largely believed that nationwide prohibition would improve the health, moral character, and industriousness of society.

Of course, things did not quite work out as planned. While the overall level of alcohol consumption may well have dropped during Prohibition, many Americans continued to drink. Bootleggers smuggled alcohol from Canada, Mexico, and the Caribbean. Thousands of speakeasies and underground clubs opened up across the country. Despite the best intentions, Prohibition resulted in the growth of organized crime syndicates. Previously the mafia had been limited to gambling, prostitution, loan sharking, theft, fencing stolen goods, and running protection rackets. Thanks to Prohibition, they were able to take control of a multimillion-dollar black market, providing them with enough money to buy their way into politics, the police, labor unions, and other powerful and influential organizations. Not only did the level of criminality and violence rise during the "Roaring Twenties," but so did corruption at every level of society. To add icing to the cake, this provided enough capital accumulation and contacts for the mob to move into weapons smuggling and the international narcotics trade.

Given its backers' intentions—to make society more sober, moral, and stable—Prohibition was an utter failure. Furthermore, government not only lost all the revenue it would have received from taxing alcohol but also had to fund the enforcement of Prohibition. Faced with growing popular opposition to Prohibition, in March 1933 President Franklin Roosevelt signed an amendment to the National Prohibition Act. This allowed the production, distribution, and sale of light beers and wines. In December 1933, the Twenty-first Amendment was ratified and Prohibition was repealed.

Without doubt, as Beck argues, the problem of overregulation has been caused by government overreach. While I accept that Beck has made a good point here, in my opinion he has told only part of the story. The private sector and the citizenry are also at fault. Most of the time, the legislature tends to be reactionary. It does nothing until some event occurs that leads to public outrage and demands that new laws and regulations solve whatever problems have arisen. Political movements, campaign groups, protesters, charities, churches, and the media all make demands on politicians to pass laws. Politicians follow the votes and issues of the day. The Nanny State is a product of a series of reactions to events and demands. In some respects, it is a case of people getting the government they ask for. It is also the case that private litigation has driven a great deal of state and federal legislation. We all know the cases of fast food restaurants being sued because their coffee was hot and someone scalded themselves. A great deal of the regulatory environment has arisen from private lawsuits in the civil courts. Many laws are simply governmental responses to these cases. It is not so much that the government thinks we are all stupid and need to be told that coffee is hot; rather, civil courts have put the onus on private companies to warn people that coffee is hot and punishes them financially for not doing so. This can hardly be blamed on the legislature, which then reacts and regulates that customers be informed that hot coffee is hot (largely to protect private companies from litigation). Jurors are culpable for the Nanny State, too. Beck would probably be the first to complain if the government proposed a cap on civil lawsuits or some committee to oversee and weed out frivolous cases. He would argue that these are private matters, and perhaps rightly so, but in that case, private law firms and the civil courts are also culpable for the growth of the Nanny State.

It is also the case that private business lobbies legislators to create a favorable regulatory environment for them, often calling for bans or regulations that put competitors out of business. Whether they get it depends on the legislator balancing how this issue will affect his or her chance of reelection; the politician has to consider how it will affect votes and campaign donations when deciding whether to back any legislation. The regulatory environment is the product of many people, working at all levels of society. Modern society is complex and pluralistic, with competing organizations in both private and public spheres, each with its own agenda and each empowered by enrolling support from the people. On any particular issue there are many valid interests at stake. You may well think, as I do, that it should be up to the individual restaurant or bar owner to allow smoking on the premises, providing they clearly inform customers that smoking is allowed. But what of the employees? They have a right to demand that they work in a smoke-free environment. In a democracy, everyone has a stake in how the laws of society are developed and how the balance between positive and negative liberty should be achieved. So who is the Nanny State? It is everyone who has ever called for or demanded regulations or laws to protect themselves, their business, their clients, their children, their neighbors, their job, or their fellow workers.

Consider the example of the criminalization of cannabis. In 1932, John D. Rockefeller wrote,

> When prohibition was introduced, I hoped it would be widely supported by public opinion and the day would come when the evil effects of alcohol would be recognized. I have slowly and reluctantly come to believe that this has not been the result. Instead, drinking has generally increased; the speakeasy has replaced the saloon; a vast army of law breakers has appeared; many of our best citizens have openly ignored Prohibition; respect for the law has greatly lessened; and crime has increased to a level never seen before.[5]

It seems that, once again, the lesson of history is that no one learns the lessons of history. Learning nothing from the disastrous prohibition of alcohol. In 1937 Congress passed the Marihuana Transfer Tax Act, largely as a result of lobbying by the wealthy businessmen Randolph Hearst, Andrew Mellon, and the Du Pont family. Serving as yet another example of how business interferes with government, the aim of this law was to destroy the hemp industry. After the invention of "the decorticator" (a machine invented by George Schlicten in 1917 that stripped fibers from the pulpy celluloid center of the stalks, saving a great deal of labor time), hemp became a very cheap substitute for paper pulp, which threatened Hearst's timber holdings and paper mills. Hemp was also competing with the new synthetic nylon as a material for clothing. This threatened the Du Pont family's interests and Mellon's investments in the nylon production industry. Mellon was the secretary of the treasury at that time.

This act was written by Harry Anslinger, who crusaded against cannabis on the grounds that, among other things, it was used in jazz clubs, where music attracted young white women and brought them into contact with both "negroes" and cannabis, the smoking of which allegedly led to immoral behavior and threatened segregation. It is now widely accepted that the information presented to the congressional hearing, which claimed that cannabis caused insanity and death, was exaggerated, false, and biased. While the law itself did not criminalize cannabis, it did impose a "nuisance tax" of one dollar per commercial transaction and required the person paying the tax to submit an affidavit containing the details of all persons involved in the transaction. This allowed that person to apply for a license to conduct the transaction. Shortly after the act was passed, the newly formed Federal Bureau of Narcotics and the City of Denver police arrested Moses Baca for possession and Samuel Caldwell for supplying cannabis without a license. Baca was sentenced to eighteen months and Caldwell for four years in Leavenworth Penitentiary.

Although this act was suspended during the Second World War, due to the demand for hemp for the war effort, it was reimposed after the war ended. In 1951, the Boggs Act increased the penalties and imposed mandatory sentences—effectively criminalizing cannabis. Despite the fact that even by 1956 Anslinger's claims that cannabis caused immoral behavior, madness, and death had been discredited, the Daniels Act was passed, further increasing the penalties for growing, possessing, or supplying cannabis. The new "justifica-tion" for the further criminalization of cannabis was that it was a "gateway drug," leading to heroin use and addiction.

In 1969, in the case of *Leary v. United States*, the Marihuana Transfer Tax Act was unanimously ruled unconstitutional by the Supreme Court because it required someone to incriminate themselves in order to obtain the license and, thereby, violated the Fifth Amendment. Under the terms of the act, a person had to identify himself or herself as "a transferee who had not regis-tered and paid" the tax in order to obtain the form to apply for the tax. As a result, Congress formally criminalized the growth, possession, and supply of cannabis under the 1970 Controlled Substances Act, despite the recommen-dations of the National Commission on Marijuana and Drug Abuse, which called for the decriminalization of the possession of small amounts of can-nabis. The chairman of the National Commission, Raymond Shafter, wrote, "The criminal law is too harsh a tool to apply to personal possession even in an effort to discourage use. It implies an overwhelming indictment of the behavior which we deem is inappropriate. The actual and potential harm of use of the drug is not great enough to justify intrusion by the criminal law into private behavior, a step which our society takes only with the greatest reluctance."

A step taken with the greatest reluctance? Apparently not. Forty years after the Controlled Substances Act was passed, we are facing a situation that echoes John D. Rockefeller's words. Millions of Americans use cannabis regularly, openly and privately; a huge illegal market has provided organized criminals with billions of dollars per year; police and courts are overwhelmed with cases dealing with cannabis possession and supply; prisons are overcrowded, while many prisoners are incarcerated for cannabis possession and supply; and as Rockefeller noted, "many of our best citizens have openly ignored Prohibition;

respect for the law has greatly lessened; and crime has increased to a level never seen before."

It also needs to be pointed out that the conservative dislike of taxes is also to blame here. Often the argument against decriminalizing something, cannabis, for example, is that it will lead to health and social problems and burden the taxpayers. Perhaps they would argue that cannabis should only be decriminalized if people did not receive any public health care for any problems associated with it. No doubt, they would argue that it is outrageous that their taxes go to subsidizing the heath care of someone who smokes cannabis (or tobacco, for that matter), or drinks alcohol or does anything else they construe as bad for your health. But this kind of argument only seems reasonable on the surface. First of all, it ignores the obvious fact that the criminalization of something requires money to pay for the enforcement of the law, including police, courts, and prisons. However, as the prohibition of alcohol showed, banning something does not stop people from doing it. If something is desirable to enough people, banning it inevitably leads to a black market and finances organized crime (including providing a source of income for terrorist organizations as well). The costs of the criminalization of cannabis far outweigh the costs of treating any associated health care problems.

It also needs to be pointed out that taxes can be levied on cannabis, once it has been legalized, and these taxes could be ring-fenced to pay for any associated health or social costs. Similarly with alcohol and tobacco, taxes should be ring-fenced for paying for associated health and social costs. In this way, consumers would pay for the public consequences of their choices. That seems fair to me. It seems to me that, on the fiscally conservative view, whether cannabis should be decriminalized or not should come down to a calculation of whether it is cheaper to enforce the laws or deal with the associated problem. However, in my opinion, the conservative objection to paying more taxes is a mask for a *moral* objection to other people doing something conservatives don't like, such as smoking and enjoying cannabis. If this is the case, the criminalization of vices is actually a taxpayer-subsidized moral crusade. It seems that conservatives in America, when they support the continued criminalization of any vice—say, drugs, prostitution, gambling, and so on—are also part of the Nanny State.

It has been conservatively estimated that the legalization of the recreational use of drugs (such as cannabis, heroin, and cocaine) would save taxpayers at least $40 billion in law enforcement costs (including policing, courts, and prisons) per year and could raise at least $30 billion in annual taxes. The continued prohibition of some drugs is costing at least $70 billion per year. Many economists support the legalization of (most) drugs.[6]

Many legal (regulated) activities, such as smoking tobacco, horseback riding, mountain climbing, riding a motorcycle, drinking alcohol, parachuting, skiing, and skateboarding, risk self-harm and costing the taxpayers money for paramedics and emergency room costs. Should these activities be illegal?

Of course not! The harsh fact of life is that any activity can risk self-harm and costing taxpayers money. Human life involves risk, and a compassionate and civilized society provides a safety net against the risk of accidents by providing emergency rescue services and hospital care. Beck seems to recognize this point with regard to wearing seat belts in a car. He considers it to be wise to wear a seat belt but argues that it should not be compulsory. So why isn't this argument extended without prejudice to include all activities that involve self-harm, the use of many kinds of recreational drugs being a good example?[7]

To put it briefly, apart from the obvious moral argument that it is the compassionate thing to do, the reason why everyone should be willing to contribute to the general safety net for the benefit of others is because accidents can happen to anyone at anytime. To provide for a general safety net for all is also to provide it for oneself. As well as being immoral, it is quite impractical to expect rescuers or paramedics to check a person's ability to pay before helping that person. Even requiring an identity check or proof of citizenship prior to aiding someone involved in an accident would be impractical. It is simply a fact of life that in a civilized and compassionate society, this basic safety net should be available to all human beings. Taxation is the price of that benefit, in order to provide everyone with a general insurance against injury. Beck argues that such benefits were not the intention of the Founders. He claims that the whole purpose of the Constitution is to tell us what government should not do, not what it should do. However, as I noted in chapter 1, in the Preamble the phrases "establish Justice, insure domestic tranquility" and "promote the general welfare" admit some room for interpretation regarding how the Framers envisioned good government.

Now, we do not want a paternalistic government that treats us like children and dictates to us what is in the general welfare or the greater good. Perhaps as an analogy to overbearing government, Beck does make a reasonable point about parents tending to be overprotective of their children. He argues that, although well intended, overprotecting children from the risk of injury tends to prevent them from learning from their mistakes, which arguably does them greater harm.[8] However, some kind of balance is required. While parents would be overprotective if they did not let their children ride a bicycle for fear of an accident or injury, it is perfectly reasonable for parents to insist their children wear helmets or bright clothing. One does not learn a great deal from having one's skull smashed in or being driven over by a truck! Parents are not being crazy for wanting their children to have a healthy diet, dress warmly on cold winter days, or not watch too much television. Human beings are not turtles, leaving their children to make their way in life without guidance and protection. The instinct to protect their children from harm is, for many parents, at least, a basic human instinct.

Of course, we don't know what the greater good or the general welfare is. We make guesses. We learn from experience. All other things being equal, those elected to public office are not any wiser or smarter than the people who elected them. In a democracy, these questions have to be raised by everyone and answered at a local level, in a decentralized way, with federal government only following the lead of the majority. Education should be the means by which people become informed about risks and consequences, but it should, as much as possible, remain up to individuals to decide for themselves which risks they are willing to take. However, we are not isolated individuals. We live with others—our family, neighbors, friends, and fellow workers—and the media provide us with information and stories from all over the world. Experiment and danger are inherent to life, revealing that evolution and change admit risky behavior, but the human ability to learn from the mistakes of others is inherent to life, as well as learning from our own mistakes. We can develop the ability to avoid or at least reduce risks in the future. This ability is called intelligence.

8

Shelter

A BASIC HUMAN RIGHT?

Glenn Beck argues that the credit crisis has made people question government pro-home policies and benefits, such as favorable interest rates and tax
deductible mortgages.[1] He claims that many people are beginning to question
their long-cherished belief in the right to own property as the basis of the right
to pursue happiness—the American Dream. He argues that Americans need
to take a step back and reconsider whether home ownership is something that
the government should be involved in.[2] He asks whether the American Dream
should be premised upon being in debt to a bank for decades.

After pointing out all the costs and hassles of owning a home, he advocates
that most people submit to being tenants, available as a migrant workforce for
capitalists, who, he feels, should have the right to hire and fire at will:

> You might think you're abandoning your community by leaving your
> hometown, but you might be helping your country by making the econ-
> omy more efficient. You are the supply. The supply needs to be where the
> demand is. But if you own a home, you limit your mobility.[3]

> It's really just common sense—if you can hire and fire at will, you are
> much more likely to take a chance on new employees, especially the
> young ones without much experience. But when "at will" instead turns
> into ironclad, virtually lifelong commitments, you're much more careful
> about whom you hire.[4]

It seems that, as we saw in chapter 5, Beck wishes to turn back the clock to the Industrial Revolution and days of unrestrained capitalism, when workers were at the mercy of landlords and industrialists. Given that he would oppose the kind of governmental regulatory oversight that would be needed to protect tenants from unscrupulous landlords, the tenement slums of Chicago and New York of the late nineteenth and early twentieth centuries should provide a reminder of the level of squalor and poverty that occurs when a migrant workforce is dependent on unregulated rented accommodation.[5] Most American cities would see a growth of ghettos and slums, while the poorest members of the population would be further impoverished and alienated from society. Of course this would further increase the profits of corporations and reduce the tax burden on the wealthy, while also removing any expectation of job security or sense of belonging for the majority of Americans.

We need to ask these questions: For whom is the economy more efficient? Whom does it benefit? Beck asserts that we should see ourselves as the supply for the labor market. He values most Americans as a national resource: a supply of labor—a commodity for capitalists. He couldn't be more wrong. For most human beings, living in a community involves developing roots and a sense of belonging. It is a fundamental aspect of who we are. People work to live, not live to work. We are not a commodity for the labor market. We are people who live social lives within a community of family, friends, and neighbors. If someone freely wishes to move and live a nomadic life, then that is their choice, but it should be a matter of personal choice rather than an economic obligation to serve the corporate drive to lower labor costs in order to maximize the return on investment. Hence, when Beck suggests that increased home ownership results in higher unemployment, we should question this. If the U.S. economy cannot sustain local economies anymore, due to the needs of global capitalism and the interests of multinational corporations, we have to ask whether global capitalism and multinational corporations are acting in the best interest of American citizens and community life.

It goes without saying that Beck argues that government should not be in the business of encouraging home ownership. However, what he has not mentioned is that the current housing policy—using tax credits and rebates to encourage home ownership—is the result of the banking industry's influence over government to encourage people to take out mortgages. It is an effective component of advanced capitalism. It gives people a stake in the economic system by placing them in massive debt and needing to work in order to pay for their home. This leads to the stability of the advanced capitalist system by providing a more compliant workforce. However, such a system is complex and involves compromises among politicians, capitalists, and workers. Powerful groups, such as political parties, trusts, associations, and trade unions, struggle to achieve greater power and influence in order to better the prospect of getting their demands met in negotiations. The advanced capitalist system is polyarchic (having many powerful participants and stakeholders in political and economic power), and the stability of the system is premised on the ability to reach compromise to resolve conflict through a combination of regulatory oversight, negotiation, and collective bargaining. For the price of higher wages (and other benefits) and better working conditions, business has a compliant workforce (who are also consumers) and the government has higher tax revenues (providing contracts for domestic development and national security needs). The existence of well-regulated and -integrated private banking, housing, and labor are essential for the stability of advanced capitalism.

But Beck wants to do away with all that. As far as he is concerned, all political and economic power must be possessed by corporations, acting in the name of the American people via a much weakened Congress and executive branch, but without any government interference or control. Unions would be outlawed or weakened to the point that they might as well not exist. Wages would be low for most people, and workers would be under the perpetual threat of capital flight, closures, and redundancies whenever cheaper imports dominate the market or a cheaper labor market is found abroad. The majority of people would live in rented accommodation, without health care or public education for their children, at the mercy of unscrupulous landlords, migrating from factory to factory, business to business, looking for low-paid work from which they could be fired at will. Unless, of course, they are Mexican, in which case, according to Beck, they must be forced to stay south of the border. As I argued in chapter 6, Beck is inconsistent about migrant labor. This is a contradiction between his "nationalism" and his ideology of free-market corporate capitalism. However, a corporate state does not discriminate about the "nationality" of its labor supply—given that it is only a commodity. It is only concerned with its cost.

Beck also considers "restrictive zoning and environmental laws" in towns and cities to be a negative way in which homeowners become "involved" in their communities. Should not citizens care about the way their neighborhoods and cities are developed? Should not citizens care about their local environment? He suggests that this is a bad thing because it "artificially" increases the price of houses and interferes with corporate development, thereby damaging the economy. What does it mean to "artificially" increase the price of houses? Apparently, it means that we should consider it to be a negative thing that the laws of supply and demand result in it costing more money to live in a clean, safe, and pleasant environment. It turns out that what Beck considers best for (most) people is to live in cheap housing, without "interfering" in how their towns and cities are developed by corporations, which will then be able to control markets and offer jobs, once they have put all the local businesses out of business.

Obviously, for Beck, local people should stop meddling in the corporate development of towns and cities. For the sake of the economy, local people should stop freely and democratically deciding to live in clean, safe, and pleasant environments. Apparently he considers it to be bad for people to improve their living conditions in a way that would actually result in their homes becoming more valuable. Once again, he reverses his free-market ideology—throwing value creation out of the equation—when it comes to anything that would interfere with corporate development and profits. Rather than having any concern for Americans' quality of life, his main concern is with anything the interferes with the power of corporations to do whatever they please within cities and towns. Contrary to Beck, I suggest that local people should have even more say in how their local communities are developed. In a free and democratic society, local residents should have the power, exercised through referenda and the ballot box, to veto any developments in their neighborhoods and cities. We need to ask: Whose economy is any proposed development good for?

Citing Houston as the paradigm, Beck is in favor of deed restrictions. These are covenants that impose a legally binding obligation upon the buyer to do or not to do something. Restrictions on higher structures or commercial uses of premises, for example, are common. Historically significant structures or trees are often protected in this way. Before 1948, it was even possible to use deed restrictions to prevent the sale of specific property to "people of the Negro or Mongolian Race," but this was deemed unconstitutional and unenforceable by the Supreme Court.[6] While I do not have any objection to deed restrictions, providing that they do not attempt racist and other unconstitutional prohibitions, it needs to be pointed out that these are private agreements. Their enforcement is a civil matter, which favors those who can afford private lawyers over those who can't. A person is limited to restricting what they can or cannot do should they purchase that property. They do not allow people to object to anything that might occur on any other property surrounding theirs. Nor do they allow people to object to what happens on undeveloped land in their local community. They also avoid any public debates, which are essential for a healthy democracy, and strictly limit the say to property owners, acting on an individual basis, on how the local community can be developed. Zoning laws allow all local citizens to have at least an indirect say, via local government, in how their community is developed. What is needed is greater decentralization and localization of political power regarding the development of cities and towns. This cannot be achieved with deed restrictions.

Beck is right to question the wisdom of pursuing ownership at the expense of the pursuit of happiness, or even defining the latter in terms of the former. But rather than insist that people should be happy with their lot as a mobile workforce—a commodity—I wish to ask: What is the relation between effective citizenship and home ownership in the United States of America? We need to look at how this question leads us to deeper questions: Should we consider shelter to be a basic human right? What would it mean for a person to have a right to shelter? I take the "right to shelter" to mean that one has a natural right to seek out warmth and protection from the elements; to be secure in one's dwelling in society; and to live without fear of intrusion, eviction, and becoming homeless. How does this relate to constitutional rights? And to an equal right to life, liberty, and the pursuit of happiness? How does it relate to the right to privacy?

Let's take a look at the right to privacy. The word "privacy" is not used in the Constitution. Yet a right to privacy has been derived from the Constitution by the Supreme Court, via appeals to the First, Third, Fourth, Fifth, Ninth, and Fourteenth Amendments. This was first introduced in *Griswold v. Connecticut* in 1965.[7] The Supreme Court examined whether a Connecticut law banning contraceptives was constitutional. A majority, 7–2, found this law to be unconstitutional on the basis that it violated the right to privacy. Justice William Douglas cited "penumbras" of guarantees in the Bill of Rights "formed by emanations from those guarantees." The First Amendment right to "freedom of speech" has been interpreted by the Supreme Court to protect the right to privacy when talking with a lawyer, doctor, or spouse. There is a "reasonable expectation of privacy." The "freedom of the press" has also been cited as the basis upon which journalists can withhold the names of their sources from state courts.[8]

While this right to privacy does apply to conversation between certain kinds of persons, rather than specifically to places, it does establish the notion of "a zone of privacy" that agents of the government cannot legally violate. The idea of the right to privacy being granted to the person can be read from the Fifth Amendment prohibition of compelling a person "in any criminal case from being a witness against himself" read in connection with the prohibition upon agents of the federal government from violating a person's right to "due process" (a prohibition applied to state governments by the Fourteenth Amendment). The right to privacy was the basis for the 1973 landmark case *Roe v. Wade*, which guaranteed a woman's right to terminate a pregnancy before the end of the first trimester.[9] In this case, the Supreme Court examined whether a Texas law banning abortion was unconstitutional. A majority, 7–2, agreed that it was. Justice Henry Blackman cited "the right to privacy" and the Fourteenth Amendment "equal right to due process" as the basis for this decision. Hence, a woman has a right to privacy when consulting her doctor; a woman has the right over her own body to decide whether to terminate a pregnancy before the end of the first trimester (twelve weeks). After that time the fetus's right to life becomes the primary concern and an abortion can only be carried out if there are medical or psychological grounds for the termination.

To see how private property is included as a zone of privacy, we need to look at the Third and Fourth Amendments. The Third Amendment states, "No soldier shall, in time of peace be quartered in any house, without the consent of the owner, nor in time of war, but in a manner to be prescribed by law." In other words, on a strict interpretation of the Constitution, during peacetime the consent of the owner is required before any soldier (a term that is taken to include all members of the armed forces and militias) can be quartered in a private residence. Even after Congress declares war, it still requires a law to permit the quartering of soldiers in any private residence without the owner's consent. And the Fourth Amendment states, "The right of the people to be secure in their persons, houses, papers, and effects, against unreasonable search and seizures, shall not be violated, and no Warrants shall issue, but upon probable cause, supported by Oath or affirmation, and particularly describing the place to be searched, and the persons or things to be seized." As Justice William Douglas argued, the Third and Fourth Amendments guarantee that a person's home is "a zone of privacy," which agents of the government cannot legally violate without legal permission. These amendments connect the concept of "a reasonable expectation of privacy" with the notion of private property.

Beck claims that home ownership was not part of the America Dream envisioned by the Founders: "it's safe to say that when our Founders were designing the American dream, a Realtor wasn't required to achieve it. . . . The American dream is not about owning a *home*, it's about owning your *destiny*."[10] If we limit the idea of home ownership to having a mortgage and a white picket fence, he is probably right. But if we look at how private property relates to the idea of a citizen of the Republic, then he couldn't be more wrong. Not only was the protection of private property fundamental to the Constitution (along with protection of the individual), but the ownership of private property was a requirement of the right to vote. The concept of property rights was a cornerstone of the foundation of the Republic and of the framing of the Constitution.

The connection between the notions of a right to privacy and private property also finds its precedent in English common law against trespassing and the right to enjoy one's own property in peace, thereby considered to be a right "retained by the people" under the Ninth Amendment. Even though today the ownership of private property is no longer a condition for being able to vote, many of the rights of citizenship cannot be fully exercised without having a residence. First of all, it is difficult to register to vote without a residence, and residence is also a requirement for running as a candidate for public office. Of course, a person can rent his or her residence from another, thus obtaining shelter and an address, but even with laws and regulations that protect the rights of tenants, there remains a balance of power in favor of the landlord as owner of the property. The owner of their own home has greater legal rights and security in the use and enjoyment of their residence than a tenant does. Ownership affords a greater guarantee of shelter and privacy.

Although one still has a "reasonable right of privacy" when using a public pay phone or meeting with a lawyer or doctor in their office, outside the home, a person's zone of privacy is greatly limited. Even though the Fourth Amendment still places limits on the power of the police to search a person and their belongings, the Supreme Court has ruled that probable cause and the expectation of obtaining a warrant is sufficient for the police to be able to stop and search a person in public if the police suspect the person may be about to commit a crime (*Terry v. Ohio*, 1968).[11] The Supreme Court considered the case of whether concealed firearms found on two men after a warrantless search by a police officer were admissible as evidence. The police officer had seen two men repeatedly walking up and down the street in front of a store, while acting suspiciously, and the officer suspected them of preparing to rob that store. He stopped them, searched them, and found that each man had concealed a revolver on his person. The Supreme Court ruled that the men's suspicious behavior constituted "probable cause" and a warrant would have been issued if there had been time to request one.

Yet the condition of "probable cause" is more stringently applied in the case of private property than it is in the case of the person's clothing or bags. The police are only permitted to enter private premises without a warrant if they have reason to believe that a person therein is in need of immediate aid, they need to chase a fugitive through private property, or they need to make an immediate search of a homicide scene for possible other victims and/or the murderer(s).[12] As Justice John Marshall Harlan put it, "Thus, a man's home is, for most purposes, a place where he expects privacy, but objects, activities, or statements that he exposes to the 'plain view' of outsiders are not 'protected,' because no intention to keep them to himself has been exhibited. On the other hand, conversations in the open would not be protected against being overheard, for the expectation of privacy under the circumstances would be unreasonable."[13]

Although in this case, the reasonable expectation of privacy was extended to public telephone booths, taxis, and offices, here we can see that a homeless person remains constantly "in plain view"—in public—and many of the actions required to seek shelter (such as using doorways, alleyways, or under bridges for shelter) could be construed by a police officer as "suspicious behavior."

While the Fifth and Fourteenth Amendments offer all citizens an equal right to due process, it is evidently easier to exercise this right if one has a residence. Bail is unlikely to be offered to a homeless person charged with a crime. It is also the case that homeless people are not issued with firearm carry permits, which, given they do not have a residence, restricts their constitutional right to possess and bear arms for self-defense. Here we can see that the ability for any citizen to exercise fully his or her constitutional rights depends greatly on having a private residence, favoring the owners of private property over tenants. Shelter in this context has two meanings: protection from the environment, from weather and danger, and protection from the government, as afforded by the Constitution.

Homeless people are people without shelter in both these senses. They are vulnerable to physical injury and harm, and they are less able to exercise their rights as citizens. Without shelter, they are less able to exercise their equal rights to life, liberty, and the pursuit of happiness; nor can they effectively participate in the democratic process. Without shelter, people are hindered from living healthy lives and being good citizens who possess the rights of citizens. Hence homeless people become alienated from civic society and often have a lower life expectancy and quality of life.

Clearly, a person has the positive liberty to purchase or rent shelter from others. However, does society have an obligation to provide shelter to those who do not have it? Do citizens have an *entitlement* to shelter? Of course there are moral arguments for a right to shelter, but these cannot be based on a strict interpretation of the Constitution. At most, given the argument above, we can derive penumbras of a negative liberty from the guarantees of the Bill of Rights and Fourteenth Amendment, protecting the positive liberty to seek shelter. Once we take the relation between the right to property and privacy into account, we can see that the right to shelter is a negative liberty. This means that no one else, especially the government, has the right to violate a person's right to seek out shelter in order to protect himself or herself from the weather, harm from others, and intrusion. If a person cannot afford to purchase or rent shelter, he or she has a right to seek out shelter wherever it can be found, say, by building a house on unused land, using and renovating an otherwise unused building, and so on—providing that person is not infringing on another person's right to shelter or privacy. It is arguable that a law prohibiting squatting in empty or unused buildings would be unconstitutional, as would be a law prohibiting the use of otherwise unused public lands to build shelter. But on the basis of the Constitution, the government has no obligation to provide shelter.

Having said that, it is clearly in the general welfare of the public and the Republic that all citizens have an opportunity to be a good citizen to the best of their ability. As I have argued above, these rights are best guaranteed to homeowners. Homelessness has social costs to the public and places a burden on taxpayers. Alienation from civic society leads to social instability, criminality, drug use, and alcoholism, all of which puts strain on police, public services, courts, emergency rooms, and prisons. All these things have to be paid for. It is simply prudent for the government to help people obtain shelter (note that a typical "homeless shelter" would not qualify because it does not afford privacy), and it is a more prudent use of taxpayers' and public resources to help people find shelter than to deal with the consequences of homelessness. For many people, the current policy of tax credits—allowing their mortgage payments to be tax deductible—is a sufficient level of government aid. For other people, some form of subsidized housing may be needed. Once we recognize a right to shelter as a basic human right and that the denial of this right leads to expensive social problems, then subsidized housing can be seen as a cost effective way of dealing with homelessness and its associated problems.

However, this does not need to place a huge burden on taxpayers' funds and public resources. It does not need to lead to the "culture of entitlements" and "dependency on government" so dreaded by conservatives and libertarians. But rather than appeal to the slogans of media pundits and propagandists that the free market will solve all our problems, despite all the evidence to the contrary, we can look for a more cooperative public solution. In large part, the housing policies of the federal government have been shaped by the demands of the banks and mortgage lenders. In my view, instead of bailing out banks, allegedly as an emergency measure to resolve the credit crisis, which still resulted in widespread foreclosures and a housing crisis, the government should have bought the mortgages from the failing banks, taken the deeds to the properties, secured the mortgages, and dealt with the mortgage holders directly. This would have allowed people to keep their homes by paying a lower amount over a longer period of time, or even being able to defer payment completely until they were in a better financial situation. It also would have helped the banks.

The government should set up, for each state, cooperative banks and credit unions to oversee statewide public lending for housing, which, after the government's initial investment, should become independent and financially self-sufficient. Being nonprofit, public cooperative banks and credit unions would be able to offer mortgages at a lower level of interest and fund their own lending, without requiring further taxpayer assistance. These cooperative banks and credit unions in each state would become the deed holders for all the householders of that state who needed a loan. The mortgage holders would be members of their cooperative bank or credit union, and the management committee of each bank would be comprised of three directors: one appointed by the federal government, one appointed by the state government, and one elected by members. They also could lend money to housing cooperatives, thus easing the tax burden on the state or city commitment to funding public housing projects, and lend money to people to renovate disused buildings. This could hardly be considered a violation of the sacred principles of the free market, given that these public cooperative banks and credit unions would be in competition with the private lending sector and when, as the credit crisis showed, the private sector hardly has demonstrated the standards of market efficiency and discipline of which media pundits and propagandists so often like to boast.

Subsidized public housing could in part be funded through property taxes at a state or municipal level to deal with specific housing problems. Property taxes are a legitimate tax, given that society protects property rights and maintains local infrastructure, such as roads, street lighting, and so on, providing these taxes are used to maintain and improve the locality from which the taxes are collected. The level of taxation should be decided by elected state and municipal legislatures and councils, directly accountable to local citizens, who may well be open to the argument that it is much more cost effective to use public funds to provide low-cost public housing rather than deal with the consequences of homelessness. Registered property owners should enjoy their right to private property without any further unwarranted intrusion from the federal, state, or municipal government. However, property that has remained unregistered for a specified period of time (say, a year), upon which property tax had not been paid, and after reasonable efforts have been made to identify an owner have failed, should become public property, available for public housing through the municipality. This would be another way low-cost housing could be provided, without placing any burden on public funds. It also would avoid many of the burdens on public funds associated with nonpayment of property taxes (given that the threat of losing property would be an incentive to register it and pay the due taxes) and also those associated with the social costs of homelessness.

In addition, derelict buildings could be renovated or the land used for public housing projects at some cost to taxpayers, but these would be an investment—given that they would remain public property, gaining revenue from rent—until residents either bought them privately, perhaps taking a mortgage through the state cooperative bank and credit union, or through a housing cooperative. In this way, various solutions to the housing problem could be applied in a cost-effective manner to provide all citizens with shelter. Of course, the media pundits and propagandists will decry these kinds of solutions as being "socialism," but this accusation is based on little more than ideological sloganeering. Behind their rants and ravings hides their real objection: It would empower people and offer competition to the private sector. And that would not do!

On a final note, it needs to be pointed out that even though property rights are fundamental to the Republic and civic society, these rights are not absolute. Although it is stated in the terms of a protection, the Fifth Amendment contains the phrase "nor shall private property be taken for public use, without just compensation." This phrase has become the basis for eminent domain. While in the Constitution this is a negative right, protecting citizens from unjust violation of their property rights, the concept of eminent domain has changed this into a positive right, belonging to the government at the federal, state, and city levels, that allows for the compulsory purchase of private property for public use. Beck only mentions this governmental violation of property rights in passing. Despite the cornerstone of the Republic and foundation of the free market being based on property rights, he is quite uncharacteristically restrained about this rampant abuse of governmental power, an abuse evident in the Supreme Court's ruling in *Kelo v. City of New London* (2005).[14]

As discussed in chapter 1, by a 5–4 majority, the Supreme Court has allowed the government to purchase private homes and businesses, against their owners' wishes, and sell them to private developers. Combined with unlimited corporate donations in elections, which effectively puts politicians into the pockets of corporations, this means that corporations can use their money and influence over local politicians to use eminent domain as a mechanism to buy up any private property they desire, regardless of the wishes of the current owners and local citizens. This gives corporations control over the development of local communities and markets. Once again, we can see how government becomes a mechanism at the disposal of corporations and big business in general, and that the real problem facing the American people is not how to keep government out of the way of business—as Beck claims—but how to keep business out of the way of government. The *Kelo* ruling by the Supreme Court has effectively brushed away the whole foundation upon which the Republic stands and has transformed the citizens of the Republic into the subjects of a corporate state. Perhaps Beck's uncharacteristic self-restraint is not so surprising after all.

9

Universal Health Care

From the day President Obama took office, Glenn Beck and the rest of the Fox News media pundits and propagandists warned America of the danger of health care reform. They warned of a government takeover of health care and told misinformed people that government death panels would be euthanizing old people and the terminally ill.[1] They decried it as the coming of socialism and the end of the American way of life! Even though the much heralded Public Option never made it out of committee before the Democratic Party compromised it into oblivion, Beck warned his audience that Maoists had taken over the White House and were plotting to turn the United States into Europe. Images of the Soviet Union and Nazi Germany were juxtaposed with Beck sketching out the lines of connection between conspirators on his chalkboard, showing how Barack Obama, George Soros, the Council of Foreign Affairs, ACORN, the Tides Foundation, and the New World Order were all implicated in a fantastic plot to construct a communist world government. Show after show, the details changed and tears were shed, but health care reform was the battleground upon which the freedom of America was to be fought, and to be won or lost.

What was the Public Option? Despite being portrayed as socialized health care—implicated in a government takeover of America—the reality of the Public Option was far more mundane. It would have worked in the same way as any company health care plan a person obtains from his or her employer. It would have operated like any insurance plan: with a pool of people paying premiums to combine their resources and collectively cover the unfortunate minority who happen to get sick at any particular time. The Public Option was not a nationalization of health care or even a single-payer system but competed in the market alongside private insurance in exactly the same way that private insurance does already. However, the more healthy people who sign up, the more money available for those who need expensive care. The majority of Americans receive their health care through their employers; generally speaking, the larger the company, the more affordable the health care plan. As an option run by the federal government, the Public Option could have pooled people from across the whole nation, and by doing so, make it more reliable and affordable than any company-based plan. All the people on Medicare, Medicaid, Veterans Administration plans, or company-based plans—estimated to be about 85 percent of the insured population—would have remained on these, unless they chose the Public Option instead.

Only about 15 percent of the insured population, people working for small companies or the self-employed, are actually participating in a "free market." Buying insurance as an individual is expensive. Plus, individuals have to undergo intense medical scrutiny to determine whether they have any costly preexisting conditions. And should individuals develop a costly condition while insured, companies often find ways to drop them. People in large pools do not have this issue because the insurance company cannot single out just one individual. People without insurance who pay at the time of delivery pay the most for their health care. While the Public Option would not have controlled costs, except through mechanisms of market leverage due to its purchasing power, it would have allowed those people currently buying individual insurance to have bought a better level of coverage for the same price, and through taxpayer subsidies would have been able to cover those people who are currently uninsured. The problem with the Public Option is that it threatened to be competitive.

It was for this reason that it had to be discredited. Hence, the media pundits and propagandists equated it with nationalized or socialized medicine. Time and time again, it was equated with the health care systems of Canada, Cuba, or the United Kingdom. Over and over, Beck brought to our attention a handful of cases in which people in the UK have received an inadequate level of heath care. This is the sum of his evidence against "socialized health care." What he has neglected to mention is that we can find numerous examples of people in the United States "private heath care" system who have also received inadequate health care, despite being insured. Private insurance does not necessarily equate to adequate coverage, and it is not unknown for private insurance companies to deny coverage. There are numerous cases of people unable to receive necessary operations or treatment due to a lack of insurance or inadequate insurance. In the United States, people have been discharged from hospitals while still in need of treatment, with massive debt due to medical costs, due to a lack of insurance, or due to inadequate insurance. If one has a preexisting condition it is almost impossible to purchase coverage, and there have been many heart-breaking cases of people with terminal illnesses denied treatment simply because they were likely to die before a legal case could be resolved in court. When we examine the merits of socialized versus private health care, it is important to recognize that both systems have their shortcomings as well as merits. Beck has offered a deeply biased argument against universal health care by focusing on the failings of "socialized health care" and the successes of "private heath care."[2] Ideology rather than evidence underpins his argument. But the truth does not matter for the media pundit and propagandist.

Indeed, without doubt, the American medical research and pharmaceutical industries have been highly innovative and provided many wonderful medical advances, diagnostic tools, and drugs. Profit has been a strong motivator for innovation. For Americans who can afford it, the U.S. private insurance system provides excellent coverage. But what of Americans who cannot afford the best insurance coverage? Let us look at the other side of the coin.

While estimates of the number of uninsured vary, millions of Americans lack insurance and many millions more are underinsured. Further, tens of thousands of Americans die each year of treatable conditions because they were denied treatment due to a lack of insurance or inadequate coverage.[3] Almost half a million of the filed bankruptcies per year in the United States are due to an inability to pay medical bills, despite the fact that 75 percent of those filing for bankruptcy had private insurance.[4] The National Coalition on Healthcare has estimated that national health care costs will double over the next decade due to increases in insurance premiums and increases in drug costs.[5] Between 2000 and 2005, insurance premiums rose by over 70 percent.[6] Those people with insurance often find that loopholes, exclusions, deductibles, copayments, and annual limits leave them having to pay huge medical bills. The 2005 Commonwealth Fund Health Insurance Survey found that over 25 percent of insured Americans delayed visiting a doctor or refilling prescriptions due to concerns with medical bills, and often this resulted in their condition worsening.[7] People are often trapped in jobs they hate or suffer poor working conditions and levels of pay simply to maintain medical benefits for themselves and their families. Only just over 40 percent of Americans surveyed expected to receive the health care they needed if they became ill or had an accident.

Beck cites the case of Massachusetts' initiative to show that, after the state implemented a public health care policy, patient visits to hospitals actually increased from 7 percent to 18 percent between 2005 and 2007.[8] Apparently he is shocked to discover that people are more likely to visit a hospital when they have an expectation of treatment without being billed. Let's assume that these people were not visiting emergency rooms because they had nothing better to do with their time. It is not too much of a stretch to conclude that, due to the implementation of this policy, quite a few people received medical care who otherwise would have avoided going to the hospital for fear of costs. But for Beck, this shows that the policy was a failure because it increased the costs to the taxpayer.

One of the things that is rarely mentioned—and certainly not by Beck—is that there are economic benefits from a public health care system. All other things being equal, employers who offer health care benefits have higher labor costs than those employers who do not offer health care benefits or those employers from countries with a public health care service. It is simply not the case that America cannot afford public health care, as Beck asserts. The economic fact of life in America is that the country needs to make choices. Perhaps the U.S. government needs to rethink its priorities and spend less money on the military and more on heath care. Perhaps instead of spending billions of dollars on the "War on Drugs" in Colombia and elsewhere, the U.S. government could spend these public funds making sure that its citizens could afford prescription drugs in America.

Is health care a luxury? Beck compares the idea of spending more money on health care to deciding to buy a Porsche or take a vacation to Fiji.[9] However, for most Americans, health care is a basic need, not a luxury. Most Americans cannot afford a Porsche, a vacation to Fiji, or good health care coverage for their families. Perhaps it would be better for Beck to recommend that Americans spend more on private health care insurance and less on cable TV.

Of course, Beck insists that the current private health care system is working pretty well. He claims that anyone who says that there are millions of uninsured Americans is a liar, part of a conspiracy to defraud the American taxpayers out of billions of dollars. Taking a figure of forty-six million Americans without health insurance,[10] Beck claims that ten million of these people are illegal immigrants (so don't matter) and eighteen million earn over fifty thousand dollars per year and simply choose not to buy insurance. This means that there are only eighteen million people without medical coverage. Only eighteen million! Even if we accept that this figure is close to the truth, it seems to me that quite a lot of Americans do not have private insurance. But not to worry, it is not as bad as it seems. Beck assures us that 33 percent of these Americans are "young and healthy" people between the ages of eighteen and thirty-four and are unlikely to get sick.[11] But, we might interject, this still leaves twelve million uninsured people, and even adults in the age range of eighteen to thirty-four get sick or have injuries; if they are uninsured, this places a burden on emergency rooms, which are, in essence, expensive front-line health care services.

Furthermore, Beck ignores the fact that half of these "young and healthy" people are women, many of whom will, while in this age range, become pregnant and need health care. In addition, he ignores the fact that many Americans have poor levels of insurance coverage. He informs us that 94.5 percent of Wal-Mart employees have health insurance, but, of course, he does not tell us what level of coverage they have. He tells us that a young and healthy person can become insured online for only fifty dollars per month. But he does not tell us about the level of coverage they would receive for this price; nor does he tell us the penalties for trying to get health care outside of their home state. If we accept his claim that all is well with the nation's health care system and that most Americans have some medical insurance, how does he explain his own claim that eighty-three million people already benefit from some sort of government health care. Hold on! Why do these people qualify for government health care? Could it be the case that they can't afford an adequate level of private insurance coverage? And if his claim that most Americans have some medical insurance, with 30 percent of the population receiving government assistance to pay for their coverage and only 3 percent of the population being chronically uninsured, then what would be the problem with extending public aid to those who are uninsured and cannot afford any insurance? Beck cannot have it both ways. Either the problem is much greater than Beck claims it is or extending public assistance to the uninsured through some kind of public system would not really be that much of a burden on taxpayers.

What is the problem with public health care? First, Beck claims that a public health care system would give free health care to those who can afford to pay for it. But this is nonsense. There is no such thing as free health care. A public health care system is free at the point of access. It is paid for by taxpayers' money. Those who can afford health care presumably have paid for it in taxes, as well as paid a contribution to the heath care of those who cannot afford it. They would either have their own coverage or bought into the Public Option. Second, Beck asserts that the increased bureaucracy involved in public health care would cost taxpayers a fortune. But is this true? If we compare the American and Canadian systems (despite his insistence that we should do no such thing!), we find that the U.S. private system spends fifteen cents on the dollar on administration costs (including billing and legal costs) while the Canadian "single-payer system" spends a little under eight cents on the dollar.[12] Of course, according to Beck, we should not compare the U.S. system with that of any other country. No two countries in the world are comparable, he asserts. Otherwise we might find ways in which a public health care system might be better, and that would not do! No, what we must do, according to Beck's ideology, is put our fingers in our ears and shout as loud as we can, "Public health care does not work!" and call anyone who says anything to the contrary an idiot or a liar. Yet as we saw in chapter 2, he was quite happy to compare the gun control laws of the United States with those of the United Kingdom to "prove" that strict gun laws increase gun crime. Are Beck's arguments consistent? Once again, they are not.

However, if we look at National Health Expenditures for Medicare, we find that they spend five cents on the dollar on administrative costs.[13] How could this be? Could a public health care system be *more efficient*? This leads us to an important question. If it turns out that public health care systems are more efficient and deliver the same level of health care for lower per capita costs, then who does the U.S. private health care system actually benefit? The answer: the shareholders. Regardless of what Beck may think about the impartiality of the research of the World Health Organization (WHO), of which the United States is both a founding member state and major contributor, the WHO ranks the U.S. health care system thirty-seventh of 193 countries, below most countries in Europe and trailing Chile and Cost Rica.[14] Yet the per capita costs of heath care in the United States are twice that of most European countries, Canada, and Japan. Do Americans receive twice as much health care as Europeans, Canadians, and Japanese? Are Americans twice as likely to get sick? Or is it the case that the drive for profits in a competitive investors' market is literally doubling the per capita cost of health care? Clearly profits comprise a huge proportion of health care costs. All other things being equal, nonprofit health care would save the American population billions of dollars per year. Even "single-payer systems" such as the Canadian system, in which the government is directly billed by doctors acting as businesses, halves the per capita cost of heath care. Even the Public Option, which was to compete in the for-profit private market, could have reduced costs.

Beck's response to the WHO study is to claim that it is "a tool of Cuban propaganda" for socialized medicine and based on the UN strategy to set itself up as the model for how to create a global government.[15] So let us put aside WHO studies for a moment, just in case they are trying to deceive the American people and promote world government.[16] Who can we turn to for information? Well, perhaps the U.S. government might be a legitimate source of information on the costs of heath care in the United States. The General Accounting Office, the Congressional Budget Office, and several state government offices have all proposed that a single-payer system could cover all Americans and still save billions of dollars. Now, perhaps the red menace runs deeper than Beck suspects. Perhaps the whole U.S. government is involved in promoting communism (after all, they do fund the UN and head the UN Security Council, so there's no smoke without fire!).[17] Is it the case that, despite all appearances to the contrary, the U.S. government is engaged in promoting communism, resisted only by Beck, Fox News, and a few patriots in the Tea Party? Or is it possible that these government agencies have merely weighed the facts and come up with a policy proposal that does not fit in with Beck's ideology? Could it be the case that the interests of the shareholders of private insurance and pharmaceutical industries are not necessarily in the general welfare of the majority of the American people? If it is the case that the U.S. private system is clearly better than any possible public system, why do private insurance and the pharmaceutical industry spend millions of dollars per year lobbying politicians and donate millions more to campaigns for presidential elections? Why the fierce opposition to the Public Option? Why not just let it compete and fail?

Now we all know that many doctors in the United States enjoy a wealthy lifestyle and do their bit for trickle-down economics, but there are many more doctors who struggle daily with private insurance companies for their patients to access health services. Many doctors, nurses, and caregivers work long hours for low pay. This is not due to wickedness or caprice on the part of private insurance companies but rather the economic necessities of a for-profit business in a competitive investors' market. It is a basic fact of economic life that for private insurance companies, the bottom line is to reduce costs and increase profits. Otherwise investors will simply put their money elsewhere. This results in the tendency to reduce coverage and labor costs and to increase profits by raising the price of private insurance. It is this economic reality of the for-profit health care business that means that, all other things being equal, private health care will always be more expensive for the same level of health care provided by a public health care system. Economics 101: It is simply a fact of economic reality that good-quality health care cannot be provided to all Americans and turn billions of dollars in profits. A for-profit health care system is simply not in the general welfare of the majority of Americans. Although I am sure that, as do U.S. senators, who receive health care paid for by taxpayers for themselves and their families for life (even if they opposed public-funded health care for other Americans), Beck has great health care coverage! Of course, Beck is entitled to purchase private insurance. No one is stopping him. And the Public Option would not have stopped him either.

Of course, Beck puts aside his prohibition on comparing different systems while he makes a great deal of the waiting lists for operations and emergency rooms in the UK public hospitals—while neglecting to mention that not only does the UK's National Health Service (NHS) cover the whole population, but anyone in the UK who can afford it can purchase private insurance as well. He also points out that the average wait for a mammogram in Italy is seventy days, but he neglects to mention that mammogram screening is provided to all women in Italy, so most women waiting for seventy days are in fact waiting for a routine check up.[18] Of course, if you have great health care coverage, then you probably never have waited in a hospital or for an operation. The experience of the majority of Americans is a little different. Most people who have visited an emergency room in a U.S. hospital will tell you that they had to wait several hours before seeing a doctor. Most Americans have to wait months for a necessary operation to be scheduled, and often their insurance provider will not cover all the costs. In both public and private systems people have to wait for treatment and operations. There are a limited number of doctors and operating rooms. It is a harsh economic reality that not all of us can get what we want or need immediately. The difference between a public and private health care system is that in a public system, medical need dictates priority, whereas in a private system, it is the ability to pay that matters.

Let's take a brief look at the British National Health Service. The NHS was founded in 1948. It provides primary care, in-patient care, long-term health care, ophthalmology, and dentistry. Health care services are free at the point of use to UK residents, although there are charges associated with dental care, eye examinations, and prescriptions. The NHS is funded by taxation and National Health Insurance contributions. According to the Department of Health, in 2008–9, £92.5 billion was spent on the NHS. The NHS runs parallel with private health care (paid for through private insurance by less than 10 percent of the population).

The three core principles of the NHS are (1) it is universal, (2) it is free at the point of delivery, and (3) it is based on clinical need, not ability to pay. While there are similarities between the NHS and a "single-payer system" like Canada's, one major difference is that hospital doctors and nurses are employees of the NHS, and hospitals and in-patient services are nonprofit. General practitioners, dentists, and opticians are self-employed and have contracts with the NHS. The Department of Health reported in 2005 that the NHS had 980,000 staff. The NHS also trains doctors and nurses.

In 2009, prescription charges were £7 (about $10) in England, £4 (about $6) in Scotland, £3 (about $4.50) in Northern Ireland, and free in Wales. Typical charges for dentistry in England are £17 (about $26) for an examination, £45 (about $69) for a filling or extraction, and about £200 (about $300) for more complicated procedures. The charge for an eye examination is £20 (about $30), and the charge for spectacles ranges between £40 (about $60) and £180 (about $270). NHS hospitals also receive funding from charities, car park fees, and the recovery of costs after personal-injury compensation claims (for example, when someone receives compensation after a road accident, the NHS is able to recover the cost for the ambulance and treatment).

In 2004, a Mori poll found that there was quite a disparity between public perceptions of the NHS and how the NHS was portrayed in the press, especially the tabloid press. While the public seem to be generally satisfied with the NHS, the press has been highly critical. This is largely explicable because the tabloid press in the UK tend to support the Conservative and Liberal Democratic opposition parties (which were elected to form a coalition government in 2010), both of which favored privatization of the NHS. Arguably, a great deal of the vilification of the NHS by the U.S. media, including Fox News and Glenn Beck, during recent media "debates" about health care in the United States is based on an uncritical acceptance of tabloid stories.

> I wouldn't be here today if it were not for the NHS; I have received a large amount of high-quality treatment without which I would not have survived.
>
> *Professor Stephen Hawking*
> *(in response to claims in the U.S. media that people*
> *suffering with motor neuron disease are considered a drain on resources*
> *by the NHS and are left to die).[19]*

Another myth Beck likes to tell us is that patients in public health care systems have their doctor chosen for them by bureaucrats. The truth is that in both the Canadian and British health care systems, the patient chooses their doctor. However, in the U.S. private health care system, customers with Health Maintenance Organization (HMO) plans have their choice of doctor restricted by the insurer. Additional fees (penalties) are imposed if customers choose an "out-of-network provider," and some doctors refuse to accept Medicare and Medicaid patients. Only customers who pay a higher premiums for Preferred Provider Organization (PPO) plans are able to choose their doctors.

However, the question of which health care system would be best for Americans is not simply an economic question. It is a moral question as well. How should poor and vulnerable people be treated when they are sick or have an accident? Should society take care of people who need help, or should persons fend for themselves and their family? The moral argument for universal health care is that it is essential for the mass liberation of the population from fear and uncertainty—fear of illness and being unable to pay for treatment, fear of unemployment and losing benefits. Health is a national security issue! Public health care does more than protect children, the elderly, and the vulnerable; it liberates people from suffocating material conditions and fear, allowing them time for greater democratic participation. Of course, whether people choose to take this opportunity is another matter, but universal health care is a condition for a free and civilized democratic society. The question between health care systems comes down to the question between civilizations. What kind of civilization does America aspire to be?

Beck asserts that "outside of a complete government takeover, there is no way to get *everyone* covered" and you "don't want the same people who run the post office cutting your chest open for an angioplasty."[20] By making these remarks, he attempts to reinforce the assumption that universal health care requires federal governmental control. This is not true. Of course a "single-payer system" like the Canadian system and a national health service like the British system are both possibilities, but they are not the only options. The Public Option would have been very different, for the reasons given above. However, if the right to adequate health care were federally mandated, it could be paid for by public funds but organized and administered at a state and municipal level. People could join a statewide public insurance option or health care cooperatives connected with their local hospitals. Networks of hospitals capable of organizing specialized treatments could be set up by the hospitals themselves without needing any centralized governmental control. This network would be comprised of associations of hospitals, research centers, and universities. Basic health care priorities and needs would be assessed by doctors, not bureaucrats and insurers, and treatment would be funded through public contributions and taxes, decided at a local level by elected legislatures. It would provide decentralized and localized delivery of health care, paid for from public funds collected at a state level.

Such a decentralized public health care system also would allow private hospitals and clinics, as well as allowing alternative treatments and therapies to be a private matter. Citizens would simply have the choice between public and private systems, and once all citizens have a right to adequate health care, the regulation of the each state's health care would be a matter for each state's legislature to decide. Congress would only need to legislate health care insofar as it could be construed as interstate and international commerce. Again, the Public Option would be one option among all the possible choices, none of which would comprise a takeover of health care by the federal government. Citizens who felt that their state was not providing adequate health care funding could either elect someone else to the state legislature or take the state to court. They could elect the Public Option or purchase private insurance. Of course, state governments may well make bad decisions about levels of funding and the administration of health care in their state. But this is not an argument against public health care. After all, the legitimacy of whole American political system is based on the premise that bad administration and regulation can always be corrected through the ballot box or the court. To argue that public health care is impossible because good government is impossible is to argue against the form of the Republic and government in general.

After the proposed health care bills bounced back and forth between the House and the Senate, while Fox News and Beck continued with their scare-mongering and distortions, Congress passed and President Obama signed into law (March 2010) the 2010 Patient Protection and Affordable Care Act and the 2010 Health Care and Education Reconciliation Act. These health care reforms have been described as a bonanza for the insurance companies and pharmaceutical industry by removing the Public Option, establishing the mandatory purchase of insurance, and using taxpayers' money in the private for-profit sector.[21] Arguably, these bills will do little to prevent increased health care costs and will allow the critics of health care reform to claim that reform was tried but did not work. Yet the media pundits and propagandists on Fox News and elsewhere have continued their onslaught against "socialized medicine" and the government takeover of health care. Even as late as August 2010, Beck was still warning Americans about the government takeover and the threat of government "death panels."[22] Efforts are underway to challenge these bills, or at least the parts of them relating to the mandatory purchase and funding of health care, as being unconstitutional.

As I have argued, a private for-profit health care system is inherently unfair because it must, due to economic necessity, put investors first, reduce costs, and maximize profits. It does this by favoring the wealthy over the poor, denying coverage to those with chronic illnesses and preexisting conditions, limiting coverage by increasing deductibles, and so on. The whole principle of treating health care as a business puts the ability to pay ahead of medical necessity and runs counter to the principle of the equal right to life. Without an equal right to life, an equal right to liberty, justice, and the pursuit of happiness is meaningless. Without going as far to suggest that they should be allowed to eat cake if they don't have any bread, Beck proposes that poor people who become sick or injured should seek out the charity of others or take out a loan to cover their medical costs. It seems that, if you cannot afford adequate coverage, your options are to either run up a massive debt (if you can find a bank that will lend you the money), place a huge burden on friends or family, or seek out a doctor willing to work for a reduced fee or waive it altogether. It is good to know that Beck's vision for the U.S. health system offers poor people so many options.

Beck states that, in the private system, healthy people *subsidize* sick people, and that investors *subsidize* research and development costs. In other words, without a hint of irony, Beck tells us that the profit motive of private insurance companies and investors is a form of *giving*, which despite the fact that insurance and medical costs have risen consistently year in and year out, promises to bring prices down at some indeterminate point in the future. In this way, according to Beck, the yearly growing profits of insurance companies and capital gains of investors is actually a way of benefiting poor people, providing, of course, they know wealthy family members, an understanding bank loans manager, or a generous doctor. But any suggestion that wealthy people should just pay some additional taxes to subsidize the health care of poor people must be rejected as "socialism." There is not any consideration of the fact that the government protects the market, protects property, and protects wealth, and, therefore, it might be considered fair that those who have better salaries, property, and wealth contribute some of it to the overall public welfare. Instead, Beck trots out the market forces argument: The profit motive drives competition and innovation. He claims that the United States has produced over half of all the new major medicines introduced worldwide in the last twenty years yet has only 5 percent of the world's population. Of course what he doesn't ask is what percentage of the world's population live in industrialized countries—which would give a more accurate proportion of America's contribution to new pharmaceutical patents. Nor does he ask what percentage of the world's population can afford these new drugs. The United States constitutes the largest market for U.S. drug companies. It may well be the case that competition between corporations has reduced the retail price of some generic drugs, but patented drugs remain expensive. Customers still need prescriptions to buy them, requiring a visit to a doctor, and the majority of new drugs are patented and expensive (in order to recoup returns for investors). While there are outbreaks of competition for market share among retailers, for the pharmaceutical companies the competition is for investment.

Beck is simply ignoring the fact that private insurance and pharmaceutical companies must compete in an investors' market—the largest return on investment wins. This requires raising prices and/or reducing costs. This results in the tendency toward an oligopoly, wherein a few huge companies dominate the market through the greatest return on investments by maximizing market leverage and economies of scale, and reduced levels of customer service for all but the wealthiest customers. Beck's own figures show that health care costs have risen across the board over the last decade in all areas except cosmetic surgery, which he considers the nearest thing in the U.S. health care system to a free market (presumably because one does not qualify for Medicaid for a boob job).[23] He hails this to prove the success of private health care: Prices for life-saving and necessary medical diagnosis and treatments have steadily risen, but the price of cosmetic surgery has decreased. This he lauds as an example of the way capitalism puts care back into the health care system. Please, don't make me sick!

10

PROGRESSIVISM

Glenn Beck considers progressivism to be a cancer that is destroying America.[1] He views progressivism as an all-pervasive movement to subordinate individuals to the needs of a totalitarian state and to redistribute wealth for the general welfare and the public good. When seeking the cause of this cancer, he cites Theodore Roosevelt's endorsement of progressive income tax to pay for things like national health insurance. Furthermore, despite it being one of the enumerated powers of Congress, he denounces Roosevelt's call for greater governmental regulation of interstate commerce as being contrary to the founding principles of the Constitution. For Beck, any form of environmental conservation is a form of government control that oppresses the right of individuals to trash the remaining wilderness of America, so he is outraged by President Roosevelt's signing of the 1906 Antiquities Act and the creation of national parks, wildlife refuges, and protected sites of "special interest" (such as the Grand Canyon). Apparently, Roosevelt trampled over personal freedom and states' rights by protecting the remaining wilderness of America—although Beck does not make it clear how conserving the American natural environment was destructive to America. Nor does he explain how the conservation of the natural landscape is part of a gradual process toward totalitarian state control. It is not clear how preserving forests, lakes, rivers, and mountain ranges, so every generation of Americans has the opportunity to explore them, is somehow undermining the liberty of Americans. Nor is it clear how exploiting and destroying the remaining American wilderness for the commercial benefit of a few Americans would be preserving the liberty of Americans at all.

National conservation and reclamation does not mean that the government considers human beings to be of less importance than spotted owls or harvest mice, as Beck claims it does.[2] It means that the possibility of the human experience of the wilderness continues from one generation to the next, offering some degree of continuity to the American experience while also restoring the natural landscape from past damage and exploitation. What is so damaging to the American way of life about preventing pollution and the destruction of the natural landscape? Beck complains about the burden that unsustainable spending and the national debt place on future generations. But what burden does the unsustainable exploitation and degradation of the environment place on future generations?

Of course, when discussing progressivism, Beck denounces the need for government regulation of any business. He conveniently forgets that he calls for employers only to employ government-approved people when it comes to discussing the employment of migrant workers, and for workers to trust governmental regulation and oversight when it comes to labor relations. He also considers the progressive call for justice to be equal for all to be "the standard popularist line," conveniently forgetting that it is one of the foundations of the republican form of government and the Constitution he pretends to adhere to (when it suits his argument to do so). He sneers at the progressive call to treat the Constitution as a living document that needs to change with changing circumstances, claiming that this is the opposite of the intent of the Founding Fathers, despite the fact that the Framers of the Constitution wrote into it a process by which it could be amended and Thomas Jefferson called for it to be rewritten every twenty years or so.[3]

Beck tries to twist the progressive call for cooperation and working to improve society as "collectivism" and a suppression of individual freedom, when it means no such thing at all, so he can, without argument, declare that there was something sinister in Theodore Roosevelt's call for "substantial equality of opportunity and of reward for equally good service" in his 1910 "New Nationalism" speech.[4] Hence he takes Roosevelt's speech declaration that "every man may hold his property subject to the general right of the community to regulate its use to whatever degree the public welfare may require it" as if this meant anything more than the assertion of the constitutional principles of the commerce clause and eminent domain. Roosevelt was a strong advocate of property rights, but he saw the need for the government to step in to protect the rights of individual Americans and small businesses from the growing power of interstate corporations. Beck's claim that Roosevelt's New Nationalism was a step on the road toward socialism is blatantly false and based on a distortion of history.

When Beck claims that government price controls of railway rates helped caused the banking crisis of 1907, he distorts history again.[5] The banking crisis of 1907 was caused by Otto Heinz's failed attempt to purchase aggressively borrowed and short-sold stock of the United Copper Company and to drive the price up, subsequently to force the borrowers to buy the shares from the Heinz family for a much higher price and allowing him to pocket the difference.[6] Well, that was the plan. Unfortunately for his scheme, he overestimated the level of borrowing and the number of shares in the Heinz family. Short sellers were able to find their shares elsewhere. This led to the collapse of United Copper, Heinz's stock brokerage, and the State Savings Bank of Butte, Montana, which had secured loans against its stock with the National Mercantile Bank. This led to runs on banks as savers panicked. This panic was averted when J. P. Morgan stepped in and used both private and federal funds to shore up the banks.[7]

Moreover, Beck distorts the facts by claiming that Roosevelt *allowed* Morgan to buy the Tennessee Coal and Iron Company (TCIR) for a fraction of its market value, as if this was a reward for Morgan's help in averting the banking panic of 1907. What Beck does not mention is that Morgan's company, U.S. Steel, purchased an insolvent brokerage company, Moore and Schley, which had secured loans against six million shares of TCIR, when the banks called in the loans. Thus U.S. Steel was able to purchase these shares for a fraction of their market value. Morgan actually tricked Roosevelt into granting the deal an antitrust immunity by convincing him that he was shoring up the firm and averting a collapse of the TCIR stock price. When the trick was discovered after the stock markets opened the following day, the federal government tried to sue U.S. Steel and apply antitrust laws but the Supreme Court blocked it. Rather than being an example of government control over banking and industry, it was an early example of how reckless and unregulated speculation led to a banking panic and how shrewd capitalists are able to manipulate crises to their advantage.

While defending tax breaks for corporations and proposing a flat rate income tax, Beck writes, "The progressive movement (which created the modern income tax under President Wilson) saw America as a democracy rather than what it really is: a Republic. The distinction is not subtle and our Founders were always clear in the belief that a democracy always led to mob rule."[8] Clearly, Beck is against democracy. Ordinary Americans cannot be trusted to run their own affairs. When he says "we the people," he means the wealthy economic elite and their representatives. It is also interesting to see that "our Founders" now seems to exclude Thomas Jefferson and Thomas Paine, both of whom were advocates of democracy. It is also interesting to see that, for Beck, America "really is" what the Philadelphia Convention deemed it to be rather than what Americans deem it to be. This would be an example of "the dead ruling over the living," which Jefferson warned against when he called every generation to rewrite the Constitution and make it a living document for themselves. Would this mean that Jefferson was progressive?

Perhaps we need to define the term "progressive." While many contemporary Democrats, such as Russ Feingold, Al Franken, Hillary Clinton, Al Gore, Nancy Pelosi, and the late Ted Kennedy, have at times called themselves "progressives," the term is often applied by conservative media pundits to anyone who expounds "leftist" political views. Bernie Sanders, Ralph Nader, Howard Dean, Noam Chomsky, and even the late Howard Zinn have all at some point been pejoratively labeled progressives. Conservative media pundits often use the terms "liberal" and "progressive" interchangeably, despite the fact that they are based on distinct political philosophies. While progressives support liberal social reforms, such as reproductive rights, same-sex marriage, and abolition of the death penalty, they tend to reject classical liberal economic commitments to laissez-faire corporate capitalism, and liberals tend to consider many progressive reforms to be examples of government overreach and interference in what should be left to the free market.

Conservative media pundits also have used the terms "socialism" and "progressivism" interchangeably, even though, given that it reforms capitalism, progressivism is not socialism at all but, rather, a political form of the transition from unrestrained industrial and finance capital to advanced capitalism. Progressivism seeks cooperative relations among capital, government, and organized labor, seeking economic prosperity, international trade agreements, integrated business-government contracting to provide public services, worker protections and rights, high wages, progressive income tax, public education, social security, subsidized housing, and public health care.

Progressives also tend to campaign for electoral reform—increasing accountability, transparency, and democratic participation—and for environmental conservation, including the development of renewable energy technologies, recycling, protection of endangered species and habitats, pollution control, and sustainable agriculture, fishing, and forestry. The contemporary progressive movement is largely a disparate collection of grass-roots campaigns and social activism groups focusing on specific issues. In the twenty-first century, progressives continue to campaign for environmentalism, social justice, equal rights, and the view that the Constitution ought to be adjusted as society evolves. As well as state political parties, such as the Vermont Progressive Party, political parties such as the Green Party and the Reform Party could well be considered to be progressive political parties. While conservative media pundits like to complain about "the liberal media," despite the fact that cable television, radio, and press in America are predominantly corporate owned (with the Internet soon to follow), there are some media that can be considered to be progressive. Examples include the *Nation*, the *Huffington Post*, the *Progressive*, *CounterPunch*, *Mother Jones*, Alternet.org, change.org, and the *American Prospect*, as well as *Democracy Now!*, the Pacifica Radio Network, and the *Young Turks*.

Progressivism is a political philosophy and movement advocating social change and reforms through governmental intervention. In America, the term "progressivism" emerged from the late nineteenth century into the twentieth century as a response to the terrible social consequences of unrestrained industrial capitalism during what is now termed as the Gilded Age (see chapter 11) and the financial crisis and depression of 1893–97. It was a response to corrupt bosses and awful working conditions, such as those practiced in the Chicago meat-processing factories (as portrayed in Upton Sinclair's 1906 book *The Jungle*).[9] It grew out of the squalor and poverty of cities, with reformers calling for an end to child labor, slums and tenement housing, harsh working conditions, and poverty. It grew out of the campaigns for better domestic and working conditions for women and universal suffrage (as established by the Nineteenth Amendment, ratified in 1920). Progressivism provided a political alternative to conservativism, socialism, and anarchism by calling for governmental regulatory oversight and constraints on both industrial and finance capital while leaving economic activity largely to the private sector, and using taxation to fund social projects, public education, and welfare. This period of social activism and reform flourished from the 1890s to the 1920s, which has come to be known as the Progressive Era.[10] It began with urban and state political and administrative reform, led by small business owners and farmers, but soon grew to be a national movement empowered by a growing middle class and unions, leading to four constitutional amendments and technical changes in the structure of the federal government. Progressive Republican presidents include Theodore Roosevelt and Herbert Hoover, and progressive Democrat presidents include Woodrow Wilson and Franklin Delano Roosevelt.

However, many progressives did not wait for government legislation and funding. They led efforts to reform local governments, schools, hospitals, housing, churches, and many other institutions. For example, at the end of the nineteenth century, Jane Addams collected private donations and ran Hull House, a residential community center in Chicago, to provide over two thousand adults with basic literacy; music and art classes; improvements in health through physical education, a public kitchen, and a bath house; a library; a theater; a kindergarten; and a coffeehouse as the center for social events.[11] Her aim for this residential community center, which at its peak comprised a neighborhood of over a dozen buildings, was to teach by example the principles of cooperation and social reform. She campaigned for the Progressive Party (founded in 1912), was a committed champion of the civic rights for women as well as for public education and the abolition of child labor, was the president of the Women's International League for Peace and Freedom in 1915—which earned her criticisms from the press for being "unpatriotic" when America joined the First World War in 1917—and was awarded the Nobel Peace Prize in 1931.[12]

> To destroy this invisible Government, to dissolve the unholy alliance between corrupt business and corrupt politics is the first task of the statesmanship of the day.
>
> *The Progressive Party platform, 1912*[13]

As I have already mentioned, from the outset, the progressive movement was reformist, seeking to improve the quality of life for Americans. Progressives hoped that governmental regulation of banks, corporations, and industries would liberate working-class Americans from the social consequences of unrestrained industrial capitalism. Rather than being a step on the road to socialism, as Beck claims, progressivism gives political form to the transition from unrestrained capitalism to advanced capitalism, which develops increasingly integrated relations among capital, the government, and organized labor. Hence, in 1907, the American Federation of Labor, under the leadership of Samuel Gompers, gave its support to Theodore Roosevelt and the Progressive Party to reform labor relations rather than nationalize industries.[14] They called for reforms such as the eight-hour work day, the forty-hour work week, minimum wage laws, improved working conditions in factories, and health and safety laws. Both as Republican president and Progressive Party candidate, Roosevelt supported capitalism and the growing interstate corporations. However, he predicted that these large corporations would gain increasing power and influence over the federal government to the detriment of American society and the national interest. Due to their growing economic leverage and economies of scale, small local businesses were increasingly unable to compete with interstate corporations. This resulted in less competition. Hence Roosevelt advocated the federal regulation of interstate corporations (for which the commerce clause applies) through enforcing already existing antitrust legislation (as also did Republican president William Howard Taft) such as the 1887 Interstate Commerce Act and the 1890 Sherman Antitrust Act. It was this kind of reform that led to the breakup of the Standard Oil monopoly.

In general, Roosevelt's New Nationalism proposed a strong federal government to regulate industry, protect the middle and working classes, and carry on great national projects, such as improvements to inland waterways. He argued that the growing interstate corporations were good for America, providing they behaved responsibly. The federal government should protect workers and children from exploitation and promote the general welfare. He advocated the further reduction of trade tariffs, the abolition of child labor, a minimum wage, compensation for work-related injuries, social security, relief for poor farmers, and a national health service. He also supported the introduction of inheritance tax and the constitutional amendment to allow federal income tax.

When Woodrow Wilson won the 1912 election, Roosevelt's paternalistic New Nationalism lost out to Wilson's much more popularist New Freedom. However, President Wilson was also a supporter of the interstate corporations and banks, providing they behaved responsibly and were federally regulated. As we can see from the Federal Reserve System, developed from the 1914 banking reforms, rather than asserting governmental control over banking and finance or nationalizing the banks, it developed as a system of integrated relations between the federal government and private banks.[15] Even though

Beck considers the progressive income tax to be tantamount to socialism through the back door, when it was passed through the Sixteenth Amendment (ratified in 1913), this further integrated the federal government, labor relations, and capital as, henceforth, the availability of public funds would be dependent on levels of wages and returns of investment. Industrialists such as Henry Ford adopted the progressive business model that, as well as building mass assembly lines, increased the wages of workers. He argued that mass-production enterprises needed mass consumption, and, therefore, workers had to be paid enough to buy the products. During this time, the Interstate Commerce Commission, the Federal Trade Commission, and the Food and Drug Administration were created. Despite fierce opposition from American interstate corporations, the Democrat-dominated Congress in 1913 strengthened labor relations and lowered trade tariffs, thereby increasing international commerce and competition until the First World War broke out the following year. Wilson only nationalized those parts of the railroads that were essential for the transportation of armaments and troops during the war, and after the end of the war, he returned them to their prior owners.

In my opinion, Beck is quite rightly outraged by Wilson's disregard for the First Amendment.[16] Wilson was intolerant of dissenters and misused the 1917 Espionage Act and the 1918 Sedition Act to silence and imprison anti-war protestors, anarchists, socialists, suffragettes, and pacifists.[17] The latter law made it a crime to say anything "disloyal, profane, or abusive" about the government, the flag, and the armed forces. Eugene Debs (union leader and Socialist Party presidential candidate in 1904, 1908, and 1912) was sentenced to ten years in prison for "obstructing recruiting" by making an anti-war speech.[18] When suffragette leader Alice Paul went on a hunger strike, after she had organized a picket of the White House and the women were subsequently arrested, imprisoned, and beaten, Wilson tried (and failed) to get her incarcerated indefinitely in a lunatic asylum.[19] In 1917, anarchists Emma Goldman and Alexander Berkman were arrested, sentenced to two years in prison, then deported to Russia for "conspiring to induce persons not to register" for the draft.[20] The poet e. e. cummings served as an ambulance driver during the war and was held in a military detention camp for over three years for saying that he felt no hatred for the Germans. There were many other terrible injustices such as this, and without doubt, this was an undemocratic abuse of power by Wilson. The 1918 Sedition Act was repealed in 1921. However, these laws were passed by Congress and upheld by the Supreme Court, and there was little opposition to them from either the press or the American public at that time. Furthermore, this was not the first time a president had called for and used such laws to suppress dissent and criticism. President John Adams, one of Beck's heroes, used the 1798 Alien and Sedition Acts to suppress and imprison critics in the press "for spreading libel and falsehoods about the government."

Wilson's authoritarianism actually ran counter to the progressive movement. As well as forming a response to the consequences of unrestrained industrial and finance capitalism, progressives called for the increased democratization of society and accountability of government. By the end of the nineteenth century, state and federal governments were securely in the pockets of Big Business, such as the growing interstate corporations and the owners of the railroads. Many of the progressive struggles for reform of the political sphere were responses to corruption in American politics. Beck sneers at the progressive fondness for "experts," but this progressive tendency to professionalization and bureaucratization in state and federal government was the result of efforts to eliminate oligarchy, patronage, corruption, and waste. Of course, Beck rejects the idea that scientists and agronomists, for example, could know if and how land has been overused and how to protect and restore it. However, the progressive idea was not that technical experts would make better decisions than politicians or citizens, but that the employment of experts and professionals would lead to better-informed politicians and citizens. Progressive Louis Brandeis, for example, used the methods and data provided by contemporary social scientists to demonstrate that long working hours actually had a high cost for society (what economists call "externals" today), as well as for individual workers, by having social consequences that caused a burden on society.[21] Reducing working hours saved public funds. Professional administrators would run city and state governmental operations but were constrained and directed in accordance with the guidelines and policy objectives of elected politicians.

Progressive reformers, such as Hazen Pingree (mayor of Detroit in the 1890s), Tom Johnson (mayor of Cleveland, Ohio, at the turn of the twentieth century), and Seth Low (major of New York, also at the turn of the twentieth century) were elected on platforms calling for greater autonomy for city administration, progressive income tax, cheap public transportation, and public education. Many cities set up municipal administrations to study the budgets and operations of government. In Illinois, Governor Frank Lowden undertook a major reorganization of state government. In Wisconsin, Robert La Follette (U.S. senator and Progressive Party presidential candidate in 1924) used the state university as the source of ideas and expertise.[22] Rather than being a conspiracy to impose "socialism" on America, the goal of the progressive movement was to enable state and city governments to serve better the citizenry by making governmental institutions, the implementation of policies, and the delivery of public services more efficient and rational. As a result of this, city and state governments were able to eliminate repetitions between departments and actually reduce the number of officials, and they were able to plan and budget. By focusing on state and city governments, many progressives by the 1920s had challenged the old tradition of political bosses and their wealthy patrons, instead developing systems of municipal administration that made politicians more accountable to the electorate and employed technical experts, professional administrators, and bureaucrats. This focus led to a shift of power away from the wealthy state oligarchs and toward the growing middle class. Hence progressives drew support from middle-class professionals, as well as from wealthy philanthropists, political activists, union leaders, and religious leaders, and created many of the local and state institutions that exist today.

This movement for better government also involved the struggle for greater democratic participation in state and federal government. The progressive movement was a grass-roots response to public and popular mistrust of politicians, corporations, oligarchs, and special interest groups. This progressive movement resulted in the development of experiments in "direct democracy," such as voter initiatives, referendums, and recalls, as well as improving "representation" through universal suffrage, direct primaries, and the direct election of senators (as established by the Seventeenth Amendment, ratified in 1913). The Oregon System was the first of these progressive experiments in direct democracy.[23] Approved by the Oregon legislature in 1902 as a result of the campaigns led by William U'Ren and the Oregon Direct Legislation League, it included the Corrupt Practices Act and introduced both voter initiatives and public referenda. In 1904, it was expanded to include direct primaries, and in 1908 it allowed voters to recall politicians and public officials. It was copied by other states in the Northwest and Midwest, and in 1911, California followed suit. Today roughly half of the states use these ballot measures. Furthermore, progressives campaigned for strict limits and disclosure requirements for political campaign contributions, the registration of lobbyists, and the publication of congressional committee proceedings.

Arguably, one of the most important consequences of progressivism is the focus on reforming and improving education, schools, and curricula. Progressive thinkers, such as John Dewey, placed universal and comprehensive public education at the top of the progressive agenda, reasoning that if a democracy was to be successful, its leaders and the general public needed a good education. Progressives have continued to debate, campaign, and use ballot measures to influence and change directions in education policy and improve levels of funding for public education. Such reform campaigns have focused on local and state education, promoting diverse and inclusive reforms, such as ending segregation and promoting equal opportunities for all children, and ending traditional disciplinarian practices, such as rote learning and corporal punishment. Progressives emphasized the professionalization of teachers through specialized teacher training and have argued that improvements in standards of public education can be achieved by improving standards of teacher training (which, of course, requires higher levels of public funding and pay). Of course, Beck objects to experts (i.e., teachers) claiming to know more about how to educate children than do parents. And he certainly is opposed to paying for public education through income tax. However, as was discussed in chapter 3, an improvement in public education requires greater levels of personal responsibility from teachers, parents, and students; it requires greater public participation in, commitment to, and funding of public education as a national priority. Progressives have argued that education is the key to better citizenship, improved political leadership, and a more advanced workforce. With the focus on adapting education to the needs of the community comes the focus on adapting education to the needs of the market as well. This commitment to improving society and the economy through improving the skills and level of education of American children has been central to progressivism since its outset in the nineteenth century, throughout the New Deal, and continues to be fundamental to contemporary progressive campaigns.

The New Deal was a series of economic programs passed by Congress between 1933 and 1936.[24] These programs were responses to the Great Depression and focused on relief, recovery, and reform, such as relief for the unemployed, recovery of the economy, and reform of the financial sector. In 1933, the New Deal largely focused on banking, railroads, industry, and farming. The 1933 Industrial Recovery Act was a temporary measure designed to restrict unfair competition and raise wages. Between 1934 and 1936, the National Labor Relations Act, the Social Security Act, and the Emergency Relief Appropriations Act were passed. The latter set up and funded the Works Progress Administration (WPA). By 1937, this government agency employed over three million Americans and had spent over $7 billion to construct public buildings, parks, bridges, schools, and roads. It funded public media, theaters, arts, libraries, and literacy projects. It also provided school lunches, clothing, and housing for the poorest American families, provided aid to poor tenant farmers, and helped migrant workers.

In 1937, the United States Housing Authority (now called the Federal Housing Administration) was set up to lend money to the states for low-cost housing for poor and homeless families, and the Farm Security Administration (now called the Farmers Home Administration) and Rural Electrification Administration were set up to help poor farmers. The 1938 Fair Labor Standards Act established the minimum wage, normalized the forty-hour work week, and abolished child labor, and the 1938 Agricultural Adjustment Act provided subsidies to farms and set quotas to maintain supply and stabilize prices as well as provide relief to farmers who had set aside fallow land to improve the quality of the soil. After Republicans gained control over Congress in 1938, the WPA was shut down, but most of the New Deal measures remained intact until the Reagan administration.

Critics like Beck denounce the New Deal as "the road to socialism," but arguably, President Franklin Delano Roosevelt took the measures necessary to prop up American capitalism instead of nationalizing the banks, railroads, and other industries. The Great Depression was the result of the failure of unrestrained industrial and finance capitalism. While historians may debate whether the New Deal prolonged the Great Depression or shortened it, it is evidently the case that it saved millions of Americans from absolute misery, starvation, unemployment, and homelessness. Furthermore, FDR appointed a fiscal conservative, Lewis Douglas, to run the Budget Office in 1933–34. During the Great Depression only about 3 percent of the population earned enough to pay income tax. The 1933 Economy Act reduced federal expenditures by $500 million. Douglas also cut the military budget by $125 million and the U.S. Post Office by $75 million, and saved $100 million by laying off federal employees. From the outset, FDR considered agencies such as the WPA to be temporary emergency measures. If FDR planned to introduce socialism to America, the actual measures introduced via the New Deal fell far short of his plan. It provided relief to millions of poor Americans, but little more than enough to keep them fed, clothed, and alive. The WPA improved some infrastructure and employment, but FDR took great care that it did not compete with the private sector. There was some relief for poor farmers and unionized workers, but there was not any radical change in agriculture and industry. The structures of industrial capitalism were hardly touched. The financial sector and monetary structures faced some new regulations, such as the 1933 Securities Act, but FDR did not propose any kind of radical system of central control or planning. It was largely business as usual.

> Some people will try to give you new and strange names for what we are doing. Sometimes they will call it "Fascism," sometimes "Communism," sometimes "Regimentation," sometimes "Socialism." But, in so doing, they are trying to make very complex and theoretical something that is really very simple and very practical. . . . Plausible self-seekers and theoretical die-hards will tell you of the loss of individual liberty. Answer this question out of the facts of your own life. Have you lost any of your rights or liberty or constitutional freedom of action and choice?
> *President Roosevelt, Fire Side Chat, 1934*[25]

However, having said that, FDR established the power of the executive branch and he increased the power of the federal government as a whole. But by doing so, he created a large array of agencies protecting various groups of citizens, especially working-class Americans, and increased the expectation of civil rights among women and ethnic minorities. On January 11, 1944, during his state of the union address, FDR declared that Americans had come to recognize the need for a "Second Bill of Rights" to "assure us equality in the pursuit of happiness." This "economic bill of rights" would guarantee, among other things, employment, fair competition, housing, health care, education, and social security. The New Deal did not just provide relief for the poorest Americans but also provided the foundation for the civil rights movement and for ordinary Americans to feel that they had the right to stand up against both government and the corporations. While its economic influence may well have been slight, its real legacy was in its political influence by paving the way for liberal reform in the 1960s and what President Lyndon Johnson called "the Great Society."[26]

With the support of a Democratic majority in Congress, the domestic programs initiated by Lyndon Johnson resembled the New Deal insofar as they were aimed at alleviating poverty and securing civil rights, but unlike the New Deal, they were initiated at a time of prosperity and continuing economic growth. As well as attempting to deal with the problems of racial inequalities, such as segregation, responding to the demands of the progressive civil rights movement and leading to the 1964 Civil Rights Act and 1965 Voting Rights Act, Lyndon Johnson and Congress continued President's Kennedy's War on Poverty and New Frontier agendas by creating federal programs such as Medicare, Medicaid, Head Start, and Food Stamps, alongside public housing and transportation programs, extending unemployment welfare and retraining programs, and improving consumer protections and safety regulations. (Medicare, Medicaid, and public education funding were expanded under the administrations of Richard Nixon, Gerald Ford, and Jimmy Carter; funding for many of these programs was cut during the Reagan administration.)

The 1964 Economic Opportunity Act funded the creation of the Office of Economic Opportunity to oversee the implementation of community-based programs, such as the Neighborhood Youth Corps, Volunteers in Service to America, the Model Cities Program, Upward Bound, and the Community Action Program. The 1965 National Foundation for the Arts and Humanities Act allowed for the creation of both the National Endowment for the Arts and the National Endowment for the Humanities. The 1965 Higher Education Act increased federal funds for universities, created scholarships and low-interest student loans, and initiated the national Teacher Corps to provide teachers to impoverished communities. (The Office of Economic Opportunity was dismantled under the Nixon and Ford administrations.)

Between 1964 and 1969, several major environmental conservation and pollution control acts were passed. These included the 1964 Wilderness Act, the 1965 Land and Water Conservation Act, the 1965 Solid Waste Disposal Act, the 1965 Motor Vehicle Air Pollution Control Act, the 1966 Endangered Species Preservation Act, the 1968 National Historic Preservation Act, the 1968 National Trails System Act, the 1968 Wild and Scenic Rivers Act, the 1968 Aircraft Noise Abatement Act, and the 1969 National Environmental Policy Act. However, despite benefiting millions of Americans, funding for social reforms and antipoverty programs was opposed by many Republicans, and due to their implementation in a top-down manner by federally appointed task forces, they did not have any connection to grass-roots progressive campaigns or activist groups. This limited their success. Furthermore, the escalating costs of the Vietnam War after 1968 further limited the available funds for these programs. However, the 1968 Bilingual Education Act offered federal aid to local school districts in assisting them to teach English to the children of immigrants (this act was allowed to expire by Congress in 2002), and the 1968

Civil Rights Act banned housing discrimination and extended constitutional protections to Native Americans on reservations.

Generally speaking, conservatives have criticized these kinds of programs for being ineffective and making poor people lazy and reliant on government. However, while these criticisms are largely based on an ideological commitment to "the free market" and a gross indifference to the plight of poor Americans, the underlying motive seems to be the traditional conservative resentment about paying taxes to help other people. Beck attacks progressivism because of its core commitment to *social justice*, which he claims is a step along the path to National Socialism and communism, toward concentration camps, gulags, and mass executions. Hence, he has denounced progressive campaigns for public health care and education as being the path to totalitarian governmental control. In order to make this connection—on his TV show "documentaries" and famous chalkboard diagrams, as lampooned by Jon Stewart on *The Daily Show*—Beck has distorted both the history of progressivism and the concept of social justice.[27]

While the National Socialists and Bolsheviks did appeal to ideas of social justice, these appeals took the form of propaganda, as they attempted to gain popular support while they established and secured their own authoritarian and centralized power base. Rather than develop democratic societies, they used violence to maintain power and developed themselves into a political elite that imprisoned and murdered their opponents and critics. This has nothing whatsoever to do with progressivism and the progressive appeal to social justice. The progressive idea of social justice refers to the idea of legally correcting inequalities, suffering, and exploitation by reforming the existing political and legal framework.[28] The progressive movement has struggled for these reforms by using peaceful, legitimate methods and tactics—through the ballot box and campaigns—that cannot be compared to those used by the Nazis and Bolsheviks. Progressives have attempted to transform society into a more democratic and fair society, based on humanitarian principles of equality, dignity, and solidarity. Progressive social justice is based on the idea that all human beings have an equal right to life, liberty, and the pursuit of happiness, the very same principles that Thomas Jefferson took to be the foundation of the United States of America.

Beck has told his Christian viewers and listeners to leave any church that advocates any kind of social justice. Somewhat bizarrely, he considers the idea of social justice to run contrary to the principles of Christianity and the teachings of Jesus Christ. Actually, the term "social justice" was coined by the Jesuit Luigi Taparelli in his book *The Constitution of Social Justice* (published 1840) based on the teachings of St. Thomas Aquinas. Pope Leo XIII, who studied under Taparelli, advocated social justice in his encyclical *Rerum Novarum* (*On the Condition of the Working Classes*, published in 1891). In this letter, he rejected both socialism and capitalism, defended labor unions and private property, and wrote that society should be based on cooperation and not competition. He declared that the role of the state was to promote social justice through the protection of rights, while the Catholic Church must speak out on social issues in order to teach moral principles and ensure social harmony. In 1931, Pope Pius XI wrote the encyclical *Quadragesimo Anno*, in which he promoted the ideas of "a living wage" and "subsidiarity." He also wrote that social justice is a personal virtue as well as being an attribute of the social order. A just society is comprised of just individuals. Today, social justice is a core concept of Catholic social teaching.[29] It is also fundamental to the Episcopalian Social Gospel and to other Christian churches, including the United Methodist Church and the Church of Jesus Christ of Latter-day Saints (of which Beck is a member).

As an aside, some commentators, Keith Olbermann included, have compared Glenn Beck to Father Coughlin. There are some similarities. Father Charles Coughlin was a propagandist and conspiracy theorist who hosted a political radio show that reached millions of listeners.[30] He was also vehemently opposed to FDR and strongly defended the gold standard. There the similarities end. At first, Coughlin supported FDR and the New Deal proposals, but he did not feel that they went far enough. He also argued that the government was too cozy with bankers and "Jewish conspirators." In 1934 he founded the "Nation's Union of Social Justice," based on a platform calling for legal protections of American workers and unions, the nationalization of major industries and railroads, redistribution of wealth, and financial reforms such as nationalizing the Federal Reserve. He was opposed to communism and considered Marxism "a Jewish atheist plot" to take over Europe and America. In this context, he defended the actions of Hitler, Mussolini, and Franco. The government restricted Father Coughlin's radio air time by denying him a permit, and also stopped him from using the U.S. Post Office to deliver his newspaper *Social Justice*. After the Pearl Harbor attack in 1941, Coughlin's isolationist stance was not only unpopular but also seen to be aiding the enemy. In 1942, the Archbishop Mooney ordered Coughlin to be silent and return to his parish. Father Coughlin was the priest at the Shrine of the Little Flower until he retired in 1966. He died on October 27, 1979.

Beck seems to be working under the misapprehension that "progressivism" means progressively bigger government. However, contrary to Beck's assertions and distortions, what progressivism really means is a progressively civilized and democratic society. Now there may well be considerable opportunities for debate about what this implies—and so there should be in a healthy and open society—but this is clearly something quite distinct from a totalitarian state. Evidently, Beck has either misunderstood or misrepresented progressivism, whereas a progressive concept of social justice is based on the idea that all human beings have equal and inviolable rights that cannot be denied on the grounds of political expediency, economic development, national interest, or the greater good. Any such denial would be an act of injustice and citizens would have a moral obligation to organize to oppose and correct such unjust acts.

Social justice arises from the rights and consent of the governed—a principle that is a foundation of the Republic and Constitution—and cannot be dictated. The Constitution is founded on the form of a republic in which all citizens have equal rights under the law. As such, the Constitution is secured upon an increasingly refined social contract between citizens to respect each others' constitutional rights. Progressivism requires that each generation cooperates to refine political and economic arrangements and institutions, based on the consent and agreement of the people subject to them, in order to correct inequalities between citizens. Government must be based on consent and equitably representative at local, state, and national levels. Members of the executive, legislative, and judicial branches are representatives and trustees of their constituents. Their use of the respective political authority is legitimate only insofar as they respect the inviolable rights of citizens and apply that power equitably between all citizens within their jurisdiction. This is the only basis of a fair and democratic system of representation, legislation, and enforcement. Laws must represent the negotiations and agreement of legislators acting with the consent of their constituents, and any negative liberty, acting as a restriction of positive liberty, must be based on reasoned agreement and public consent. Otherwise it would be an unjust law and the citizenry would have the moral right to disobey, resist, and oppose it.

However, political freedoms, such as those enumerated in the Bill of Rights, are meaningless when the political system is dominated by a wealthy class—the economic elite. The notions of equality under the law and equal rights are fairly meaningless when the legislature and courts protect the interests of a wealthy economic class over and above all other citizens. When representatives only represent the interests of this class, the system no longer takes the form of either a republic or a democracy but takes the form of a plutocracy. This is an inherently unjust, corrupt, and illegitimate tyranny that the majority has a moral right to resist and oppose. The progressive concept of social justice is not about economic equality at all—hence it differs from socialism—but is about *political equality*. In the republican form of government, as promised in the Constitution, all citizens must be politically equal. Obviously, political equality is quite impossible when there are enormous economic inequalities—hence the use of progressive income tax to aid the poorest members of society to improve their economic condition—but the goal of progressivism is that of equality of rights under the law and equality of access to the political institutions of government, as promised in the Declaration of Independence and the Constitution. Rather than being a cancer that is undermining the foundations of America, the progressive movement is actually the means by which the promise of the American Revolution is to be fulfilled through an ongoing, generational process of correcting political and economic inequalities, through the reform of political and economic institutions and arrangements, in such a way that all human beings have an equal right to life, liberty, and the pursuit of happiness.

PRESIDENT ROOSEVELT, STATE OF THE UNION ADDRESS, JANUARY 11, 1944:[31]

It is our duty now to begin to lay the plans and determine the strategy for the winning of a lasting peace and the establishment of an American standard of living higher than ever before known. We cannot be content, no matter how high that general standard of living may be, if some fraction of our people—whether it be one-third or one-fifth or one-tenth— is ill-fed, ill-clothed, ill-housed, and insecure.

This Republic had its beginning, and grew to its present strength, under the protection of certain inalienable political rights—among them the right of free speech, free press, free worship, trial by jury, freedom from unreasonable searches and seizures. They were our rights to life and liberty. As our nation has grown in size and stature, however—as our industrial economy expanded—these political rights have proven inadequate to assure us equality in the pursuit of happiness. We have come to a clear realization of the fact that true individual freedom cannot exist without economic security and independence: "Necessitous men are not free men." People who are hungry and out of a job are the stuff of which dictatorships are made.

In our day these economic truths have become accepted as self-evident. We have accepted, so to speak, a second Bill of Rights under which a new basis of security and prosperity can be established for all—regardless of station, race, or creed. Among these are

> the right to a useful and remunerative job in the industries or shops or farms or mines of the nation;
> the right to earn enough to provide adequate food and clothing and recreation;
> the right of every farmer to raise and sell his products at a return which will give him and his family a decent living;
> the right of every businessman, large and small, to trade in an atmosphere of freedom from unfair competition and domination by monopolies at home or abroad;
> the right of every family to a decent home;
> the right to adequate medical care and the opportunity to achieve and enjoy good health;

the right to adequate protection from the economic fears of old age, sickness, accident, and unemployment;

the right to a good education.

All of these rights spell security. And after this war is won, we must be prepared to move forward, in the implementation of these rights, to new goals of human happiness and well-being. America's own rightful place in the world depends in large part upon how fully these and similar rights have been carried into practice for all our citizens. For unless there is security here at home, there cannot be lasting peace in the world.

11

THE MYTH OF THE FREE MARKET

Glenn Beck talks of "liberty, capitalism, inventiveness, and the progressive principle of natural selection" in which struggle and competition are the routes to success.[1] He argues that any kind of public safety net prevents people learning from their mistakes. It is for this reason that he is opposed to taxpayer-funded welfare, education, health care, public housing, or any mechanism by which wealth is redistributed from the "fortunate" to the "unfortunate." Echoing the Social Darwinism of the late nineteenth century, Beck considers social justice to be a road to ruin and evil. It is for this reason that he claims to be against progressive taxation. He considers it to be unfair because those Americans in the top 50 percent of earners pay 97 percent of the total contribution income tax.[2] He cites 2006 IRS figures to back up this claim.

Let us assume that this statistic is correct, yet let's turn it on its head. What does it mean? It means that 50 percent of working Americans earn so little money that they are only able to contribute 3 percent of the total income tax. That means that half of working Americans do not earn enough money to pay income tax!

Beck also cites a 2005 Congressional Budget Office report that shows that the top 20 percent earn 55.1 percent of the pretax income yet pay 86.3 percent of the total income tax contribution. He considers this to be unfair on the top 20 percent. Again, let's accept this figure as accurate and turn it on its head. This means that 20 percent of Americans earned over half the nation's total income, while 80 percent of American workers earned less than half of the nation's total income. This shows that there is massive inequality within the American economic system and illustrates that 20 percent of the population effectively owns over half of the nation's wealth. Is this really an indication of national prosperity? Whose prosperity? These figures also conceal the fact that the tax system has become corrupt. Due to their ability to take advantage of expensive tax attorneys, loopholes, and offshore banking, the wealthiest Americans pay less of a percentage of their income as tax than do ordinary American middle-class workers. Does this seem fair? Not really.

Unfortunately, there is insufficient space here to go into a detailed argument in defense of a progressive income tax, but the premise of the argument is straightforward. The market did not come into existence all by itself, as if by magic or natural forces. It has been constructed by the efforts of our predecessors over many generations.[3] Those efforts would have been meaningless and futile without a concept of private property and the political institutions that protected it and encouraged the further development of the market by protecting patent rights and scientific discovery. The market has a history. It needed to reach stages of its historical development before certain enterprises were even possible. If Bill Gates had been born in eleventh-century Medieval Europe, he probably would have been put to work taking care of the pigs and would have remained impoverished his whole life, no matter how intelligent or hard working he was. Yet in the twentieth century, after the invention of computers and programs, as well as the supporting industries and growth of the human need for computer operating systems, upon which a new market could flourish, Bill Gates was able to put his intelligence and efforts to work and become extremely wealthy through founding and developing the Microsoft Corporation.

Yet Bill Gates did not pay for any of these past efforts to develop the conditions required for a global computer software market. He simply took advantage of them. Once we recognize this historical fact, we can see that there is an argument that those people *who benefit most* from the current market conditions should *pay proportionately more tax.* Obviously, we can't pay back all our predecessors for their efforts. Instead, we pay forward in order to provide the next generation with schools, hospitals, universities, space programs, better infrastructure, a cleaner environment, better public services, and so on, all of which will help further develop the market, improve the national level of prosperity, and provide greater revenue for the development of the nation. It is an investment in the future of the nation. It is on this premise that progressive income tax is fair (and patriotic).

However, Beck would not buy into this argument. Instead, he favors a value-added tax to replace the income tax.[4] He considers this to be fair and argues that this means that everyone will contribute to the national tax bill. However, such a tax would disproportionately penalize poorer Americans, who will find that their overall income is dramatically reduced due to the increased cost of living. Effectively, it would mean that 50 percent of all working Americans would become poorer, while the wealthiest 20 percent of Americans would become even richer. In addition, if Beck had his way, Americans would no longer have access to public education, or welfare provisions, or mortgage relief. So they would not only have even less net income, but their children would not go to school, they would live in rented accommodation, and they would probably have to work two or three low-paid jobs just to pay the bills, or rely on private charity. Furthermore, as Beck is against any kind of public health care, the number of uninsured or inadequately insured Americans would dramatically increase. Within a single generation, poverty would escalate in America.

Beck is also against Social Security. He describes it as a "ponzi scheme."[5] He ignores that the way Social Security is supposed to work is that contributions from wages throughout a person's working life collect interest to pay for that person's pension when they retire. Social Security should for the most part work like a private pension plan, but be nonprofit. In fact, in virtue of being nonprofit, there should be more money available for its contributors when they need it. However, the problem with Social Security is not inherent to it. The problem is that successive Congresses have taken this money and spent it. If this was done in private insurance, it would be called embezzlement, but unlike private insurers, Congress can replace the money in the Social Security fund with government bonds. The future problems this will cause depend on the future value of these bonds—which is dependent on the national debt, among other things. This is not a flaw in the Social Security system but a flaw in how it has been managed by successive governments. Media pundits and propagandists have been spreading the lie that it is the system itself that it is inherently flawed, due to the gradually aging population, and that pensions would be better served by the private sector, despite the numerous cases of embezzlement within the private sector.

Rather than demanding that the government pays this money back to the Social Security fund, Beck's "solution" is to cut Medicare and Medicaid. Pensioners would not only lose their Social Security but also have to pay for their medical expenses. This means that, as well as becoming poorer and less able to provide for their own retirement, more and more Americans would have to take care of their parents or see them die on the street. This in turn will further increase the burden on lower-income families and drive them even deeper into poverty. Not to miss the opportunity, he also suggests firing unionized public sector workers, which will increase unemployment and poverty (given that he would cut unemployment welfare). Of course, reducing the military budget is out of the question, and Beck also wants money to be found to build that seven-hundred-mile fence across the southern border (presumably without using illegal immigrant labor).

Beck claims that politicians are "hijacking private business and stealing our money," but he is silent about how private business has hijacked government.[6] He rejects any notion of regulating banking and financial services. He denounces this kind of progressive call for reform as being based on the idea that experts know better how to do things than people who are not experts. Apparently, things are best left in the hands of people who do not know what they are doing. Well, you don't need to be an expert to know how deregulated banking and financial services have worked out! But what Beck really objects to, of course, is income tax and experts deciding how to redistribute our money, although "our" refers to only the 50 percent of the population who have enough income to pay income tax. Hence, he complains that the 1991 Medicare Prescription Drug Benefit Plan *took* American taxpayers' money to give it to low and average income elderly Americans, thereby *stealing* from wealthy Americans, their children, and their grandchildren. Apparently, public provision for helping old Americans afford medicine is theft and corruption.

Is Beck just mean-spirited about paying taxes or is there some rationale behind his "solution" to the national debt? Beck puts his faith in the free market and unrestrained capitalism.[7] However, apart from a few local businesses and local farmers' markets, in America, the market is dominated by major multinational corporations. Using their economic leverage from economies of scale, cheap foreign labor, and their investors' capital, these corporations have accumulated massive wealth. With mergers and the consolidation of corporations, furthering the control and domination over markets and political institutions, public policy has become dominated by strategic corporate planning. Corporations have almost seized total control over the water supply, industry, commerce, utilities, agriculture, entertainment, media, finance, medicine, transportation, infrastructure, and most other aspects of daily life. The so-called "trickle-down" economics theory has been used to justify accumulated ownership of all the means of production, distribution, and consumption by cartels of corporations, which have increasingly outsourced jobs to countries such as India and China in order to take advantage of cheap labor and unregulated workplaces. Small local businesses and farmers are unable to compete. Rather than trickling down, wealth is horizontally divided among investors and corporations, both of which buy products and services from corporations, which through mergers and acquisitions form trusts, dividing up the market into niches. This has resulted in a loss of market competition, the destruction of local economies, and the suppression of the free market. Instead of being the owners of their own businesses—which would form the basis of a free market—most working Americans are the employees of a corporation. Due to unrestrained capitalism, the free market has become a myth.

As corporations have grown into massive multinational corporations, investors have become even more distant, and markets have shifted from being a competitive consumers' market, wherein the best and cheapest products or services win, to an competitive investors' market, wherein the highest return on investment wins. With increased corporate consolidation, customers have lost out and investors have gained. While this may well have resulted in higher profits, it reduced corporate accountability and means that corporate interest is no longer even related to customer satisfaction, let alone the public interest or good. The government not only protects corporate rights and privileges—such as property and patent rights—but also limits liability and allows corporations to purchase other companies and corporations. By limiting liability (investors can only lose their investment and are not liable for corporate debts), government *artificially* protects investors while simultaneously maintaining the myth of the free market. What this has achieved is that investors have become distanced from corporate management, leading to a rise in corporate unaccountability and irresponsibility, which combined with "the golden handshake" has ended up creating the conditions that undermine market discipline and competitiveness. This has not only shifted liability further away from investors and toward creditors but also shifted risks and costs to society as a whole—leading to privatization of profits and the socialization of costs. The corporation has become abstracted into a legal entity that is over and above its owners, while corporate directors and executives are not even held accountable for the loss of shareholders' investments (anyone remember Enron?). This has created a recipe for disaster that has reared its head in crisis after crisis, from the banking crises of the late nineteenth century to the recent banking crisis and the bailouts. As predicted by Adam Smith in his book *The Wealth of Nations*, it is folly to put managers in charge of other people's money because this generates irresponsible investment.[8] Smith coined the idea of "the invisible hand of the free market," but he also was opposed to corporations in general because they increased the tendency for the creation of cartels and monopolies that undermine free market competition.

As an aside, Beck informs us about the 1794 Whiskey Rebellion, wherein whiskey producers were outraged about a tax imposed on them to pay for the War of Independence. He tells us that the tax was "6 cents per gallon for large whiskey producers and 9 cents per gallon for small producers."[9] And then he triumphantly declares that President Washington led an army to put down this rebellion "without a shot being fired."[10] Putting aside Beck's oversimplification of this event, given that the rebellion did involve violent conflict but was suppressed before the federal peacekeepers arrived, what I find interesting is that he does not seem to notice how this tax effectively put small producers at a disadvantage against large producers, given that the large producers could afford the flat fee and avoid the higher per gallon tax. Here, perhaps, we see Congress making its first of a long series of laws designed to advantage Big Business by making it harder for small businesses to compete. And, perhaps coincidentally, upon retirement from the presidency, after many small producers had gone out of business, George Washington moved into the whiskey business, investing in a full-scale industrial still. Contrary to Beck's insistence that the problem with America is that Big Government interferes with the people's business, I contend that the situation is the reverse: the problem is that Big Business interferes with the people's government.

Media pundits and propagandists like Beck accuse progressives of advocating socialism, and he is critical of anyone who argues that socialism was never properly implemented.[11] Yet his arguments in defense of free-market capitalism, despite the current "economic crisis," are based on his claim that free-market capitalism has never been properly implemented, due to political interference and corruption.[12] Once again, Beck's arguments exhibit a double standard. However, this is little more than sloganeering. Most progressives actually advocate *advanced capitalism*, a post-Ford model of capitalism. In this model, the state and business develop close and integrated relations to regulate the market and provide public services through the public contracting of private companies. Far from being socialist, advanced capitalism involves increased levels of privatization based on complex relations between government and business through a process of public tendering and regulation. The government places restraints on business in order to protect consumers, workers, the environment, and market competition. In exchange, business receives government contracts paid for from taxpayers' funds, protection of property and patents, and a skilled and healthy workforce; in addition, due to antitrust legislation, businesses can operate in a cooperative market as well as receive copyright protections and other benefits. Government also acts as the mediator between business and organized labor. In this way, economic growth remains stable while workers have safe working conditions, and wages increase in proportion to economic growth. This gives workers a stake in the economy.

Providing access to the housing market and a public safety net—such as Social Security, Medicare, Medicaid, and unemployment welfare—gives the poorest citizens a stake in the stability of the system. With access to public education, children can learn the skills that will be needed by the market in the future, which gives children a stake in the future of society. When government invests in education, the resulting educated population benefits future governments, by providing increased tax revenue and reduced welfare costs. The Public Option would have provided all citizens with access to affordable health care, again giving them a stake in society and providing society with a healthy workforce, which reduces revenues lost to sickness. As the economy grows, all citizens benefit to some degree, and this leads to increased social stability, government revenue for public services, and further economic growth.

However, the operations of advanced capitalism represent "a redistribution of wealth" for the advocates of unrestrained capitalism. Hence, they call for an end to all taxpayer-funded services—apart from the police and military—and the deregulation of all markets. What has happened as a result of deregulation? There has been a transformation from industrial capitalism to finance capitalism. The processes of production have become subordinated to the accumulation of profits and capital. This has led to a redistribution of wealth from producers to investors in step with the consolidation of capital into massive multinational corporations. The market has shifted from being a competitive consumers' market to becoming a competitive investors' market. This has led toward capital accumulation forming a corporate oligopoly, capital flight and outsourcing, the repression of workers and trade unions, increased levels of social alienation, increased inequality, rising unemployment, higher prices, lower wages, and economic instability.

Meanwhile, year after year, corporations make record profits and investors receive a greater rate of return. As the deregulation of banking and financial services has repeatedly shown, speculative and irresponsible lending has resulted in savings and loans crises since the 1980s. The recent banking crisis was a direct result of further deregulation during the Clinton and Bush administrations. Once investment banking and brokerage firms were able to merge, leading to massive banking conglomerations, the kind of scandal and crisis caused by Enron was inevitable; wherein investment and brokerage firms were complicit in Enron's misrepresentation of their profits, due to warning signs and conflicts of interest being ignored in the corporate pursuit of profits and increased share value in a competitive investors' market. Here is where ideology rears its ugly head and turns its blind eye. Despite history showing that regulation was imposed in the 1930s to prevent exactly the same kind of abuses and consequences that have resulted from deregulation since the 1980s, the call for further deregulation blindly continues. It is this kind of ideology that underwrites the recent Republican claims that any kind of regulation to fix the damage caused by the deregulated financial sector will cause damage to the economy. The myth of the free market has become an irrational and pathological creed that is blind to all the facts.

Similarly, the 1996 Telecommunications Act has allowed massive levels of corporate consolidation and reduction in market competition, price increases, worker layoffs, and mismanaged investments, and a reduction in customer service. This trend continues, as we can see from the January 2011 FCC and Department of Justice approval of the massive merger between Comcast and NBC. This merger means that, for the first time, a single company will own both the means to access the Internet for millions of people and the content that is passed through it. It can now block or disrupt its competitors, raise prices, control the content of media, stifle criticism, and further abuse the political system.

Beck's ideological commitment to deregulation runs to such an extreme that he complains that "we can't drill for oil, develop nuclear power, or burn clean coal because of the environmental impacts."[13] Who are the "we" here? How many Americans drill for oil, develop nuclear power, or operate coal power stations? Very few. So it turns out that he is outraged that the freedom of a few Americans is limited in order to protect everyone from environmental impacts (i.e., pollution, climate change, and nuclear reactor explosions or meltdown). Is Beck really advocating completely unregulated nuclear power stations, oil platforms, petroleum refining, transportation, and storage, and the operation of coal-fired power stations, mines, and waste management? Unregulated nuclear power stations and radioactive waste disposal? Obviously, common sense would suggest that some regulation of the nuclear power industry is a good idea. After we admit that fact, then it is a matter of degrees.

How much regulation and oversight is needed? This is a matter of negotiation, debate, expert testimony, and agreement, subject to revision—in other words, an open and transparent democratic process. Of course Beck has a right to criticize any government policy, such as Cap and Trade, but his efforts to debunk global warming are little more than cherry picking from scientific results, misinterpreting them by citing a few controversial papers in isolation from the vast body of scientific evidence that confirms not only the existence of global warming but also supports the hypothesis that it is being increased by human industrial activities.

This book, however, is not the place to discuss global warming. What is of concern here is the obsession with deregulation regardless of its consequences. Sometimes Beck's complaints about regulation border on the level of sheer ridiculousness. For example, he complains about a California law requiring that cans of tuna be labeled with warnings about mercury levels, alongside a federal law requiring the use of compact fluorescent lightbulbs (CFLs) by 2012, despite the fact that they contain about thirty times more mercury than a tin of tuna, as if one regulation contradicts the other.[14] This is a very strange complaint. After all, apart from a few eccentric individuals, people do not eat lightbulbs. Yes, in the event of a CFL being broken, care must be taken to air out the room and clean up the powder and broken glass. If people were in the habit of sprinkling the powder and glass fragments on their food, then I suppose that some kind of warning label about mercury levels would be required.

No matter how the facts show that laissez-faire capitalism has resulted in a global economic crisis and a government that serves corporate interests rather than the citizenry, media pundits and propagandists continue to assert that unrestrained capitalism is the only way to get out of the crisis that government has supposedly caused. It is now argued by Beck and other pundits on Fox News, as well as many of the Republicans in Congress, that regulation is the cause of the economic crisis and unemployment. Their circularity of logic and denial of facts are quite astounding, as they argue for further deregulation to solve the problems caused by deregulation. Without irony, they accuse the government of being "socialist" for giving trillions of dollars to Wall Street while accusing the government of trying to take over the financial sector by passing regulations to prevent the worse excesses of finance capitalism, offer customers some modest protections, and prevent the crisis from being repeated. Ignoring the fact that these regulations have been basically written by the same industries that are being regulated, Beck repeatedly explains the bailouts and regulation of failed banks and other industries as being a government takeover, which, again without a hint of irony, he explains is part of a Marxist plot to impose a New World Order based on socialism. Hence, according to Beck, the problem is that Americans just do not understand that capitalism is not about making money, it is about freedom.[15] This explains, he tells us, why two-thirds of Americans in a recent poll don't trust capitalism. He argues that the current crisis is not a failure of capitalism, but a failure of Americans to understand the principles set down in the Constitution by "the Founding Fathers." What underlies this argument is the ideological aim of rolling back all progressive legislation and returning America to the conditions of the Gilded Age.

The term "Gilded Age" was coined by Mark Twain and Charles Dudley Warner in their 1873 book *The Gilded Age: A Tale of Today* as a play on the term "golden age" and the era's ostentatious display of wealth.[16] In American history, the Gilded Age refers to the era of rapid economic, industrial, and urban growth in the United States during the late nineteenth century.[17] Telegraphs and railroads spread across America (the First Transcontinental Railroad was completed in 1869). Wealthy philanthropists built hospitals, schools, universities, colleges, libraries, museums, and theaters, and funded arts and science. During this time, interstate corporations grew, spread, dominated business, and began to influence governmental regulation and policy at both the state and federal levels. This began a period known as the Second Industrial Revolution, a new wave of immigration, and the growth of urban sprawl and slums throughout the Northeast, as America became the world's leading producer of steel.[18] Corporations built and owned industrial towns around their mines, railroads, and factories. The "robber barons" rose to power and used their wealth to control local and state governments.[19] Interstate corporations formed powerful cartels—trusts—and dominated agriculture, industry, mining, and the railroads.[20] Industrialists and financiers such as John D. Rockefeller, Andrew W. Mellon, Andrew Carnegie, and J. P. Morgan accumulated unprecedented personal fortunes and influence over the federal government.[21]

In 1901, United Steel became the first billion-dollar corporation. The massive accumulation of capital led to the formation of Wall Street and the stock market, beginning the transformation from industrial capitalism to financial capitalism—from a producers' market to an investors' market.[22] Political corruption and patronage were rife, and federal forces were used to protect the interests of the owners of factories, mines, and railroads, who tended to be governors, mayors, and senators as well. Judges were in the pockets of the wealthy oligarchs, who also owned the newspaper presses and publishing houses. Voter intimidation and electoral fraud were commonplace. The populations of New York, Philadelphia, and Chicago each exceeded one million people. Poverty increased as more migrant and itinerant labor moved into city tenements, without clean water, sewers, hospitals, lighting, policing, or schools. Violent criminal gangs took over the slums and inner cities. Workers were exploited to provide cheap labor and unions were violently oppressed. As discussed in chapter 5, it was at this time that unions were formed to struggle and battle for workers' rights and protections.[23] The Gilded Age came to an end with the banking crisis of 1893 and the subsequent four years of economic depression. The Progressive Era was a response to the many social problems caused during the Gilded Age.[24]

Corporations have one goal: to make money for shareholders. While they have become good at this, this goal is not necessarily compatible with the well-being of a democratic society or the ecology of the Earth. Massive environmental degradation and destruction—poisoning air, water, and the food supply while further destroying forests and wilderness—have been the consequence of unrestrained capitalism. Corporations spend billions of dollars on advertising, public relations, and presenting a good image and discrediting critics. They have grown so wealthy and powerful that corporations are threatening to undermine the political institutions of government at every level. They have overridden the regulatory mechanisms designed to keep them in check and are at the stage of development in which government has become little more than an instrument for protecting, satisfying, and expanding corporate interests. Rather than acting as an impediment to Big Business, Congress has largely been happy to write laws and regulations that benefit corporations and investors, even at the expense of national sovereignty. For example, NAFTA allows foreign investors to sue the American, Canadian, and Mexican governments when local laws or international environmental agreements reduce a corporation's profits in order to compensate for their "loss." According to the corporate ideology, people have no right to education, health care, housing, employment, pensions, or even food and water, but investors have a right to expect returns on their investments. NAFTA constitutes a coup d'état over the sovereignty of the people and their governments.

This pro-corporate ideology is not confined to Congress. Since 1919, the Supreme Court has made it clear that the foremost duty of a corporation is to maximize its profits and shareholder dividends rather than improve the wages and living standard of its workers.[25] This concept of shareholder primacy is at odds with the public interest and democratic principles of governance and established the legal basis for unrestrained corporate power. Here we see how the Supreme Court has legislated from the bench and become an obstacle to progressive and democratic reform in America. The Supreme Court has become the instrument by which corporations can veto any state or federal legislation or overrule the executive branch of government. The Supreme Court has even ruled that regulations that reduce a corporation's profitability can be construed as a violation of the Fifth Amendment! For example, the Court overruled a state law that prohibited underground mining under or near residential areas on the grounds that it was an unlawful seizure of private property by not allowing the mining company to extract the coal.[26] This decision enshrines "the principle of regulatory taking" in law, which demands that companies receive compensation for lost profits as a result of legislation. Hence, somewhat perversely, the Supreme Court struck down a Massachusetts law compelling cigarette manufacturers to tell the public what is in them on the grounds that the ingredients are a "trade secret" and private property.[27]

The Supreme Court also has repeatedly upheld the right of corporations to free speech, overriding states' rights to legislate advertising, including prohibiting the advertising of cigarettes near schools.[28] Corporations have even been allowed to invoke Fourth Amendment protection against warrantless inspections by federal work and safety inspectors.[29] Yet as we have seen, the Court has no problem with the private property of citizens being seized under eminent domain and sold to private developers. Nor does the Court object to corporations being allowed to read personal emails, listen to phone calls, install hidden cameras, and request random drug tests of their employees. It is not that the Supreme Court has stopped at giving corporations the same rights as persons—an absurd enough result in itself—but it has given corporations *greater* rights than those afforded citizens.[30] Under such circumstances, democratic oversight and regulation of corporations becomes impossible, and the republican form of government is undermined if people are no longer citizens equal under the law. The Republic has become a corporate state and citizens have become its subjects.

However, given the protections and privileges afforded by incorporation, it is reasonable that the public both receives benefits from corporations and has some degree of oversight over corporate activities.[31] If business wishes to remain strictly private, then let it forgo investor liability limitation and patent protections! All states (except Alaska) have the legal right to revoke corporate charters, and Congress has the constitutional authority (and obligation) to regulate interstate commerce. Yet state and federal governments have not only remained passive in the face of growing corporate power, they have also nurtured that growth and helped remove any opposition to it. But the law is clear. State legislatures have the right to revoke corporate charters of corporations registered within the state if they commit criminal acts, act against the public good, and/or fail to pay their taxes. However, the problem is that should a corporation have its charter revoked in one state, it can always reincorporate in another state. This has led states to be reluctant to enforce the law and thus risk losing tax revenues.

State-based corporate law is clearly a problem. This clearly indicates that perhaps it is time for a federal charter registry that prevents any state from allowing reincorporation if another state has revoked a charter due to criminal activity, to protect the public good, or due to tax evasion. This is both reasonable and constitutional (under the Commerce Clause) if such corporations operate outside of their state. Once we recognize that corporations were only initially granted charters providing that they agreed to abide by specified conditions and serve the public good, we can see the legal basis for challenging unrestrained corporate power. The refusal to do this shows the extent to which corporations have gained dominance over both federal and state governments. Yet unrestrained corporate power is the greatest threat to democracy, communities, and the possibility of a free market.

Without doubt, Beck would object to any governmental interference in the private business of corporations. However, corporations in the United States began as quasi-government organizations created by state governments to build infrastructure such as roads, canals, and railroads.[32] Their powers and rights were written into their charters as issued by the state legislature. Investors were responsible for any debts owed by corporations and were liable for any fines resulting from legal action taken against corporations. Over the course of the nineteenth century, corporations became increasingly privatized and the rules for incorporation became looser. Further deregulation resulted in corporations being considered independent entities, with the same constitutional rights as citizens, all the while receiving public funds through contracts for public works projects. By the end of the nineteenth century, corporations had risen to the point of becoming the dominant institutional power in America. And despite Teddy Roosevelt's concern, the power of corporations increased throughout the twentieth century.

At the turn of the twenty-first century, corporations have unprecedented power over government and society. Initially, corporations were strictly prohibited from interfering in politics, but today they have unrestrained and unmonitored rights to spend money on lobbyists and political campaigns. Moreover, through think tanks, policy centers, universities, media, public relations, and lobbyists, the corporate takeover of America has been relentless and all-pervasive. Over the last century, corporations have consolidated power over all levels and branches of government, mass media, and the electoral process. As we enter the second decade of the twenty-first century, the Internet has become the new frontier of corporate ownership and control. Politicians are beholden to corporations for any chance of election or reelection. Unlimited campaign spending by corporations during elections, in addition to the corporate opportunities that await congressmen (many of whom are millionaires from the corporate sector), has resulted in only pro-corporate candidates running or being elected to public office (with a few exceptions). Congress is swamped with tens of thousands of corporate lobbyists, many of whom were former congressmen now enjoying lucrative salaries and benefits, and the national interest has become synonymous with corporate strategy and business development.

The erosion of the public sector alongside the rise of corporate power has resulted in an increased public dependency on corporations, which makes government dependent on corporations to supply public services and products, and further binds the political process to corporate interests. Decades of deregulation and Supreme Court rulings in favor of giving corporations greater rights than citizens have resulted in unrestrained corporate power in America. While corporate quarterly profits break records during a recession, more and more ordinary working- and middle-class Americans find it difficult to pay for basic needs such as groceries, housing, utilities, and health care.

The citizens of the United States must effectively control the mighty commercial forces which they themselves have called into being.

Theodore Roosevelt, 1910[33]

Without any democratic control over corporations, there is no reason to believe that any system of federal chartering, oversight, or legislation would afford any effective oversight or restraint upon corporate power. The fundamental problem facing democracy is how to place corporations under public oversight and control and, if need be, revoke their charters and seize their assets (after returning investments and debts).[34] While corporations may act independently of government oversight and regulation, while enjoying limited liability and a right to spend unlimited money on political campaigns, unrestrained corporate power and a corporate state are the inevitable outcomes. How can an abstract legal entity—an artificial construction of state law—be afforded constitutional protections, such as the right to free speech under the First Amendment?

Ironically, the defenders of a strictly constructionist reading of the Constitution—that is, taking it literally—are often among the first to defend the assertion that these rights are afforded to corporations, even though corporations are not mentioned anywhere in the text of the Constitution. Furthermore, the equal right to life, liberty, and the pursuit of happiness announced by Jefferson in the Declaration of Independence was premised on a natural rights theory in which human beings receive their rights from their Creator, namely, Nature's God. However, corporations are creatures of the state legislature. It is clearly a category mistake to confuse persons and corporations within the terms of the U.S. Constitution. What is needed is an amendment to the Constitution clarifying that the enumerated rights belong to persons, not corporations. I shall discuss this in the next chapter.

> I hope we shall crush in its birth the aristocracy of the moneyed corporations which dare already to challenge our government to a trial of strength and bid defiance to the laws of our country.
>
> *Thomas Jefferson*, 1816[35]

Many people want to know why the government seems to have no problem finding trillions of dollars to bail out capitalists—who have been preaching market discipline and self-reliance—but supposedly America cannot afford universal health care. Beck considers health care to be a luxury. Why is it always working- and middle-class Americans who make the sacrifices? Rather than wanting to be led and fed by the state, it seems to me that Americans want to know why capitalists weren't forced to suffer the consequences of their own failures, as a genuine capitalist system demands they should. In my view, many Americans simply do not believe in the myth of the free market any longer.

To be fair, Beck has been fairly consistent in his criticisms of the bailouts. However, there has been something of an evolution to his narrative since September 2008. When the bailout was first proposed during the Bush administration, Beck was scathing about the banks, the old boys' network, and the Federal Reserve, and he blamed corporate greed and political corruption.[36] Yet in the run-up to the congressional vote on the 2008 Emergency Economic Stabilization Act (EESA), he declared the bailout to be inevitable, that a $2 trillion bailout would be necessary, and he reversed his position, declaring: "The real story is the $700 billion that you are hearing about now is not only, I believe, necessary, it is also not nearly enough, and all the weasels in Washington know it."[37] He supported EESA, as long as it was without earmarks, but shifted the focus of the blame to Freddie Mac and Fannie Mae and government-assisted housing loans.[38]

After EESA had passed and been signed into law on October 3, Beck reversed his reversal and was unequivocally against the bailout, for which he blamed Congress and the cultural lack of personal responsibility.[39] His narrative shifted the blame from banks and predatory lending to irresponsible borrowers, progressive Big Government interference in the free market, and welfare, community development loans, and ACORN.[40] This kind of revisionism has become commonplace among conservative right-wing media pundits and propagandists. They deny that government can create jobs, claiming that is the task of the market, yet they blame the government when the market fails and unemployment rises. They criticize the government for not doing enough to avert the crisis, and then criticize the government for whatever it does to try to avert the crisis. The same "trickle-down" economics theory that underscored the call for deregulation—citing the invisible hand of the free market as the self-correcting mechanism of unrestrained capitalism—has been used by media pundits and propagandists, as well as politicians, for the rationale behind the bailouts. Here we see how ideology has created a culture of denial. They have simply denied that the deregulation of banking, credit, and other financial services had anything to do with the economic crisis. It was argued that bankers and speculators are the creators of wealth, and that regulation harms business, when the case for deregulation was being made, yet when deregulation led to an economic crisis, the argument for the bailouts was that these banks were "too big to fail" and would recreate the wealth to get out of the crisis.

Critics of capitalism "prefer increased state control" rather than take personal responsibility, asserts Beck, because "having a cap on success is an appropriate price to pay for also having a cap on failure."[41] This is a perverse reversal of the fact that the capitalists being criticized did not actually succeed, but failed—and then took government bailouts, to be paid for by future generations of Americans who had no say whatsoever as to whether the bailouts should have been paid or not. It seems to me to be quite reasonable to say that if private corporations are going to be given taxpayers' money *for failing*, while their top executives take huge bonuses, then the government should regulate the capitalists who cannot be trusted to act responsibly in an unregulated system.

My own view is that all the banks and businesses that failed should either have been left to fail in accordance with market discipline or nationalized. When the government is in effect handing out welfare to corporations, at taxpayers' expense, the public has a right to demand some level of democratic oversight, as well as a higher level of taxation on these companies to recoup the bailout money. But following Beck's "logic," the failed capitalists are "a success" and working Americans should stop being so resentful, tighten their belts, and make sacrifices for the good of the country—even though he denounces all calls for "the greater good" to be against individual freedom if it would benefit the public. By demanding that failed banks be regulated and that some level of public health care is provided from taxpayers' money, American citizens are, according to Beck, "socialists" and "sheep willing to be shorn and molded by their master," on the slippery slope toward "the regimes of Hitler, Mussolini, Stalin, Lenin, Castro, Chavez, or Kim Jong-Il."[42] It seems that Beck thinks that bankers are acting freely in accordance with the Constitution when they take public funds, putting their country in crippling debt, but ordinary Americans are ignorant slaves if they want subsidized prescription drugs. Furthermore, despite the fact that the government runs the National Aeronautics and Space Administration (NASA) and Advanced Research Projects Agency (ARPA), which invented the Internet, we are supposed to believe that it is impossible for a government agency to lead innovation or even be able to run the U.S. Post Office or Amtrak.[43] We are supposed to believe, without question, that the government can run the U.S. Armed Forces, the CIA, and Homeland Security, but it is too inherently incompetent and corrupt to run a heath care Public Option, Social Security, and the Department of Education.

As I have argued in this chapter, the use of the myth of the free market has been central to the rhetoric calling for further deregulation. Citing government inefficiency, market competition, and anti-union rhetoric, organizations like the Heritage Foundation have been promoting pervasive deregulation, ignoring the history of why industries were regulated in the first place.[44] Post-deregulation has not only seen waves of mergers, loss of competition, increased prices, reductions in customer services, and a reduction in wages and workers' rights, but also resulted in monopolies and price manipulation, as well as disruptions to supplies that were essential for the economy and society in general. For example, after the 1992 Energy Policy Act, the deregulation of utilities resulted in the deliberate withholding of electricity supply to create shortages and drive up prices and profits, while it disincentivized maintaining and upgrading equipment and the network infrastructure. Since 1992, customers throughout America have experienced massive price increases for electricity and a loss of any accountability for the stable supply of electricity, vital for the economy and communities. The blackouts in California in 2000 and in the Northeast in 2003 should provide cautionary tales about the flawed policy of deregulating utilities.

Despite all the past failures of deregulation, including the crisis of 2008, the advocates of corporate ideology continue to promote their propaganda for further deregulation, rolling back antitrust laws, and total privatization of all public services. Yet all this is based on nothing more than an abstract idea of the free market that does not exist in the real world. It is the product of the imagination of laissez-faire economists that has been used by propagandists to justify or conceal the corporate power grab over the world's economies and the corporate takeover of political institutions.

Rather than advocating centralized government control, the progressive argument is that decentralized smaller business, utilities, and industries bring great benefits to customers and local economies, by increasing both market competition and discipline, while keeping wealth in local communities. This would result in a higher level of customer service, better quality products, and stable prices and supply. It also would lead to greater local accountability and input into economic development, as well as better working conditions, higher wages, and a greater level of investment in local infrastructure. In the case of utilities, this would provide opportunities to develop local sustainable electricity generation technologies, owned by local people through cooperatives, and also provide greater national security (with a decentralized network, it is harder to cause widespread disruptions to the power grid). Municipalities that own their own utilities or are supplied by an energy cooperative have lower prices, better service, a more stable supply, and greater investment in infrastructure.[45]

Opposed to progressivism and blinded by the ideological myth of the free market, conservative right-wing media pundits and propagandists assert that America should be based on unrestrained corporate capitalism, protected by a fiercely militaristic and nationalistic government, which equates the interests of the ruling corporations with the national interest and is unrestrained by any due process if national interests are threatened. According to the corporate ideology, people are entirely subject to corporate interests, without any legal protections that override private contracts. Health and safety at work protections, or environmental protections, are considered to be illegitimate governmental violations of unrestrained corporate power. Compliant governments not only provide corporations with a "friendly" regulatory environment but also, at taxpayers' expense, put police and military forces at their disposal to protect corporate interests.

Within this vision of America, only the rights of the economic elite and their trusted servants would be protected by the law; politicians would only serve the interests of their corporate paymasters. Ordinary Americans would have no rights, and unions would be outlawed. Any "enemy of the state" or "suspected terrorist"—as determined in secret by the government—would be subject to warrantless surveillance and searches, open to arrest, indefinite detainment, torture, trial by secret military courts, and execution, whenever the government deemed it expedient to do so. Hence, corporate ideology tends toward fascism. With the federal and state governments acting as the handmaiden for unrestrained corporate power, with the Supreme Court waiting in the wings to strike down any democratic initiative, the corporate takeover of America is almost complete. The final stage is the complete control over the media. That is the subject of the next chapter.

12

WE, THE PEOPLE

Mainstream corporate media do not present a wide spectrum of political views. Instead, they present a spectrum of centrist to right-wing positions. The accusation of liberal bias in the media—"the liberal media"—was a worn-out cliché by the end of the 1970s. Today, it is laughable. Cable TV has blurred the distinction between news, entertainment, and propaganda in favor of a pro-corporate agenda. On talk radio the situation is even more extreme, with some hosts calling for armed rebellion against Washington, D.C., or the reformation of the Confederacy, their narratives rife with anti-government, anti-liberal, and anti-immigrant rhetoric. The level of hate speech that now dominates political discourse in talk radio reflects the growing polarization of American politics and the erosion of public debate. While appealing to only a small minority, extreme right-wing discourse has a profound effect on how public debate is represented in the media; it moves the "mainstream" view further to the right, presenting a center-right position as being the moderate position and the view of the "average American."

Cable news networks, such as Fox News, present themselves as the voice of mainstream America, even though their audience demographic represents only a very small percentage of the American population. Critics have given example after example of how Fox News, while promoting itself with the slogan "Fair and Balanced," selects topics that favor the conservative right agenda, distorts facts to fit the message of the day, blurs the distinction between reporting and commentating, discredits and smears the political opposition to the Republican Party, and suppresses any information that can problematize or contradict its reporting.[1] Of course, it is reasonable to surmise that, while there are a fraction of Fox News viewers who are sufficiently ill informed to believe that Fox News is, as it touts, "Fair and Balanced," most viewers know that Fox News' reporting is biased. All news reporting is biased. However, when viewers share this bias, they find slogans such as "Fair and Balanced" to be comforting, and they watch Fox News because it reinforces their own prejudices and opinions. This slogan is shared code for "we are right, everyone else is wrong." Critical or opposing viewpoints, or even troublesome facts, are rejected because they make the viewer feel uncomfortable and threatened. It is this factionalization of media into self-reinforcing and isolated camps of ideological viewpoints—fed to viewers as gratefully received propaganda—that is perhaps the most pernicious influence of cable TV news on public debate in America. As Jeff Cohen, founder of Fairness and Accuracy in Reporting (FAIR), put it, "It is not easy to come up with a slogan more insincere than 'fair and balanced.' Fox News accomplished this with 'We Report. You Decide.'— Which insinuates: *While our competitors lay their ideology on you, we give you the facts, ma'am.* This one is absurd because no TV news operation offers more punditry and less reporting than Fox. . . . A more accurate slogan would be 'We Opine. You Recline.'"[2]

Ten corporations dominate mass media: Disney (ABC), AOL–Time Warner (CNN), News Corporation (FOX), Viacom (CBS), Vivendi Universal, Sony, Liberty, Bertelsmann, AT&T-Comcast, and General Electric (NBC). These corporations own all the commercial television networks, all the major Hollywood studios, and most of the cable TV systems and channels. Both free speech and investigative journalism have suffered as a result—as well as local news and public debate, especially during elections. The marketplace of ideas has become a market, full stop. Sound bites and propaganda have become the norm—interspersed between entertainment and commercial advertising. Ratings dominate. Since the Federal Communications Commission relaxed the rules on media consolidation in 2003 to allow the same company to own both broadcast and print media in the same niche, allowing one company to own radio stations capable of reaching up to 45 percent of the national audience— despite massive public opposition and even the Supreme Court declaring it against the public interest—news has become a product. Dominated by the pursuit of ratings (the means to sell advertisement space and gain commercial sponsorship), the tendency is toward sensationalism rather than factuality. Jeff Cohen sums this situation up nicely: "Generating heat is far more important than shedding light."[3] This has a profound effect on the political process.

Media corporations have a troubling level of influence over political campaigns, given that they have the power to silence a candidate, or to select what to cover and when to cover it, or to editorialize for or against candidates. Corporations have become the gatekeepers for the selection of candidates to the extent that the electorate only gets to choose between pro-corporate candidates. It does not end there. Lobbyists use their clients' money to buy access to congressmen, who are also funded by corporations to attend "fact-finding"

weekends or conferences. Corporations also hire the services of public relations firms, opinion pollsters, trade associations, think tanks, policy centers,
and campaigners to bombard politicians with pro-corporate opinions, spin,
and perspectives, often backed up only by poor or selective research. These
kinds of activities do not have to be reported in accordance with the 1995 Lobbying Disclosure Act. With their combined unlimited campaign and lobbying
expenditure, is it surprising that corporations have come to dominate politics
at every level? Furthermore, lobbyists work ceaselessly to influence regulatory
agencies to interpret and apply legislation in a way that benefits their clients.
Sometimes lobbyists are able to persuade regulatory agencies to postpone the
application and enforcement of legislation or regulations. Even when hard-
fought citizens' campaigns for public protections and oversight have been
won, laws are often subverted, diluted, stalled, or simply not enforced. Hired
"experts" often dominate public hearings, either using blatantly manufactured
facts or statistics, or using marginal findings, in attempts to discredit areas of
massive scientific consensus.

No better example of this can be found in the seemingly tireless attempts
to construct "scientific controversy" in the case of global warming caused by
industrial pollution. Glenn Beck used this tactic in his *An Inconvenient Book*,
presumably taking advantage of the possibility that the majority of his readers
know even less about the science involved than he does, to convince his readers
that there is a massive international scientific conspiracy to defraud the public
about global warming. This is further compounded by the fact that the media
no longer investigate or even fact check the statements made in these kinds of
public hearings. Moreover, there is an absence of media follow-ups or correc-
tions when news stories are shown to be either false or misleading. Instead, such
stories are simply dropped. If the task of media is to act as a watchdog on
governmental policies and the activities of the wealthy and powerful, then the
mainstream media have failed.

The Center for Responsive Politics reported that business interests contrib-
uted more than $1.23 billion in the 2000 elections, and $1.03 billion in the
2002 midterm elections.[4] The candidate who raised the most money won 94
percent of all elections. Business accounts for 73.3 percent of all spending. In
contrast, organized labor unions only account for 7 percent of all spending.

The 1907 Trillman Act banned direct corporate contributions to campaigns in federal elections, but there are so many loopholes in this law that it
simply has not been enforced, and corporations have been able to go around
it by using soft-money contributions, organizing Political Action Committees (PACs), and bundling contributions from individual employees. State
legislators have been known to sit on committees regulating their own
business interests and many have financial ties to the businesses lobbying
state legislators.[5] This forms something of a vicious circle of conflicts of interest that has resulted in rolling back environmental and consumer protections,
the privatization of schools and prisons, increased corporate spending on

campaigns for state judicial elections of judges and attorneys general, and abusing eminent domain to force citizens to sell their private property to corporate developers. The basic problem is straightforward: As long as politicians need huge sums of money to get elected and reelected, then they will inevitably pander to whoever foots the bill. Citizens' campaigns for changes in laws and regulations are often frustrated by the fact that all three branches of government and the mainstream media are already dominated by corporations. With increased media consolidation, a great deal of local, state, and federal governmental processes, such as the work of regulatory agencies and legislatures, are simply ignored. This leaves crucial operations of government uncovered. This completely erodes the possibility of public oversight and political accountability. Of course, this state of affairs benefits the corporations that have hijacked the political process in order to gain a favorable regulatory environment. It is for this reason that the citizens' campaigns cannot rely on internal congressional reform.

After the 1972 Federal Election Campaign Act (which compelled disclosures of campaign contributions) and the forming of the Federal Election Commission to enforce this law, it was effectively subverted in 1975, when the FEC ruled that corporations were allowed to organize PACs to collect and bundle employee campaign contributions as well as use corporate funds for campaign advertising in favor of a particular candidate or against their opposition—without requiring shareholder approval. Combined with the 1976 Supreme Court ruling that any limits on campaign expenditures are unconstitutional, this FEC ruling opened the door to the corporate domination of election campaigns.[6] This door was wedged open by the Supreme Court in 2010 when it ruled that unlimited campaign expenditure should be allowed on the grounds of the First Amendment, and that the prohibition of corporate-funded political broadcasts within sixty days of a federal election or thirty days of a primary election was unconstitutional.[7] This weakened the 2002 Bipartisan Campaign Reform Act (BCRA), which banned soft-money donations for "party building" and imposed restrictions on election broadcast ads on the run up to elections and primaries. These restrictions were upheld by the Supreme Court in 2003.[8] However, apart from the restrictions of soft-money donations, this bill was largely thrown out by the Supreme Court ruling in 2010.

Through the use of PACs, corporations are increasingly dominating the funding of the campaigns to elect judges (thirty-eight states have judicial elections) and influence the nomination and appointment of federal judges. Organizations such as the U.S. Chamber of Commerce, the National Chamber Litigation Center, the Washington Legal Foundation, and the Federalist Society have actively funded, promoted, and advanced a pro-corporate agenda within the courts and legal system. This involves not only advocating or opposing new regulations and legislation but also rolling back long-established laws and regulations for which there is widespread consensus, such as health and safety at work laws or anti-discrimination laws. This often involves distorting the Constitution to reinterpret it in accordance with a conservative right agenda. Take, for example, Justice Scalia's recent remarks that the equal protection under the law for all citizens clause in the Fourteenth Amendment does not prohibit sexual discrimination.[9] Scalia claims that preventing sexual discrimination was not part of the intent behind this amendment in 1868, and he considers it wrong to apply the Fourteenth Amendment to strike down sexually discriminatory state and federal laws.

Indeed, Scalia is probably right in saying that the Fourteenth Amendment was not written to prevent sexual discrimination, but so what? Since 1920, when the Nineteenth Amendment was ratified, women have been granted the right to vote. The clear intention of this amendment was to afford women the full rights of citizenship. If the intentions behind the words of the Constitution have any meaning at all, it would be hard to deny that the Nineteenth Amendment corrects and clarifies the Fourteenth Amendment. While the Constitution does not prohibit sexual discrimination between private citizens, since 1920 it has evidently been the case that the Fourteenth Amendment can be used to strike down discriminatory state and federal laws against women. Despite any pretensions to hold to an "originalist" perspective, it is clear that Scalia is selective about how he reads and interprets the Constitution in accordance with his own conservative right ideology and agenda. This is judicial activism and is part of the current attempt at rolling back over ninety years of progressive legislation and reform to promote and protect women's rights.

While in my view it is obvious that the 2010 Supreme Court decision was pro-corporate judicial activism against BCRA, it did raise a very important question: Is it reasonable to allow media corporations to comment on an election campaign and candidates without restriction while at the same time prevent other kinds of corporations from enjoying this right? If media corporations are just another corporation—news is a product, same as soup or hats—then they should be treated the same as any other corporation. However, the court did not think through its own ruling. One of the problems with corporate media is that it is a business, pure and simple. Sometimes being a good business and being a free press are incompatible. In many respects, we cannot blame media corporations for this state of affairs. Their responsibility is to their shareholders, not the public. News and editorials need to be mainstream and as uncontroversial as possible to avoid offending sponsors and advertisers. Investigative journalism is expensive. Local news is expensive. By blurring the line between news and entertainment, ratings go up.

Media corporations are reactionary. In a real sense, the public gets what they want. If there is anyone to blame here, both the citizenry and the government are at fault. It is the responsibility of the people and their representatives to make sure that the publicly owned airwaves are used in the public interest and for the public good, whatever we deem that to be. Why don't the public *demand* factual and investigative journalism, rather than celebrity-centric gossip and crime story sensationalism? In part, the public enjoy gossip and sensationalism. However, in good measure the public also want real news. People are demanding better media. There is a growing shift toward alternative Internet-based media and a growing public awareness that mainstream media disseminates propaganda and misinformation.

It is quite absurd to treat corporate media conglomerates as if there is no difference between them and "the free press" of the eighteenth century to which the First Amendment refers. Putting the word "news" in the name of a company does not qualify it as a "free press." The 2010 Supreme Court ruling neglects to attend to this crucial point: No amount of campaign reform will make any significant progress toward free and fair elections without a free press, and there cannot be a free press while media are controlled by only a few people with clear commercial interests at stake. Allowing corporations to dominate media stifles free speech. What is needed is widespread media antitrust legislation to break up media conglomerates, to reintroduce media competition and diversity, and to afford the public greater access and control over media. This is not the same as government control. It is a matter of increasing the diversity of views and the number of people to whom media gives a voice to say whatever they want to say. That is free speech and a free press. This is essential for the possibility of engaged and critical public debate. American progressives need to campaign for media antitrust legislation. However, given the Internet is largely the last remaining bastion of the free press and public access media, it is essential that Net Neutrality is protected.

The Internet is the next frontier in the struggle between democratic and corporate America. Net Neutrality is not government control over the Internet or a Marxist plot to overthrow the capitalist system, as Beck would have us believe, but it is the means by which no one can control the Internet and its content.[10] Beck has either misunderstood or misrepresented what Net Neutrality is. What is Net Neutrality? It is the principle that states that there should not be any restrictions imposed by Internet service providers and governments regarding transmission speed and the content of data. It is the foundational principle of the Internet. The efforts to protect it are in opposition to corporate attempts to own the Internet, to charge variable rates for different data transmission speeds, and to control content, possibly blocking access to competitors, and charging whatever they wish to access the Internet. Net Neutrality allows everyone to have the same access to the Internet and to communicate at the same speed. Beck twists the meaning of Net Neutrality to mean that the government intervenes and regulates Internet traffic by imposing the "Fairness Doctrine" in order to silence critics of the government. He attacks a nonprofit organization called Free Press for being behind a Marxist plot to take over the Internet by promoting Net Neutrality.[11] This is false. Contrary to Beck's assertions, what Net Neutrality requires is that the Internet remains decentralized and uncontrolled.

In a democracy, media competition and diversity are *essential*. Media conglomerates stand in opposition to the freedom of the press and diverse public debate. With Net Neutrality, it would be impossible for anyone to take over the Internet. Net Neutrality advocates claim that government should only play a regulatory role, by enforcing antitrust legislation to prevent a few major corporations from owning the Internet and controlling both its rate of data transmission and content.[12] If a few corporations control both the pipeline and the data that passes through it, then a loss in market competition and abuses of power are inevitable results. Antitrust legislation and enforcement are necessary to break up these mass media giants and prevent media corporations from being owned by other corporations. This is necessary for media diversity and competition upon which the market of ideas and public debate depend. In many respects, America has turned full circle back to the early-twentieth-century progressive call for trust busting! This is why the FCC ruling (January 2011) to allow the merger between Comcast and Universal is disastrous for the possibility of preserving Net Neutrality.[13] It is yet another example of how the government serves corporate interests, rather than those of the people. It has effectively turned the Internet over to predatory capitalism.

One of the often missed implications of the First Amendment is that, as well as founding the separation of Church and State, it also founds a separation of Press and State as being necessary for free and diverse public debate and critical discourse. What develops from the accelerating vicious circle of corporate ownership of media and domination of politics is an increased political indifference to the activities of "parent corporations"—turning a blind eye—which has resulted in the largest corporations being above the law. This undermines the Republic and transforms it into a corporate state. The reporting of public hearings and regulatory agencies are now largely left to citizens' groups, marginalized media watchdogs, and political campaign reform networks. Here the Internet and Net Neutrality are essential media for public information, communication, and grass-roots campaign organization. Net Neutrality is vital for the public to resist the domination of mass media by media corporations and their owners. Independent media are necessary for the public to oversee the activities of government agencies and effectively petition government. It is for this reason that both Net Neutrality and media reform are necessary for the future of democracy. Any successful campaign against corporate control over the media must have its own alternative media to disseminate information and coordinate activities.

The public still "owns" the airwaves, which are leased to corporations, and the public can remind corporate media that it has a legal obligation to serve "the public interest, convenience, and necessity." More should be done to pressure politicians to make corporations respect this obligation (i.e., compel better coverage of local news and issues). It is also the case that Public Broadcasting Service and National Public Radio need greater public funding (so as to avoid the need for donation drives) in order to provide successful publicly owned channels for twenty-four-hour news media and public debate. This greater funding—along with publicly funded low cost and high speed Internet access—can be raised by charging media corporations much higher fees to use the public airwaves. The problem facing America is one of a struggle for political accountability—how to make the so-called representatives of the people accountable to the people rather than to powerful corporations and the economic elite. The ownership of media is central to this struggle, and its outcome will define the future of America.

The situation is stark, but far from hopeless. In many respects, we are witnessing a repeat of the 1870s, when the wealthy elite rode roughshod over the political institutions of that time and used them to further their own ends. Grassroots movements of farmers, workers, and reformers rose up and heralded what became known as the Progressive Era. This movement was either ignored or vilified by the press of their day. Campaigners had to create their own newspapers (what became the Reform Press Association) and set up a network of thousands of public speakers who traveled across America, spreading ideas and bringing news and expanding their movement and networks. While nonprofit media outlets such as the Pacifica Radio network, the host of *Democracy Now!*,[14] are important for providing information and critical commentary, the Internet provides the possibility of grassroots political campaigns being organized by any group of citizens with access to computers and a server. Today, through the Internet, we are almost seeing history repeat itself, except on a much larger scale. People across America and throughout the world are creating alternative media comprised of websites, newsletters, blogs, petitions, newspapers, video blogs, social network sites, online self-publication, and online TV and radio. These online activities are combined with protests, petitions, cooperatives, meetings, movies, books, art, music, and theater to create powerful alternative media. These alternative media reach, inspire, and *enroll* millions of people. The virtue of the Internet is that it is participatory to the extent that anyone with a computer and a connection can join in.

Arguably, what we are witnessing is the growth of a powerful, progressive, and critical alternative media of the kind that the Framers had in mind when they considered the First Amendment and the free press. Once again, we can see how the progressive movement is realizing and continuing the American Revolution. Public participation in mass media requires Net Neutrality and affordable access to the Internet. Just as the fullest understanding of the Second Amendment holds that it is the citizenry acting as the militia, collectively defending themselves as a free people, that is the condition for a free state, the fullest understanding of the First Amendment holds that the citizenry needs to become the free press and actively participate in public debate and the dissemination of knowledge, ideas, skills, and inspiration, as well as criticism of abuses of governmental and corporate power. The citizenry can *democratize the media by becoming the media.* How can "We, the People" save America from media pundits and propagandists? Vigilant, critical, passionate, and democratic participation by citizens in the institutions of government, in media, and in civic society is the way that the American people can save America by themselves, of themselves, and for themselves.

What can Americans do about the corporate takeover of America? Public campaigns to crack down on corporate crime and corruption should continue and be intensified. However, in a political culture dominated by corporations, including all three branches of government and the media, this kind of political campaigning will more often than not amount to little more than isolated prosecutions and punishments for a few of the worst offenders who get caught. It will only result in the prosecution of a handful of individuals without achieving the required structural changes to the way that government lets corporations do business and put their own interests above the public (including their customers and workers). What is needed is a much deeper reform of the whole political system to prevent corporations from dominating the political institutions of government.

In my view, the use of PAC money and corporate funds on "independent political broadcasts," without obtaining shareholder approval, to either support or oppose a candidate does not qualify as free speech for two reasons: (1) corporations are not persons and cannot speak, and (2) other people's money is being used without their consent or even knowledge to promote candidates favored by directors or managers rather than by the shareholders. However, to date, the Supreme Court stands as an obstacle to any hopes to constrain corporate influence over the democratic process. This is why it is essential to amend the Constitution to clarify that only persons, and not corporations, have rights. If employees or shareholders want to donate their own money to campaigns, that should be their right as individuals, but it should be illegal for corporations to form PACs to solicit money from employees and also to spend any money on political campaigns without the consent of shareholders.

Amending the Constitution to clarify that the enumerated rights only apply to persons, not corporations (which are artificial creations of state law), can form the basis of a much broader and far-reaching public campaign to liberate political institutions and politics in general from corporate interference and control.[15] This is a necessary step to achieve the kind of political oversight and transparency required to keep corporations out of politics and under the rule of law. Without this constitutional amendment, time and time again, the Supreme Court and its pro-corporate judges will be able to allow the Constitution to be used as a tool to strike down laws and regulations passed by the representatives of the people, as well as override voter initiatives directly passed by the people, and place corporate "rights" over and above those of the people. Only once the Constitution has been amended, will it be possible to address adequately the scope and depth of corporate crime and corruption, to have diligent enforcement of the law, and impose appropriately severe punishments (fines, revocation of charters, nullification of share value, and seizure of property) for corporate infringements of the law. The aim is not to interfere with private business. The aim is to stop private business from interfering with public politics. This requires nothing more or less than placing corporations under the rule of law.

It is not easy to amend the Constitution. However, as its twenty-seven amendments prove, neither is it impossible. Article V of the Constitution provides four different procedures to amend the Constitution:

1. A two-thirds majority in both Houses of Congress propose an amendment to be ratified by three-quarters of the states' legislatures. This procedure has been used for twenty-six of the twenty-seven amendments.
2. A two-thirds majority of both houses of Congress propose an amendment to be ratified by state conventions in three-quarters of the states. This procedure was used to ratify the Twenty-first Amendment to repeal Prohibition.
3. Two-thirds of the state legislatures can ask Congress to call a national convention to debate and propose an amendment to be ratified by three-quarters of state legislatures.
4. Two-thirds of the state legislatures can ask Congress to call a national convention to debate and propose an amendment to be ratified by state conventions for three-quarters of the states.

There has not been a national convention since the Philadelphia Convention drafted the Constitution in 1787. It is time that a national convention is convened to propose an amendment to clarify that the enumerated rights belong to persons, not corporations. People of all political persuasions should unite to pressure their state legislatures to call upon Congress to form a national convention wherein each state sends its own delegates, chosen by methods decided by each state, to debate in public and propose this amendment to the states for ratification. While ratification could be left to the states' legislatures, it seems more appropriate for it to be left to state conventions (i.e., referenda). The national convention formed and ratified in this manner would be an expression of the renewal of the democratic power of the citizenry. It would be a response to the Jeffersonian call for each generation to rewrite the Constitution. It would be a renewal of the Constitution itself as a living expression of the ideals of "We, the People."

Once the Constitution has been amended, real political campaign finance reform becomes possible at every level of government. It will become possible to deny corporations unlimited spending power and the right to form PACs. It is one thing for investors or employees to donate to political campaigns, but it is quite another for managers to be able to bundle these donations and use massive corporate funds to dominate media with advertisements that favor one candidate and discredit others. The current system effectively allows corporations to select candidates and manipulate elections in exchange for future favors returned. This is effectively a form of legalized corruption. It has to stop. It is also essential that lobbying is further restricted so that corporations do not have an inordinate level of access and that other constituents are able to see their representative or senator. It is essential that detailed records of the activities of lobbyists are available as a matter of public record. Without this kind of campaign reform and oversight over lobbyists, citizens' voices are drowned out or simply ignored during elections and any attempt by the legislature to regulate or investigate corporate activities will meet internal conflicts of interest from politicians who depend on corporations for reelection. Corporations can also deduct their lobbying expenses from their taxes. This loophole creates a huge imbalance between corporations and citizens, who cannot deduct their expenses from their taxes when traveling to see their congressman. This loophole needs to be closed.

Arguably, free air time for candidates, spending limits, and/or public funding for election campaigns would reduce candidates' need for corporate financial aid, but in my view, what is really needed is a shift from dependency on corporate media and expensive, polished media campaigns toward grassroots activism, alternative Internet-based media campaigns, and greater participation by the citizenry in election campaigning. People need to stop trusting the images, spin, and sound bites fed to them by mainstream corporate media. They need to switch off the media pundits and propagandists. As customers, as consumers, people retain a great deal of power in the marketplace if they organize to shape corporate policy through consumer boycotts or changing our patterns of consumption. But this kind of activity can only be effective as part of a larger citizens' mass movement to democratize America through grassroots organization. This is only possible if "We, the People" stand up and assert the right to self-governance through democratic political institutions and to participate in how those institutions are developed. Democracy is at stake. The people need to step up and become a democracy, by the people, from the people, and for the people. Only the people can do this. A democracy is never given to the people as a coming-of-age present. A democracy is won or lost.

Bringing together a national network of local activists and politicians to learn from each others' experiences and ideas, and to cooperate and strengthen community struggles by sharing knowledge, skills, and resources, can form the basis for a successful grassroots political campaign. Also, although union membership has been steadily decreasing, over sixteen million Americans still belong to an organized labor union, and this affords an opportunity to involve working men and women in public debate and democratic participation in grassroots campaigns. Coalitions and alliances among activists, unions, community-based organizations, policy centers, churches, and specific issue campaigns can lead to highly organized grassroots movements that can change legislation through effective political struggle and citizens' participation at all levels. Through citizens' participation "We, the People" can rebuild the public sphere, reclaim political institutions, and elect their real representatives to public office. Through local grass-roots campaigns, citizens can

- support and strengthen local businesses and farmers' markets;
- organize consumer boycotts, fair trade, and cooperatives;
- resist corporate takeover of local economies and communities;
- elect candidates to school boards;
- protest nuclear power plants, GMO foods, factory farms, private prisons, and so on;
- support political campaigns at all levels—participatory democracy in action;
- support independent candidates running against party incumbents;
- support third party candidates;
- organize local associations and charities to improve communities;
- network and connect with other grass-roots movements with overlapping concerns and interests;
- organize literacy drives and support public libraries;
- change patterns of consumption;
- liaise and cooperate with unions and citizen advocacy groups;
- support nonprofit alternative media; and
- improve civic society and the quality of local community life.

America stands at a crossroads between becoming a democracy or a corporate state. Before Americans can hope to live in a democracy, citizens must challenge the dominant corporate ideology and predatory capitalism, which are only concerned with the next quarterly profits report. We need to *overcome the tyranny of the bottom line.*[16] Business needs to be put in its place, as serving people, not the other way around. "We, the People" need to reclaim the legal control over corporations—as creatures of state law—and remind them that they are chartered only on the premise that they serve the public good. Corporations are only granted the rights and privileges that the people and their representatives grant them, and corporations need to be reminded that their charters can be revoked by the citizenry through the state legislatures. The struggle facing "We, the People" is that of winning back the right to self-governance. This is not just a problem facing Americans, it is a global problem. "We, the People" need to take back sovereign power over the state and government.

Progressivism is not the cancer destroying America. Corporatism is the cancer destroying American. The American people need a progressive message calling for "We, the People" to claim their government and their country through grass-roots movements, community organization, democratic mass participation at all levels, and by fostering civic virtue, critical political discourse, and public engagement in civic society. Indeed, as Beck says, "Both the media and the people have failed the Republic."[17] Unfortunately, he only considers this as far as it relates to taxation and public spending. He also ignores how his own media punditry is part of the problem in the way that, frequently, he has used frightening rhetoric, outlandish claims, and images of martial law, the collapse of America, and even the end of the world, to convey the idea that democracy is "mob rule" and government is an entirely *negative* force that is attempting to control all aspects of American life. His rhetoric aims at discrediting democracy by connecting it with images of violence, anarchy, and shadowy conspiracies. His whole approach to public participation is *negative*—no taxes, no regulation, no greater good—and thus appeals to the rhetoric of the Tea Party. But, given that his *positive* discussion of civic virtue remains entirely religious and individualistic, it is relegated to the private realm of family and church. Hence, while appealing to the fiscally and socially conservative Christian right, in terms that support his corporate ideology, Beck's "conservative libertarianism" actually implies the self-destruction of the public realm—the destruction of the possibility of democracy—via the total privatization of civic life and the corporate domination of America.

Nowhere are Beck's double standards, hysteria, and disdain more evident than when he is discussing democracy. When the members of the Tea Party invoke their First Amendment right to peaceful assembly and to petition their government, Beck calls them patriots, but when public workers in Wisconsin invoke the same right to petition their state government—to protest against laws eroding their pensions and removing their right to collectively bargain—he calls them "dope smoking hippies," communists, anarchists, and "the enemy within."[18] Beck connects the public sector workers' protests in Wisconsin to the protests in Cairo (calling for the resignation of Hosni Mubarak and for national elections) as being part of a global conspiracy to use insurrection, violence, and chaos as the pretext to impose the New World Order under one world government.[19]

He warns his viewers to beware what is concealed behind "the Masks of Democracy" because the protests in Egypt—as well as others in the Middle East—are part of an "Islamic socialist" conspiracy between Marxists and Islamic fundamentalists to destroy capitalism and "the Western way of life."[20] Beck claims that teachers, firefighters, police, and other public workers of Wisconsin (and elsewhere) are being manipulated, as "shields" and "useful idiots," by unions that have been infiltrated by radical leftists, anarchists, and Islamic fundamentalists.[21] He tells us that American labor unions are aiding and abetting terrorists and the enemies of America, and that the protests of Wisconsin public sector workers are taking America down the path toward revolution, totalitarianism, and a reign of terror.[22] Unless Americans wake up and defend freedom—like Davy Crockett and the heroes of the Alamo—the fires burning across the Middle East will come to America and lead to global chaos and millions of deaths.[23]

Beck tells his viewers that the blueprint for these protests and their intended consequences can be found in an anarchist pamphlet called *The Coming*

Insurrection by The Invisible Committee.[24] He explains that the aim of this plot is to cause instability—leading to a global crisis—in order to create "the perfect storm," which will justify the imposition of the New World Order, with the evil, socialist puppet master George Soros (alias "Spooky Dude") pulling the strings. After all, every comic book plot needs an evil genius behind the scenes! Furthermore, in accordance with Beck's twistifications, democratic protests in the Middle East and Wisconsin alike—both being funded by George Soros—are part of a plot by Iran and the Muslim Brotherhood to encircle and destroy Israel, create a Islamic caliphate, and prepare for the prophesized End of Days, when the al-Mahdi or the Twelfth Imam, who Beck compares to the Anti-Christ in the Book of Revelation, will return.[25] He asserts that leftists and union leaders are mistaken to believe that "the enemy of my enemy is my friend" by considering Islamic fundamentalists to be useful allies in their plot to destroy Israel and America—the beacons of freedom—and impose socialism on the world. Hence the "economic terrorism" of strikes and protests, organized by American union leaders as part of a strategy of "redistribution of wealth," are not only aiding and abetting Islamic fundamentalists and terrorists but are also leading to a nuclear war between Iran and Israel and the end of the world. It is for this reason, he tells us, union leaders and all those who seek "redistribution of wealth" in America are on the side of evil and in league with "the father of lies," a.k.a. Lucifer.[26]

Of course, this is all nonsense, you might say, and I would agree with you. Beck is clearly playing on his audience's fears and prejudices with this far-fetched conspiracy theory, and no thinking person would take it seriously. However, what is revealing is how his narrative reveals a deep-seated anti-democratic rhetoric that needs to slander and vilify democracy. He tells us that democracy is opposed to "the Republic" and anti-American. Hence his arguments against progressivism are riddled with this kind of anti-democratic narrative, which attempts to superimpose democracy and anarchy and make them appear identical. The aim of this rhetoric is to "divide and conquer" the working and middle classes in order to pit workers in the private sector against unions and public workers. At the heart of the struggle between democracy and the corporate state is a struggle between two incompatible and competing conceptions of liberty. Beck's understanding of liberty illustrates this. If Americans choose to protect their environment, spend public funds on health care and education, and put the public good before corporate profits, then, according to Beck, they are acting slavishly against the founding principles of America. But if the American people passively stand by and watch America's wildernesses trashed and their government taken over by corporations, they are preserving liberty.[27] It seems that liberty means the blind pursuit of money and power, regardless of the consequences. Is that really what Jefferson had in mind when he wrote the Declaration of Independence?

Beck asserts that the current situation in America is "a fight of us versus them. 'Us' comprises those who believe in liberty, as described in the opening lines of the Declaration of Independence. 'Them' comprises those who believe that the definition of *liberty* must evolve with the time."[28] However, the opening lines of the Declaration of Independence do not describe liberty, apart from declaring it as an inalienable right of all men, endowed by their Creator, along with the right to life and the pursuit of happiness. It also declares all men to be created equal, yet Beck does not have any time for equality. In my view, Jefferson would have been appalled with the idea that his words should be taken as absolute and unquestionable doctrine that supported moneyed interests over the rights of the people. The American Revolution is an *experiment* in self-governance. Of course we need to have an evolving understanding of what liberty means—that is part of what it means to be free. We have to learn what equality, life, and the pursuit of happiness mean, as we go along—that is also what it means to be free.

It is because he promotes a message based on appeals to individualism, personal responsibility, and acceptance that Beck's message appeals to so many Americans. It sounds virtuous and honorable. However, combined with his fearmongering imagery and anti-democratic rhetoric, this message implies a retreat of the citizenry into private family life and out of the political realm (apart from supporting Tea Party candidates). Beck talks of faith, hope, and charity, but what he actually promotes are obedience and fatalism. This message discredits the people's right, through democratic mass participation, to resist the corporate takeover of America, to defend their rights, and to demand better government. My argument is that this message, by promoting a level of public apathy and cynicism that will erode the political institutions upon which the possibility of good government and democracy depend, erodes the belief in the possibility of good governance achieved through democratic participation. Anything that weakens the democratic aspirations of Americans also disables the main obstacle to unrestrained corporate power. It is for this reason that I have been debunking Glenn Beck rather than simply changing the channel or turning off the television set.

In June 2011, Fox News pulled the plug on the *Glenn Beck* TV show. Fox also announced that Beck will do some production work on special documentaries for Fox News. He also has claimed that he will be reaching out to a younger audience through his radio show, tours, books, and websites, and he has started his online subscription-based TV channel called GBTV. He is a businessman and enjoys the limelight. Who knows what he will do next? Beck says he hates politics, but I find it hard to believe that he will be content to work quietly behind the scenes during the run-up to the 2012 election. Perhaps he might even consider running on a Tea Party ticket for the presidency! Time will tell. But at the end of the day, Glenn Beck is not the cause of what has gone wrong with American media and public debate—he is a symptom, and soon will be replaced by a new media pundit and propagandist, selling whatever the new message his or her corporate paymaster wishes him or her to sell to the American people. That is, if the American people are willing to buy it.

In the spirit of fairness, I shall give Glenn Beck the last words: "It is not just the political class who has mastered the art of deception. There are other potentially deadly masters who will seek to exploit your frustration and sense of desperation. Many will warn you of government tyranny; they'll talk of secret societies, vast conspiracies, shadow governments, and the need for violent action. I urge you to stay away from these individuals and their ideas."[29] Wise words, indeed.

NOTES

Preface

1. Brian Stelter and Bill Carter, "Fox New's Mad, Apocalyptic, Tearful Rising Star," *The New York Times*, March 29, 2009, http://www.nytimes.com/2009/03/30/business/media/30beck.html?pagewanted=1/.
2. Glenn Beck, *Arguing with Idiots: How to Stop Small Minds and Big Government* (New York: Threshold Editions, 2009) (hereafter cited as *AWI*).
3. *Glenn Beck* (TV show), Fox News Channel, December 8, 2010; videos and transcripts of Glenn Beck's TV program can be found at the Fox News website, http://www.foxnews.com/on-air/glenn-beck/index.html/, and at Beck's own website, http://www.glennbeck.com/; see also *The Daily Beck*, http://www.watchglennbeck.com/.
4. *Glenn Beck* (TV show), December 9, 2010.
5. Ibid., February 20, 2009.
6. Bob Egelko and Henry K. Lee, "I-580 Shootout Suspect Mad at Left-wing Politics," *San Francisco Chronicle*, July 19, 2010; and "Highway Shooter Targeted Tides Foundation, ACLU," *Bay City News*, July 20, 2010; John Hamilton, "Jailhouse Confession: How the Right-Wing Media and Glenn Beck's Chalkboard Drove Byron Williams to Plot Assassination," *Media Matters for America*, October 8, 2010, http://mediamatters.org/research/201010110002/.
7. Brian Stelter, "Spotlight from Glenn Beck Brings a CUNY Professor Threats," *The New York Times*, January 21, 2011. For Glenn Beck's response and continued targeting of Frances Fox Piven, see the *Glenn Beck Program*, January 24, 2011, 4.56 p.m. EST; audio from Glenn Beck's radio show can be found at his website, http://www.glennbeck.com/.
8. Dana Milbank, *Tears of a Clown: Glenn Beck and the Teabagging of America* (Garden City, NJ: Doubleday, 2010); Alexander Zaitchik, *Common Nonsense: Glenn Beck and the Triumph of Ignorance* (New York: Wiley, 2010).

Chapter 1. Twistifications and the Constitution

1. *Marbury v. Madison*, 5 U.S. (1 Cranch) 137 (1803).
2. *AWI*, chap. 12.
3. *AWI*, 267. Beck uses the terms "Founding Fathers" (or "the Founders") and "the Framers" interchangeably. However, I shall be following historical convention and use the term "the Founders" to refer to those people who were influential and involved in the American Revolution and the founding of the United States of America as signatories of the Declaration of Independence and/or leaders in the War of Independence, and "the Framers" to refer to the delegates of the Philadelphia Convention in 1787. Hence Thomas Jefferson, who was absent from the Philadelphia Convention, and Thomas Paine are considered to be among the Founders but are not included among the Framers.
4. *AWI*, 268.
5. *The Constitution of the United States of America* (Bedford, MA: Applewood Books, n.d.).
6. An online copy of *Agrarian Justice* can be found at http://www.constitution.org /tp/agjustice.htm/.
7. Federalist Paper No. 41 and Federalist Paper No. 45, respectively; the Federalist Papers can be found online at http://www.foundingfathers.info/federalistpapers/.
8. Federalist Paper No. 46.
9. Federalist Paper No. 26 and Federalist Paper No. 22, respectively.
10. Federalist Paper No. 23 and Federalist Paper No. 33, respectively.
11. Federalist Paper No. 34.
12. Although the Supreme Court and Chief Justice Marshall ruled that the Maryland law imposing a tax on the Second Bank of the United States was unconstitutional (*McCulloch v. Maryland*, 17 U.S. 316, 1819). The Supreme Court ruled that the "necessary and proper" clause allowed Congress to pass laws concerning matters not specifically enumerated in the Constitution, providing that they were useful in aiding Congress in the furtherance of its constitutionally granted powers.
13. *United States v. Butler*, 297 U.S. 1 (1936).
14. *South Dakota v. Dole*, 483 U.S. 203 (1987). The Supreme Court did place limits on the federal government's power to impose conditions. Such conditions must be unambiguous, do not violate any constitutional limit, must relate to existing federal programs and projects, and must be in the general welfare.
15. *AWI*, 278.
16. In fact, the three-fifths ratio was first proposed in a 1783 amendment to the Articles of Confederation in order to shift the tax burden from each state from real estate to number of population. However, at that time, the delegates of southern states objected to that proposal. Cf. Hannis Taylor, *The Origin and Growth of the American Constitution* (1911; reprint, Ithaca, NY: Cornell University Library, 2009), 51.
17. Universal white male suffrage became the norm by 1840, during the presidency of Andrew Jackson. Prior to this date, some states had removed property restrictions for white males, and states that joined the union after 1790 dropped property restrictions on voting rights. However, up until 1850, several states replaced property restrictions with the requirement that only taxpayers could vote, and the poll tax was used in some states to disenfranchise poor African Americans from voting until 1964, when the Twenty-fourth Amendment was ratified and outlawed such practices.

18. *AWI*, 275. The term "bills of attainder" comes from old English law. They allowed the seizure of property as part of a punishment. They were used by the British Crown during the American Revolution to seize the property of the rebelling colonists. Article I, Section 9 of the Constitution prohibits bills of attainder. Beck considers HR 1575, the End Government Reimbursement of Excessive Executive Disbursements Act (or the End GREED Act) to be a "bill of attainder." However, this bill did not pass the House, so the question of its constitutionality is moot.

19. *AWI*, 278.

20. George Washington to Joseph Reed, 1775, in W. B. Allen, ed., *George Washington: A Collection* (Indianapolis: Liberty Fund, 1988), 20.

21. Fritz Hirschfeld, *George Washington and Slavery: A Documentary Portrayal* (Columbia: University of Missouri Press, 1997).

22. In his will, Washington decreed that his slaves be freed after his wife's death. His wife freed them, fearing that this condition might lead the slaves to kill her. Cf. John C. Fitzpatrick, ed., *The Last Will and Testament of George Washington and Schedule of his Property to Which Is Appended the Last Will and Testament of Martha Washington* (Washington, DC: Mount Vernon Ladies' Association of the Union, 1939), 2–4.

23. Peter S. Onuf, *Statehood and Union: A History of the Northwest Ordinance* (Bloomington: Indiana University Press, 1997).

24. Gary Nash and Graham Hodges, *Friends of Liberty: A Tale of Three Patriots, Two Revolutions, and the Betrayal that Divided a Nation: Thomas Jefferson, Thaddeus Kosciuszko, and Agrippa Hull* (New York: Basic Books, 2008), 248; Nash and Hodges argue that after Kosciuszko's death, Jefferson had a change of heart and did not wish to become embroiled in the contentious issue of abolition.

25. An online version can be found at the University of Virginia Library's electronic text database, http://etext.lib.virginia.edu/toc/modeng/public/JefVirg.html/.

26. Gordon Brown, *Toussaint's Clause: The Founding Fathers and the Haitian Revolution* (Jackson: University Press of Mississippi, 2005).

27. Henri Gregorie, *An Enquiry Concerning the Intellectual and Moral Faculties and Literature of Negroes* (Beloit, KS: McGrath, 1967).

28. Barbara Heath, *Hidden Lives: The Archaeology of Slave Life at Thomas Jefferson's Poplar Forest* (Charlottesville: University of Virginia Press, 1999).

29. Annette Gordon-Reed, *Thomas Jefferson and Sally Hemings: An American Controversy* (Charlottesville: University of Virginia Press, 1998); Eyler Robert Coates, *The Jefferson-Hemings Myth: An American Travesty* (Charlottesville, VA: Jefferson Editions, 2001).

30. An online copy of this letter can be found at Teaching American History, http://www.teachingamericanhistory.org/library/index.asp?document=459/.

31. An online copy of this letter can be found at From Revolution to Reconstruction, http://odur.let.rug.nl/~usa/P/tj3/writings/brf/jefl81.htm/.

32. Thomas Jefferson to John Cartwright, 1824, From Revolution to Reconstruction, http://odur.let.rug.nl/usa/P/tj3/writings/brf/jefl278.htm/.

33. *AWI*, 272.

34. Federalist Paper No. 10.

35. L. H. Butterfield, ed., *The Adams Papers: Diary and Autobiography of John Adams*, 4 vols. (New York: Atheneum, 1964), pt. 1, sheet 23; this can be found online at http://www.masshist.org/digitaladams/aea/cfm/doc.cfm?id=A1_23/.

36. *AWI*, 270.

37. *AWI*, 272–73.
38. *AWI*, 297.
39. *AWI*, 275.
40. *AWI*, 274.
41. *Ex parte Merryman*, 17 F. Cas. 144 (1861).
42. Thomas Jefferson to Abigail Adams, 1804; see Lester J. Cappon, ed., *The Adams-Jefferson Letters: The Complete Correspondence Between Thomas Jefferson and Abigail and John Adams* (Chapel Hill: University of North Carolina Press, 1988).
43. It is also the case that the Constitution does not state how many judges should sit on the Supreme Court. The fact that there are nine judges is not constitutionally obligatory. There could be more. They could even be selected from the whole population of citizens at random.
44. *AWI*, 248.
45. *Hamdi v. Rumsfeld*, 542 U.S. 507 (2004).
46. *Hamdi v. Rumsfeld*, 548 U.S. 557 (2006).
47. *Boumediene v. Bush*, 553 U.S. 723 (2008).
48. An online copy can be found at Library of Congress, http://www.loc.gov/loc/lcib/9806/danpre.html/.
49. *AWI*, 289.
50. *AWI*, 290.
51. *Kelo v. City of New London*, 545 U.S. 469 (2005).
52. Hugo Grotius, *On the Law of War and Peace* (Whitefish, MT: Kessinger, 2004).
53. *Citizens United v. Federal Election Commission*, 130 S.Ct. 876 (2010).
54. *AWI*, 292.
55. *AWI*, 293.
56. *Gonzales v. Raich* (previously *Ashcroft v. Raich*), 545 U.S. 1 (2005).
57. *Glenn Beck* (TV show), March 3, 2009.

Chapter 2. The Militia Clause

1. Speech before the Virginia ratification convention, June 14, 1788, http://conservativeminds.org/patrick-henry/patrick-henry-on-the-need-for-a-militia/.
2. Noah Webster, *An Examination into the Leading Principles of the Federal Constitution* (1787; reprint, Farmington Hills, MI: Gale ECCO, 2010).
3. *AWI*, chap. 2.
4. *AWI*, 35.
5. *District of Columbia v. Heller*, 554 U.S. 570 (2008).
6. *United States v. Miller*, 307 U.S. 174 (1939).
7. "Handgun Crime Up Despite Ban," BBC News, July 16, 2001.
8. Home Office, "Firearms Offences and Intimate Violence," 2005/2006, http://rds.homeoffice.gov.uk/rds/pdfs07/hosb0207.pdf/.
9. Linda L. Dahlberg, Robin M. Ikeda, and Marcie-jo Kresnow, "Guns in the Home and Risk of a Violent Death in the Home: Findings from a National Study," *American Journal of Epidemiology* 160 (10): 929–36, http://aje.oxfordjournals.org/content/160/10/929.full/.
10. For example, see the media watchdog Keep and Bear Arms, http://www.keepandbeararms.com/.
11. *AWI*, 39.

12. Julian Boyd, ed., *The Papers of Thomas Jefferson*, vol. 1, *1760–1776* (Princeton, NJ: Princeton University Press, 1950), 344.

13. "That the people have a Right to mass and to bear arms; that a well regulated militia composed of the Body of the people, trained to arms, is the proper natural and safe defense of a free state, that standing armies, in time of peace, are dangerous to liberty, and therefore ought to be avoided." Within Mason's declaration of "the essential and unalienable Rights of the People," drafted by Thomas Jefferson, George Mason, and others, and later adopted by the Virginia ratification convention, 1788.

14. *Arver v. United States*, 245 U.S. 366 (1918).

15. *The Declaration of Independence* (Bedford, MA: Applewood Books, n.d.).

16. For an online copy of this speech, go to Presidential Rhetoric, http://www .presidentialrhetoric.com/historicspeeches/jefferson/stateoftheunion.1808.html/.

17. Obviously, there are enormous problems with the questions of how to achieve and enforce such an international ban. The discussion of this topic is well beyond the scope of this book. However, perhaps a first step that the U.S. government could take would be to assert unilaterally the doctrine that the preemptive use of nuclear, biological, or chemical weapons would be illegal and a war crime, thus making it illegal for any military personnel to give or obey any order to participate in an attack using such weapons. Neither Congress nor the president could order the first use of such weapons, under any circumstances. This initiative would take the step of asserting that such weapons should be reserved for proportionate retaliation, until such time as an international ban and mechanisms for enforcement have been negotiated and agreed upon.

Chapter 3. Public Education

1. *AWI*, chap. 3; see also *Glenn Beck* (TV show), April 14, 2010.

2. *AWI*, 63.

3. *AWI*, 77.

4. *AWI*, 62–63.

5. The federal funding of education did not start in 1980. Under President Lyndon Johnson's Great Society reforms, the 1965 Elementary and Secondary Education Act provided federal funds for poor schools and initiated the Head Start Program. The 1965 Higher Education Act not only provided scholarships and low-interest loans for college students but also founded the Teacher Corps to provide teachers for the poorest schools. The 1968 Bilingual Education Act provided federal funds to teach English in schools.

6. *AWI*, 69.

7. Polly Curtis, "Children Being Failed by Progressive Teaching, Say Tories," *The Guardian*, May 9, 2008.

8. Naomi Aoki, "Harshness of Red Has Students Seeing Purple," *Boston Globe*, August 23, 2004.

9. National Center for Educational Statistics website, "The Nation's Report Card: Trends in Academic Progress in Reading and Mathematics 2008," http://nces .ed.gov/nationsreportcard/pubs/main2008/2009479.asp/.

10. Beck does not give any reference to these quotations; they are from the second article of Dewey's 1897 essay "My Pedagogic Creed."

11. *AWI*, 69.
12. *Fields v. Palmdale School District*, 2005.
13. *AWI*, 77.
14. *AWI*, 73.
15. *AWI*, 72–74.
16. *AWI*, 70–71.

Chapter 4. Beyond Petroleum

1. *AWI*, chap. 4.
2. *AWI*, 86.
3. *AWI*, 90.
4. *AWI*, 94.
5. *AWI*, 1.
6. *AWI*, 87.
7. For an interesting documentary on how oil and automobile companies bought up and suppressed the patents for deep-cycle fuel cells, and also influenced both state and federal government policies to prevent affordable and efficient electric cars becoming available on the market, see *Who Killed the Electric Car?* directed by Chris Paine. The official website for this documentary is http://www.whokilledtheelectriccar.com/.
8. For historical examples, see Aaron David Miller, *Saudi Arabian Oil and American Foreign Policy* (Chapel Hill: University of North Carolina Press, 1991); Multinational Oil Corporations and U.S. Foreign Policy CREPORT together with individual views, to the Committee on Foreign Relations, United States Senate, by the Subcommittee on Multinational Corporations (Washington, DC: Government Printing Office, January 2, 1975); an online copy can be found at http://www.mtholyoke.edu/acad/intrel/oil1.htm/.
9. For updated statistics and figures on U.S. oil consumption, see the U.S. Energy Information Administration website, http://www.eia.gov/.
10. U.S. Geological Survey, Fact Sheet 0028–01, http://pubs.usgs.gov/fs/fs-0028-01/fs-0028-01.htm/.
11. U.S. Geological Survey, "Short-Term Energy Outlook," http://www.eia.doe.gov/emeu/steo/pub/.
12. *AWI*, 94.
13. K. A. Kvenvolden and C. K. Cooper, "Natural Oil Seepage Rates," *Geo-Mar Lett* 23 (2003): 140–46, http://walrus.wr.usgs.gov/reports/reprints/Kvenvolden_GML_23.pdf/.
14. Alyeska Pipeline Service Company, "The Facts: Trans-Alaska Pipeline System," 2007, http://www.alyeska-pipe.com/Pipelinefacts/FINALfacts%202007.pdf/.
15. *AWI*, 95.
16. Sarah Graham, "Environmental Effects of Exxon Valdez Spill Still Being Felt," *Scientific American*, December 19, 2003, http://www.scientificamerican.com/article.cfm?id=environmental-effects-of; Samuel Skinner and William Reilly, "The Exxon Valdez Oil Spill, National Response Team," May 1989, http://www.akrrt.org/Archives/Response_Reports/ExxonValdez_NRT_1989.pdf/.
17. "NOAA Ocean Science Mission Changes Course to Collect Seafloor and Water Column Oil Spill Data," May 6, 2010, http://www.noaanews.noaa.gov/stories2010/20100506_spillsampling.html/.

18. Justin Gillis, "Giant Plumes of Oil Forming Under the Gulf," *The New York Times*, May 15, 2010, http://www.nytimes.com/2010/05/16/us/16oil.html/.

19. David Biello, "Is Using Dispersants on the BP Gulf Oil Spill Fighting Pollution with Pollution?" *Scientific American*, June 18, 2010.

20. National Oceanic and Atmospheric Administration website, http://www.noaanews.noaa.gov/stories2010/20100608_weatherbird.html/.

21. U.S. Travel Association website, press release, July 22, 2010, http://www.ustravel.org/news/press-releases/bp-oil-spill-impact-gulf-travel-likely-last-3-years-and-cost-227-billion/.

22. For examples, see William H. Kemp, *The Renewable Energy Handbook: A Guide to Rural Energy Independence, Off-Grid and Sustainable Living* (Tucson, AZ: Aztec Press, 2005); Rex A. Ewing and Doug Pratt, *Got Sun? Go Solar: Get Free Renewable Energy to Power Your Grid-Tied Home* (Masonville, CO: PixyJack Press, 2005); Bob Ramlow with Benjamin Nusz, *Solar Water Heating: A Comprehensive Guide to Solar Water and Space Heating Systems* (Gabriola Island, BC: New Society Publishers, 2006); Paul Gripe, *Wind Power: Renewable Energy for Home, Farm, and Business* (White River Junction, VT: Chelsea Green, 2004); Bill Mollison, *Permaculture: A Designer's Manual* (Sisters Creek, Tasmania: Tagari Publications, 2004).

23. See also Glenn Beck, *An Inconvenient Book: Real Solutions to the World's Biggest Problems* (New York: Threshold Editions, 2009), chaps. 1 and 7.

24. This could even include oil companies, if those companies were local companies owned by and employing local people rather than national or multinational corporations.

25. Mark Harrington, "Trees Uprooted at Brookhaven Lab for BP Solar Project," *Newsday*, November 29, 2010, http://www.newsday.com/long-island/suffolk/trees-uprooted-at-brookhaven-lab-for-bp-solar-project-1.2503396/.

Chapter 5. Union Bashing

1. *AWI*, chap. 5.

2. *AWI*, 114–15.

3. *AWI*, 113.

4. Frank Morn, *The Eye that Never Sleeps: A History of the Pinkerton National Detective Agency* (Bloomington: Indiana University Press, 1982).

5. Arthur Gordon Burgoyne, *The Homestead Strike of 1892* (Pittsburgh: University of Pittsburgh Press, 1980); Leon Wolf, *Lockout: The Story of the Homestead Strike of 1892: A Study of Violence, Unionism, and the Carnegie Steel Empire* (London: Longmans, 1965).

6. David O. Stowell, *The Great Strikes of 1877* (Champaign: University of Illinois Press, 2008).

7. Rosemary Laughlin, *The Pullman Strike of 1894: American Labor Comes of Age* (Greensboro, NC: Morgan Reynolds, 1999); David Ray Papke, *The Pullman Case: The Clash of Labor and Capital in Industrial America* (Lawrence: University Press of Kansas, 1999).

8. Eugene Debs, *Writings of Eugene V. Debs: A Collection of Essays by America's Most Famous Socialist* (St. Petersburg, FL: Red and Black, 2009).

9. *Adair v. United States*, 208 U.S. 161 (1908).

10. George G. Suggs, *Colorado's War on Militant Unionism: James H. Peabody and the Western Federation of Miners* (Norman: University of Oklahoma Press, 1991).

11. Senate address on May 8, 1937.
12. George Wolfskill, *The Revolt of the Conservatives: A History of the American Liberty League 1934–1940* (Chicago: Houghton Mifflin, 1962).
13. *AWI*, 113.
14. *AWI*, 114.
15. U.S. Department of Labor, Union Members Summary, http://www.bls.gov/news.release/union2.nr0.htm/.
16. *AWI*, 114.
17. U.S. Department of Labor, 1994 Worker Representation and Participation Survey, http://www.dol.gov/oasam/programs/history/reich/reports/dunlop/appendixa.htm/.
18. Richard B. Freeman, "Do Workers Still Want Unions? More than Ever," Economic Policy Institute, http://www.sharedprosperity.org/bp182.html/.
19. National Labor Relations Board, http://www.nlrb.gov/sites/default/files/documents/119/nlrb2008.pdf/.
20. Beck, *Inconvenient Book*, chap. 17.

Chapter 6. Illegal Immigration

1. *AWI*, chap. 6.
2. *AWI*, 133.
3. *AWI*, 150–51.
4. Center of Immigration Studies' website, http://www.cis.org. The CIS describes itself as "an independent, non-partisan, non-profit, research organization" and declares its mission to be "providing immigration policymakers, the academic community, news media, and concerned citizens with reliable information about the social, economic, environmental, security, and fiscal consequences of legal and illegal immigration into the United States." It states that its members are animated by a vision of a "low-immigration, pro-immigrant" vision of America. Generally, the CIS argues for an enforcement-first policy combined with a reduction of welfare and other benefits for illegal immigrations to encourage them to return to their country of origin. This has been termed by Mark Krikorian, CIS's executive director, to be a "strategy of attrition."
5. *AWI*, 136.
6. Steven Camarota, "Senate Amnesty Could Strain the Welfare System," CIS, 2007, http://www.cis.org/articles/2007/welfarerelease.html/; and "The High Cost of Cheap Labor," CIS, http://www.cis.org/articles/2004/fiscalexec.html/.
7. *Plyler v. Doe*, 457 U.S. 202 (1982).
8. *AWI*, 138.
9. *AWI*, 147–49; see also Beck, *Inconvenient Book*, chap. 22.
10. *AWI*, 134.

Chapter 7. The Nanny State

1. *AWI*, chap. 7.
2. *AWI*, 153.
3. *AWI*, 154–59.
4. *AWI*, 156.

5. Letter on Prohibition, quoted from Daniel Okrent, *Great Fortune: The Epic of Rockefeller Center* (New York: Viking Press, 2003), 246–47.

6. Mark Thornton, "Prohibition vs. Legalization: Do Economists Reach a Conclusion?" *Econ Journal Watch,* April 2004.

7. If he is a libertarian, Beck should consider the question of whether one indulges in recreational drugs to be a matter of personal choice, and as a strict constructionist, he should point out that the federal government has not any constitutional authority to regulate narcotics.

8. *AWI*, 165.

Chapter 8. Shelter: A Basic Human Right?

1. *AWI*, chap. 8.

2. *AWI* , 175.

3. *AWI*, 183.

4. *AWI*, 32.

5. Deborah Hopkinson, *Shutting Out the Sky: Life in the Tenements of New York, 1880–1924* (New York: Orchard, 2003); Jacob A. Riis, *The Battle with the Slum* (New York: Dover, 1998); Peter H. Rossi, *Down and Out in America: The Origins of Homelessness* (Chicago: University of Chicago Press, 1991).

6. *Shelley v. Kraemer*, 334 U.S. 1 (1948).

7. *Griswold v. Connecticut*, 381 U.S. 479 (1965).

8. Twenty-nine states and Washington, D.C., have shield laws protecting the sources of journalists from being revealed in state court. At present, there is not any federal shield law, but in July 2008, a limited federal shield law passed the House and still awaits a vote in the Senate.

9. *Roe v. Wade*, 410 U.S. 113 (1973).

10. *AWI*, 187.

11. *Terry v. Ohio*, 392 U.S. 1 (1968).

12. *Flippo v. West Virginia,* 528 U.S. 11 (1999).

13. *Katz v. United States*, 389 U.S. 347 (1967).

14. *Kelo v. City of New London*, 545 U.S. 469 (2005).

Chapter 9. Universal Health Care

1. *Glenn Beck* (TV show), August 9, 2009. The first use of the term "death panel" in the context of health care reform has been attributed to Sarah Palin, when, on her Facebook page (August 7, 2009), she wrote, "The Democrats promise that a government health care system will reduce the cost of health care, but as the economist Thomas Sowell has pointed out, government health care will not reduce the cost; it will simply refuse to pay the cost. And who will suffer the most when they ration care? The sick, the elderly, and the disabled, of course. The America I know and love is not one in which my parents or my baby with Down Syndrome will have to stand in front of Obama's 'death panel' so his bureaucrats can decide, based on a subjective judgment of their 'level of productivity in society,' whether they are worthy of health care. Such a system is downright evil." Fox News pundits took this statement as fact and used it to criticize "the government take over of health care" or "Obamacare." See Brendan Nyhan, "Why the Death Panel Myth Wouldn't Die:

Misinformation in the Health Care Reform Debate" *Forum* 8, no. 1 (2010), http:// www-personal.umich.edu/~bnyhan/health-care-misinformation.pdf/.

2. *AWI*, chap. 11.

3. "Harvard Medical Study Links Lack of Insurance to 45,000 U.S. Deaths a Year," *The New York Times*, January 27, 2009, http://prescriptions.blogs.nytimes.com/2009/09 /17/harvard-medical-study-links-lack-of-insurance-to-45000-us-deaths-a-year/; Andrew D. Wilper et al., "Health Insurance and Mortality in U.S. Adults," *American Journal of Public Health* 99, no. 12 (December 2009), http://pnhp.org/excessdeaths /health-insurance-and-mortality-in-US-adults.pdf/; Reed Abelson, "Census Numbers Show 50.7 Million Uninsured," *New York Times*, September 16, 2010, http://prescriptions .blogs.nytimes.com/2010/09/16/census-numbers-show-50-million-uninsured/; "Income, Poverty, and Health Insurance Coverage in the United States: 2009," *U.S. Census Bureau Report*, September 2010, http://www.census.gov/newsroom/releases /archives/income_wealth/cb10-144.html/.

4. Robert W. Seifert and Mark Rukavina, "Bankruptcy Is the Tip of a Medical-Debt Iceberg," *Health Affairs* 2 (2006), http://content.healthaffairs.org/content/25/2 /w89.full/.

5. National Coalition on Health Care website, http://nchc.org/.

6. National Coalition on Health Care, "Insurance Companies Prosper, Families Suffer: Our Broken Health Insurance System," U.S. Department of Health and Human Services, February 18, 2010, http://nchc.org/facts-resources/insurance-companies-prosper-families-suffer-our-broken-health-insurance-system/.

7. The Commonwealth Fund, http://www.commonwealthfund.org/Content/Surveys /2005/2005-Biennial-Health-Insurance-Survey.aspx/.

8. *AWI*, 238.

9. *AWI*, 238–39.

10. Taken from *USA Today*, March 31, 2009.

11. *AWI*, 239–41.

12. John Canham-Clyne, "A Rational Option," *Boston Review*, October 1995; this article can be found online at http://bostonreview.net/BR20.4/Clyne.html/.

13. Personal health care expenditures, by source of funds and type of expenditure: United States, selected years, 1960–2007, http://www.cdc.gov/nchs/data /hus/hus09.pdf#127/; however, see the American Medical Association paper on "Administrative Costs of Health Care Coverage" for a discussion of the problems associated with administrative cost estimates from both governmental and private sources at http://www.ama-assn.org/ama1/pub/upload/mm/478/admincosts.pdf/.

14. World Health Organization, "The World Health Report," http://www.who.int /whr/2000/en/.

15. *AWI*, 251. See also Beck, *Inconvenient Book*, chap. 15; *Glenn Beck* (TV show), December 9, 2009.

16. Cf. *Glenn Beck Program*, February 18, 2011; "Beck Attacks WH Council for Community Solutions, Ties Community Organizing to United Nations, Islamists, Communism," Media Matters of America, http://mediamatters.org/mmtv/201102180014/.

17. *Glenn Beck* (TV show), January 9, 2009.

18. *AWI*, 243.

19. Rachel Weiner, "Stephen Hawking Enters U.S. Health Care Debate," *Huffington Post*, December 8, 2009, http://www.huffingtonpost.com/2009/08/12/stephen-hawking-enters-us_n_257343.html/.

20. *AWI*, 237.
21. Bob Herbert, "They Still Don't Get It," *The New York Times*, January 23, 2010, http://www.nytimes.com/2010/01/23/opinion/23herbert.html?_r=1/; Randall Amster, "The Road to Health Care Is Paved with Bad Intentions," *Huffington Post*, January 8, 2010, http://www.huffingtonpost.com/randall-amster/the-road-to-healthcare-is_b_415838.html/.
22. *Glenn Beck* (TV show), August 17, 2010.
23. *AWI*, 264.

Chapter 10. Progressivism

1. Glenn Beck, *Common Sense* (New York: Threshold Editions, 2009), chap. 5 (hereafter cited as *CS*).
2. *CS*, 76.
3. *AWI*, 214.
4. Theodore Roosevelt, *The New Nationalism* (New York: Outlook Company, 1910); for an online reproduction of his speech, see http://teachingamericanhistory.org/library/index.asp?document=501/.
5. *AWI*, 119–20.
6. Robert F. Bruner, *The Crisis of 1907: Lessons Learned from the Market's Perfect Storm* (Hoboken, NJ: John Wiley and Sons, 2007).
7. Ron Chernow, *The House of Morgan: An American Banking Dynasty and the Rise of Modern Finance* (New York: Grove Press, 2010).
8. *CS*, 40.
9. Upton Sinclair, *"The Jungle": The Uncensored Original Edition* (1905; reprint,Tucson, AZ: Sharp Press, 2003).
10. Leon Kink and Thomas Paterson, *Major Problems in the Gilded Age and the Progressive Era: Documents and Essays* (Florence, KY: Wadsworth, 2000); Lewis L. Gould, *America in the Progressive Era, 1890–1914* (New York: Longmans, 2001).
11. Jane Addams, *Twenty Years at Hull House* (1910; reprint, Chicago: Create Space, 2009).
12. Louise W. Knight, *Citizen: Jane Addams and the Struggle for Democracy* (Chicago: University of Chicago Press, 2006).
13. Teaching American History, Progressive Party Platform, http://teachingamerican history.org/library/index.asp?document=607/.
14. Stuart Bruce Kaufman, *Samuel Gompers and the Origins of the American Federation of Labor, 1848–1896* (Santa Barbara, CA: Greenwood Press, 1973).
15. Allan H. Meltzer, *A History of the Federal Reserve*, vol. 1, *1913–1951* (Chicago: University of Chicago Press, 2004).
16. *AWI*, 221.
17. William Preston, *Aliens and Dissenters: Federal Suppression of Radicals, 1903–1933* (Urbana: University of Illinois Press, 1994).
18. Ernest Freeberg, *Democracy's Prisoner: Eugene V. Debs, the Great War, and the Right to Dissent* (Cambridge: Harvard University Press, 2008).
19. Katherine H. Adams, *Alice Paul and the American Suffrage Campaign* (Urbana: University of Illinois Press, 2007).
20. Howard Zinn, *A People's History of the United States* (New York: Harper Classics, 2010) , chaps. 12 and 13.

21. Gerald Berk, *Louis D. Brandeis and the Making of Regulated Competition, 1900–1932* (New York: Cambridge University Press, 2009).

22. Nancy C. Unger, *Fighting Bob La Follette: The Righteous Reformer* (Madison: Wisconsin Historical Society Press, 2008).

23. Allen Hendershott Eaton, *The Oregon System: The Story of Direct Legislation in Oregon* (Memphis: General Books, 2010).

24. Paul K. Conkin, *The New Deal,* American History Series (Wheeling, IL: Harlan Davidson, 2002); Anthony J. Badger, *The New Deal: The Depression Years, 1933–1940* (Lanham, MD: Ivan R. Dee, 2002).

25. The American Presidency Project, http://www.presidency.ucsb.edu/fireside.php/.

26. John A. Andrew, *Lyndon Johnson and the Great Society,* American Ways Series (Lanham, MD: Ivan R. Dee, 1999).

27. Jon Stewart, *The Daily Show,* Comedy Central, March 18, 2010.

28. David Miller, *Principles of Social Justice* (Cambridge: Harvard University Press, 2001).

29. Pontifical Council for Justice and Peace, *Compendium of the Social Doctrine of the Church* (Washington, DC: USCCB Publishing, 2005).

30. Donald Warren, *Radio Priest: Charles Coughlin, The Father of Hate Radio* (New York: Free Press, 1996); C. J. Tull, *Father Coughlin and the New Deal* (Syracuse, NY: Syracuse University Press, 1965).

31. The Presidency Project, http://www.presidency.ucsb.edu/ws/index.php?pid=16518/.

Chapter 11. The Myth of the Free Market

1. *CS,* 12.

2. *AWI,* 190.

3. David S. Landes, *The Unbound Prometheus: Technological Change and Industrial Development in Western Europe from 1750 to the Present* (New York: Cambridge University Press, 1969); Leo Marx, *The Machine in the Garden: Technology and the Pastoral Ideal in America* (New York: Oxford University Press, 1964).

4. A value-added tax (VAT) is a tax on consumption. It differs from a sales tax. For a sales tax, the revenue is collected at the point of purchase by the customer, as a percentage of the total price, whereas for a VAT, tax revenue is paid each time value is added in the supply chain; it is levied at each stage in manufacture, supply, and purchase of any product. The value added is calculated as the sale price charged to the customer minus the costs (including materials, labor, and other taxable expenses).

5. *CS,* 26–28.

6. *CS,* 58.

7. *AWI,* chaps. 1 and 9; *CS,* chap. 3; and see Glenn Beck, *Broke: The Plan to Restore Our Trust, Truth and Treasure* (New York: Threshold Editions, 2010).

8. Adam Smith, *The Wealth of Nations* (1776; reprint, St. Paul, MN: Thrifty Books, 2009).

9. *AWI,* 278.

10. For detailed accounts, see Stephen R. Boyd, ed., *The Whiskey Rebellion: Past and Present Perspectives* (Westport, CT: Greenwood Press, 1985).

11. *AWI,* 28–29.

12. *AWI,* chap. 1.

13. *CS,* 70.

14. *CS,* 73–76.

15. *CS,* 43–44.

16. Mark Twain and Charles Dudley, *The Gilded Age*, Modern Library Classics (New York: Modern Library Edition, 2006).

17. Sean Cashman, *America in the Gilded Age* (New York: New York University Press, 1993); Charles W. Calhoun, *The Gilded Age: Perspectives on the Origins of Modern America* (Lanham, MD: Rowman & Littlefield, 2006).

18. Walter Licht, *Industrializing America: The Nineteenth Century (The American Moment)* (Baltimore: Johns Hopkins University Press, 1995).

19. Matthew Josephson, *The Robber Barons: The Great American Capitalists 1861–1901* (Piscataway, NJ: Transaction Publishers, 2010).

20. Alan Trachtenberg, *The Incorporation of America: Culture and Society in the Gilded Age* (New York: Hill and Wang, 2007).

21. Cf. Chernow, *House of Morgan.*

22. Charles R. Geisst, *Wall Street: A History* (New York: Oxford University Press, 1997).

23. Cf. Kaufman, *Samuel Gompers.*

24. Cf. Kink and Paterson, *Major Problems in the Gilded Age.*

25. *Dodge v. Ford Motor Company*, 204 Mich. 459, 170 N.W. 668 (1919).

26. *Pennsylvania Coal Co. v. Mahon*, 260 U.S. 393 (1922).

27. *Philip Morris, Inc. v. Reilly*, 113 U.S. 129 (2000).

28. *Lorillard v. Reilly*, 533 U.S. 525 (2001).

29. *Marshall v. Barlow's, Inc.*, 429 U.S. 1347 (1977).

30. The Supreme Court has treated corporations as persons since granting them Fourteenth Amendment rights in *Santa Clara County v. Southern Pacific Railroad Company*, 118 U.S. 394 (1886).

31. For an excellent study of this, see *The Report of the Citizens Works Reform Commission*, published as Lee Drutman and Charlie Cray, *The People's Business: Controlling Corporations and Restoring Democracy* (San Francisco: Berrett-Koehler, 2004), http://citizenworks.org/.

32. Drutman and Cray, *People's Business*, chap. 1.

33. "New Nationalism" speech.

34. See the Corporate Accountability Project's website, http://www.corporations.org/.

35. Thomas Jefferson to George Logan, 1816. A copy of this letter can be found online at the Internet Archive, http://www.archive.org/stream/writingsofthomas10 jeffiala/writingsofthomas10jeffiala_djvu.txt/.

36. *Glenn Beck* (CNN Headline News), interview with Ron Paul, September 9, 2008.

37. *Glenn Beck* (CNN Headline News), September 22, 2008.

38. Ibid., September 23, 2008.

39. Ibid., October 8, 2008.

40. Ibid., October 13, 2008.

41. *CS,* 44.

42. *CS,* 45.

43. *CS,* 15–16.

44. Heritage Foundation's website, http://www.heritage.org/.

45. "New Rules Project: Customer-Owned Electric Utilities: Generation, Transmission, and Distribution," http://www.newrules.org/energy/rules/communitybased-energy-development-cbed/encouraging-community-owned-energy-systems/.

Chapter 12. We, the People

1. Fairness and Accuracy in Reporting (FAIR), "Fox: The Most Biased Name in News," July 2001, http://www.fair.org/index.php?page=1067/; see Robert Greenwald's 2004 documentary exposé *Outfoxed: Rupert Murdoch's War on Journalism*, http://www.outfoxed.org/; and Jeff Cohen, *Cable News Confidential: My Misadventures in Corporate Media* (Sausalito, CA: PoliPoint Press, 2006) (hereafter cited as *CNC*).

2. *CNC*, 73.

3. *CNC*, 120.

4. For their website, go to http://www.opensecrets.org/.

5. Diane Renzuli and the Center for Public Integrity, *Capital Offenders: How Private Interests Govern Our States* (Washington, DC: Public Integrity Books, 2002).

6. *Buckley v. Valeo*, 424 U.S. 1 (1976).

7. *Citizens United v. FEC*, 130 U.S. 876 (2010).

8. *McConnell v. FEC*, 540 U.S. 93 (2003).

9. Reported in the *California Lawyer*, January 2011.

10. *Glenn Beck* (TV show), April 6, 2010.

11. Free Press is a U.S.-based nonprofit organization (launched in 2002) that claims to be working to reform the media through education, organizing, and advocacy. It promotes diverse and independent media ownership, improving public media, better quality journalism, and public access to communications. It claims to be the largest media reform organization, with nearly half a million members. Its website can be found at http://www.freepress.net/.

12. Advocates for alternative media and campaigns for media reform and Net Neutrality include Fairness and Accuracy in Reporting, http://www.fair.org; Media Matters for America, http://mediamatters.org/; Mother Jones, http://motherjones.com/; the *Nation*, http://www.thenation.com/; Common Dreams, http://www.commondreams.org/; AlterNet, http://www.alternet.org/; BuzzFlash.com, http://buzzflash.com/; the *Huffington Post*, http://www.huffingtonpost.com/; the New Rules Project, http://www.newrules.org/; U.S. Public Interest Research Groups, https://www.uspirg.org/; Center for Policy Alternatives, http://www.stateaction.org/; Progressive Democrats of America, http://pdamerica.org/; Dream Change, http://www.dreamchange.org/; and the Center for Digital Democracy, http://democraticmedia.org/.

13. Federal Communications Commission website, http://www.fcc.gov/transaction/comcast-nbcu.html/.

14. *Democracy Now!* website, http://www.democracynow.org/.

15. The following organizations support a constitutional amendment clarifying that corporations are not persons, and only persons have rights: Common Cause, http://www.commoncause.org/; Move On, http://www.moveon.org/; Campaign Legal Center, http://www.campaignlegalcenter.org/; Democracy Matters, http://www.democracymatters.org/; Democracy 21, http://democracy21.org/; Voter Action, http://www.voteraction.org/; Public Citizen, http://www.citizen.org; Center for Corporate Policy, http://www.corporatepolicy.org/.

16. Drutman and Cray, *People's Business*, 128.

17. *CS*, 37.

18. *Glenn Beck* (TV show), February 21, 2011.

19. Ibid., February 17, 2011.

20. Ibid., February 3, 2011.

21. Ibid., March 3, 2011.

22. Ibid., March 4, 2011.

23. Ibid., March 30, 2011.

24. The Invisible Committee is an anonymous group of French writers who analyzed the current state of crisis in Western society and explained how violent and revolutionary acts of resistance, protest, and sabotage could lead to the destruction of the state and capitalism. The French police and courts charged and convicted nine students in the town of Tarmac for "terrorist enterprises" for sabotaging trains and writing this pamphlet. *The Coming Insurrection* by The Invisible Committee can be found online at http://zinelibrary.info/files/cominginsurrection.pdf/.

25. *Glenn Beck* (TV show), March 29, 2011.

26. Ibid., March 21, 2011.

27. *CS*, 61.

28. *CS*, 58–59.

29. *CS*, 90.

INDEX

ABOUT THE AUTHOR

KARL ROGERS, Ph.D., is a professor of philosophy and a cofounder and director of the John Dewey Center for Democracy and Education, affiliated with the Institute of Advanced Study, University of Minnesota, Minneapolis. Dr. Rogers's published works include *Participatory Democracy, Science and Technology: An Exploration in the Philosophy of Science; Modern Science and the Capriciousness of Nature;* and *On the Metaphysics of Experimental Physics.*